MILLS COLLEGE
LIBRARY

Mills College Library
Withdrawn

MEN OF CHAOS

by Hermann Rauschning

THE VOICE OF DESTRUCTION

THE CONSERVATIVE REVOLUTION

MEN OF CHAOS

—

MEN OF CHAOS

by Hermann Rauschning

G. P. PUTNAM'S SONS, NEW YORK

COPYRIGHT, 1942, BY HERMANN RAUSCHNING

All rights reserved. This book, or parts thereof, must not be reproduced in any form without permission.

Designed by Robert Josephy

MANUFACTURED IN THE UNITED STATES OF AMERICA

943.085
R 248m

139892

CONTENTS

PREFACE   vii

Part I—THE WHIPPERS-IN OF THE REVOLUTION

1. "The Ploughing Up" and The Ploughmen   3
2. "What Fellows They Are!"   11
3. The Fight for the Requisites of Power   15
4. The Poultry Farmer   21
5. The Eternal Pagan   32
6. The Little Monster   42
7. Winning the Revolution   51
8. The Revolutionary in Disguise   62
9. The Bull   67
10. Witches' Sabbath in America   81
11. Raw Material   87
12. The Genuine Nazi   93
13. Siegfried and Hagen in the Party   103
14. Underlings of the Revolution   109

Part II—REVOLUTIONARIES AGAINST THE GRAIN

1. The New Talleyrand   117
2. The Cross-Spider   123
3. The Executor of the Will   134
4. Blood Nobility and New Nobility   142
5. "Una Terribile"   147

Part III—DIPLOMATS, DELUDED AND DELUDING

1. "Little Man, What Now?"   155
2. A Foreign Minister   162
3. Keeping All Avenues Open   167
4. The Administrator of the Legacy   172
5. Tragic Conflict   178

Mills College Library

MILLS COLLEGE Withdrawn
LIBRARY

6. The Lure of Adventure 183
7. Leviathan and Behemoth 189
8. Grotesque Misconception 195

Part IV—CAPTAINS OF INDUSTRY AND
ECONOMIC VISIONARIES

1. Captains of Industry 207
2. Essen Conversations 211
3. A German Industrialist 215
4. A Barrel of Saar Wine 223
5. The Exact Process 230
6. Technocrats 235
7. Work is a Vice 242
8. A Planning Office 247
9. A Visit in Exile 258

Part V—OLD GENERALS AND YOUNG
OFFICER ADVENTURERS

1. The Fetish 265
2. The Power Behind the Scenes 270
3. Hitler Boy Quex 275
4. The Points 281
5. Lost Balance 291
6. A Necessary War 292
7. Military Security 298
8. From Schlieffen to Trotsky 301
9. Hannibal's Elephants 305
10. Technicians of Destruction 311
11. The Limits of the Possible 315
12. Hitler's Dodge 318
13. A Peace Party 321

Epilogue 326

INDEX 335

PREFACE

IN THE FOLLOWING account of conversations and meetings with both well known and unknown men of Germany, I have set out to do more than provide a supplement to my talks with Hitler, published nearly three years ago. It seems to me that it is not enough to give a mere description of the background against which is set the dubious figure of a man who has started great developments, but who is himself destitute of all the qualities of real greatness. I have tried to give a cross-section of that inflamed, feverish Germany of nearly ten years ago, in which lie the roots of the events of today. I have tried to afford an insight into the thoughts, the hopes, and the fears of men who, whether known or unknown, share the responsibility for what is happening today in the world.

Those talks with Hitler aroused astonishment and a good deal of incredulity. Events have since shown, however, that they were neither an exercise of fancy nor an exaggeration of Hitler's significance. But one objection seemed justified: Was it really Hitler's ideas and Hitler's will that determined the course of events in Germany? Was he not merely the puppet manipulated by other men in the background? Were not Hitler's utterances in reality of no importance? Was it not a shifting of responsibility to push him into the foreground?

Certainly the master of our fate is not Adolf Hitler. The man is not a Titan. We have to deal with other forces than a single individual. Great effects cannot proceed from small causes. Great effects may be produced by small operations; but behind these are the true causes, and those must be proportionate to the effects.

My motive for calling up the past once again, after the passage of these many years filled with monstrous events and

vii

tragic collapses, is that I see in the over-simplified judgments of events in Germany a great danger for the future.

Behind the events which took place in Germany before the war there is something which concerns us all. For the chaos of destructive forces which motivated those events remains the true characteristic today, despite the seeming unity of will of the German people. Military defeat and the capitulation of the system which now rules Germany will not necessarily mean the elimination of the destructive motives, and these motives and forces are not limited to Germany in their effects. They are the elements, rather, of a progressive historical crisis in which all nations are involved.

It is the danger of these destructive forces let loose in the world today which is the essential theme of the following conversations, and I would like to present this, not by scientific analysis, but through the medium of meetings with living personalities—with men who are part of this chaos.

Not all of the motives, nor a complete picture of German development, are illustrated by the following conversations and meetings. But they give the background of the major power-politic events, which threaten to remain also the background of the coming struggle for the peace.

That we are in the midst of a universal revolution hardly anyone will want to contest. The elements of this revolution are visible today in every country. It is the eternal tragedy of revolutions that their start or their abrupt entry into new phases remains unobserved. The result is that they are promoted by the very people who are most hotly opposed to them. In all revolutions we have to distinguish between the conscious and the unconscious revolutionaries. Hitler was made. But he was made by the revolutionary situation. This man was born of the mental chaos of universal destruction, of a society in which all spiritual values had been effaced or shattered. It was the confusion of the only half-understood revolution, the conflicts of aims and ideas, that gave him power as the most radical of the men of the revolution in Germany.

I have set out, not to explain, but to enable the reader to see for himself how a whole nation which, taken all in all, was no worse than other nations of Europe, a nation of hard-working, capable people, was precipitated into this chaos. I have no desire to expose and denounce the nation in whose error and responsibility I have had my share. My purpose has been to supply material for the understanding of what has happened.

One day even the cynics and nihilists will realize that their principles, on which they may be able to live their personal lives, produce nothingness when they become general maxims of human society. Even they will want to change their ways, and will seek for values that endure. The process that is now at work in Germany, amid the fighting and the bombing and the privation, is a process of cleansing. The counter-picture to the external destructive movement, of which National Socialism became the common denominator, is a great creative process, a spiritual and moral process of transformation. That is the other side of German reality.

A word about the form of these reports and their basis. Critics have questioned the authenticity of my talks with Hitler. Certainly none of the following conversations took place exactly in the words here given. Talks of which notes are afterwards taken are always abbreviations. Nevertheless they are not invented conversations. They contain essential passages, extracted perhaps from long and tiring debates, of which many were concerned with quite other matters, troubles of the moment, and questions of detail, but in which outstanding things were said that may be well worth placing on record. I can affirm that my conversations, reconstructed from notes and from recollections, are true records in the fullest sense. Internal evidence must bear witness to the truth of these reports of personal meetings, just as for the Hitler talks.

With this I come to a last but not unimportant point, namely the question: Are these conversations and the earlier Hitler conversations authentic? Did the author write these conversations himself? What kind of man is he? He belonged to the National Socialist Party; he heard of the Reichstag fire, without making immediate public protest. Is not such a person already condemned by his past?

Some readers may reject the author because of his former political allegiance. For those who are not frightened away from a closer examination, I would like to give a few facts about myself because a mass of inaccurate information has been spread about me personally; and in this case, the personal is part of proper judgment.

I joined the Party in the summer of 1931, immediately following the devaluation of the British pound which caused further stress in the Danzig economic situation. I came into politics from Agrarian politics. Between 1929 and 1930 the milk prices in Danzig fell about 40 per cent for the producers. Wheat prices fell more than 50 per cent, the price of sugar beets about 45 per cent; hogs were practically unsaleable; the foals of our best breeding stables had no market. This of course certainly does not justify a revolution. But it does justify extraordinary measures. In the United States it led to the New Deal, to the "constitutional revolution" as Edward S. Corwin calls it. The points of departure and the goals were the same among many German politicians, at least among my friends who shared my opinions.

Added to these general considerations there were circumstances in Danzig that furnished particular motives. There was a growing tension between Poland and Danzig. In our own small community party political conflicts grew. Young workers pursued Communism. Even in our villages, uniformed units of the "Red Front" appeared. The worst condition, however, was the weak leadership which had no understanding of the critical symptoms. It had no understanding of the strata that in Germany, up to then, had represented the soil: the conservatives, the Deutsch-National. They were not conservative; they were reactionary. They did not understand that to be conservative in the true sense means to be revolutionary. Compared with this, National Socialism seemed like revolutionary conservatism. At least we thought we would be able to make it into such a movement.

I had come into contact with the old Conservative circles, among which I had generally counted myself, before I moved to the territory of the Free City. Until 1926 I lived in the one time Prussian part of the new Poland. I organized there the means of a free German culture. I founded a German library. I published a German scientific periodical and a popular monthly. It was not the groundwork for a fifth column movement nor any other type of irredentist politics. It was merely the attempt to base the life of the German minority on a cultural organization.

My conflict with the political leaders of the Germans in Poland developed from the same attitude which later also brought me into conflict with the Polish policy of the Third Reich. Together with my friends I saw the future of Europe assured by overcoming the political and economic frontiers and by limiting nationalism to cultural fields, for the preservation of its values. If such trends of thought were accepted, then the difficult question of the Free City of Danzig would also be solved. One of the explosive spots of Europe could then become a joining arm. It was these thoughts which later guided me in my foreign policy for Danzig.

Such a policy necessitates the good will of all participants, not merely those on one side. Among the leading political circles of Germans in Poland there was little approval of such a policy, and as little understanding of it among the Poles. It was these double restraints which led me to give up politics in 1926 and move to the Free City of Danzig where, in addition

to my practical occupation with agriculture, I devoted myself
to historical study. I published at that time, out of my experiences in Poland, a major examination of the first ten years of
Polish policy toward its German minority: *The De-Germanization Policy in Poland: Ten Years of Polish Politics*. A year
later I published a large historical work on music.

The motives for which I joined the Party were not the same
as those which swept a large number of wiser men into the
ranks of the National Socialists. I recognized that the crisis at
that time was not merely a passing economic crisis, but rather
the beginning of a great dynamic world process in which there
were only two possibilities. One way was to assimilate the
fruitful revolutionary motives at the right time and to fuse
them with the elements of the old order. This is the way of
the conservative revolution (as my book, *The Conservative
Revolution,* points out). It is the way of Great Britain and
America, with the leitmotiv: "Only that is conservative which
moves forward, and only that is progressive which does not
break with the past." The other alternative was to permit oneself to be overrun by the revolutionary forces, with all the
dangers of total destruction which means a break of historic
continuity. If one desired the first solution, the only road that
could be traversed in Germany as well as in Danzig was *with*
a mass movement and not against the masses. In fact, there
was no choice possible. It was National Socialism. That is
what it looked like to us at the time.

But such a decision did not carry with it the interpretation
that is put upon it today. It was not the sanctioning of all acts
of terror, of aggression, and plans for world conquest. Nor did
this exclude the freedom of the spirit, the ideals and principles
of democracy.

As to my intentions and principles in conducting the policy
of Danzig when I was president of the Senate and administrator of the government of that small State which for a time
stood so much in the foreground of public interest, I think it

best to refer the reader to an objective and precise presentation
of the facts recently published in the *Nazi Conquest of Danzig*
by H. L. Leonhardt (University of Chicago Press, 1942).

I take from this my avowal to the eternal principles of
democracy and every form of free human society. On April 7,
1935, on the occasion of the Peoples' Day Elections, I publicly
opposed the National Socialists with this statement whose last
sentence I quote from Leonhardt. I leave it to the judgment of
the reader whether such an avowal has less power of conviction if it is taken at a time, as mine was, when I was in danger
of my life, or if it is proclaimed at a time when it brings civil
advantages and public acknowledgment. With this avowal I
would like to introduce the following conversations in the firm
conviction that the overwhelming number of Germans, who
have become silent under external pressure, will acknowledge
with me these principles as the elements of a new, humane
order:

"I therefore declare myself opposed to your List I*, and in
favor of a clear legal order, based on the inalienable principle
of equality before the law; in favor of free, inviolable co-
operation, based on the moral responsibility of the individual
in social, economic, and political duties; in favor of the legal
idea of self-government upon which Baron von Stein and
Bismarck based the public and constitutional life of the German nation and which has become an integral part of all
leading institutions of our German past; in favor of freedom
of thought and of culture, opposed to any constraint paralyz-
ing their creative power and transcending the natural obligation toward one's own people; in favor of a community of the
people not based on external uniformity, but daily won anew
in the conflict of ideas and of characters, yet supported by mutual esteem and a respect for the honor even of an adversary,
and by common effort to attain the same goal; in favor of

* *Die Wahlliste der Nationalsozialisten in Danzig.*

liberty of conscience unshackled by any claim to blind obedience; in favor of the Christian faith, which lies at the heart of
our morality and of our culture, and whose sacred domain we
cannot abandon without destroying our true selves and falling
into idle sophistry."

I

THE WHIPPERS-IN OF THE REVOLUTION

"THE PLOUGHING UP" AND THE PLOUGHMEN

IS IT STILL of any use to depict the characters of the leading Nazis? Their time is over. The play is drawing to its end. Their part in it is finished.

But what part did they play in this tragedy? That of gangsters, it is said. Both inside and outside Germany they are known as criminals. People talk of their unprecedented corruption. By kicking and elbowing they forced their way up to the sources of power and pleasure. Is that all we can say about them? A new gang of bosses have come to the top, as I once heard a Berlin workman remark. "The rotation of the élites," says the man with a scientific education, echoing Pareto.

Everyone among the Nazis had a different idea of National Socialism. Everyone thought of it as a springboard for his own ambitions, for his own personal egoistic ambitions or those of his group. This was equally true of the party members, the middle-class supporters, and the men in the background who pulled the strings. It was true above all of those who claimed to be "in the know." But was it not true that National Socialism, with all its program points and its doctrinaire teachings, was simply a springboard for ambitions? Just a means to an end?

This question and its answer came up in the course of a conversation I had with Keppler, who was then Hitler's economic adviser and later became an Under-secretary of State.

"Don't let yourself be diverted from the main issue," said Keppler, "by present appearances of aimless chaos and arbitrary organization. By the main issue I mean the deposition of politics from its old importance and the transformation of the system of free markets and private enterprise into a controlled economic system. It's obvious this can't be done overnight, and that we must operate behind a smoke-screen. What we are working out here is the new mechanism of production."

Revolutions are not born of doctrines. Nor do social and economic changes suffice to produce them. Revolutions become possible only when the bastions and dykes by means of which men seek to protect themselves from one another disintegrate and collapse. When the supreme conceptions and moral values lose their authority, revolutions become inevitable. It takes a long time for that loss of authority to permeate from the higher ranks of society down to the broad masses, and finally to throw whole peoples off their customary path. The roots of every revolution, those of the nihilist revolution included, lie deep in the past.

We Germans are thorough in everything, even in cynicism. We turn it into a system, a philosophy. I don't want to be taken or a narrow-minded moralizer. Skepticism and cynicism are as inseparable from humanity's autumn as the sere and yellow leaf from Nature's. But we are concerned here with something different—no longer merely the attitude of mockery that refuses to take anything seriously, no longer merely the resigned turning away from a more or less hostile environment, but a doctrine—cynicism as a principle of action, as a political maxim.

The first in the long procession of intelligent cynics who, because they had no spiritual foundation left, were able to treat the gravest matters in Germany as gamblers, was, it seems to me, von Kühlmann, Foreign Secretary during the last war. A highly gifted man, an accomplished diplomat, with a consummate mastery of the technique of his calling, fertile in ideas, versatile—but in character a nihilist. He had a great opportunity of preserving Germany from the worst. But this counted less than his own career. He took the line of least resistance. This Kühlmann spirit is deeply embedded in all ranks of the public service. It is just as widespread in the highest quarters of society as in the lower ranks and among the "groundlings," where, in the form of crass opportunism, it paved the way for the revolution.

The share of the broad masses of the German people in the responsibility for the revolution and the war lies not where it is constantly sought, in a supposedly ingrained militarism, but in this opportunism, under the influence of which they imagine always that they are choosing the lesser evil, but make with deadly certainty for the greater one.

When I wrote *The Voice of Destruction* several years ago I was reproached for having concentrated the whole blame for the events in Germany on Hitler, leaving in the background those who were really responsible for them. It was alleged that the real responsibility rested on the military caste, the Junkers, and the big industrialists—on the forces of reaction, capitalism, and Prussian militarism.

It is quite true that it is impossible to hold any single individual responsible for this revolutionary catastrophe. The so-called new order which has come into existence in the past nine years in Germany is something far beyond the powers of a single human being to create, and equally beyond the scanty capacity and attainments of the Nazi party members. It depended on the co-operation of the German people, with all their proved capability and creative power.

Nevertheless this man Hitler, with his extraordinary temperament and pathological demonic possession, acted as a catalytic agent in the mother-lye of the revolutionary forces. He is neither a lunatic nor a cork always floating on the surface. He is something more, and it was all the more necessary to reveal that extra something because he is not to be overcome by the mere contempt of his enemies. But this man Hitler would never have become anything, except perhaps a half-crazy extra waiter for the Sunday afternoons in some suburban café garden, had it not been for the forces behind him, which he used and which used him. What share of responsibility must, then, be borne by the German military caste?

Nothing could be more incompatible than the delirious speeches, the dervish dances and wizard's drums of the party bosses on the one hand, and on the other the cold-blooded, laconic, practical, clear-headed German officers. How can we explain their tolerance of the Nazis?

It was the national element that attracted them. Here at last were the "people"—the little men, the representatives of the masses—and yet they were not pacifists or anti-militarists. They were nationalists.

The men of the Nazi party, the old, original members, were in truth the only real revolutionaries in Germany. It was their historic function to revolutionize Germany. Undoubtedly some of them were aiming at something very different from what they actually achieved. They were patriots in their own way. In their ideas Germany played a part never allotted to her by the moderate, well-tempered bourgeoisie.

But they came into office in such a very short time and without any practical experience. They refused to be impressed by experts. They forced their will on the staffs and crushed the toughest resistance. They had no respect for the rules of administrative work. They entered like a gale through the window and blew the papers about on all the desks. The result was fearful disorder. They had no interest in procedure, routine, departmental jealousy, and other illusory difficulties. But they broke the opposition of the bureaucracy.

Little has been written about the struggle which the Nazis fought out with the bureaucracy after coming into power, but I think it may be described as perhaps the cleverest and smartest of their political achievements. It was a struggle over each single individual in the bureaucracy; an almost soundless struggle, carried on by means of all sorts of allurements, coarse or refined, all sorts of corruption, material or mental. It was carried on by means of the appeal to a generous patriotism, and by working on the low but intensely strong motives of vanity, apprehension, and the desire to get on in the world.

One of the levers used to compel the capitulation not only of individuals but of whole staffs was the fear of being suddenly thrown aside as superfluous ballast. For the officials of the Foreign Ministry this prospect grew more and more tangible with every day of the consolidation of the Nazi power. Hitler had created nucleus organizations in the party for every branch of the public administration; the party plan had at first been that these should be able to take over *"schlagartig,"* like lightning, all the functions of the government departments. Later Hitler allowed the existence of these organizations to serve as a continual threat and deterrent to official obstruction. His tactics were justified in the result.

The gentlemen of the Foreign Ministry capitulated with the rest. They gave way one after another. Was the Ribbentrop Office, or Alfred Rosenberg's "Foreign Office," to be allowed to take over the functions of the Ministry? Better meet Hitler on small points and so make sure of the means of "preventing the worst" in important matters. Better give way betimes than have the whole conduct of affairs turned over to those wild men, Rosenberg and Ribbentrop. Such was the line of thought I found in confidential discussions. "What would you have us do?" men would ask with a shrug of the shoulders. "Would you permit yourself the luxury of manly independence of spirit? Whom would you be serving if you did? Nobody but Adolf."

When I asked a friend of mine, a big businessman and a Liberal, for his help against the Nazis, he advised me to come to a compromise with them as quickly as possible. "I should be sorry if anything happened to you. Do you remember the game they played with your colleague, Count Kalkreuth? He had looked after the Nazis, and been careful to stroke them the right way. And what has been his reward for the line he took? They have done him down. They are charging him with corruption. Because the poor man happened to buy a few loads of feeding-stuff for his farm cheap, instead of paying through the nose for it a few days later. He happened to know the prices were shooting up. Well, I ask you, haven't we all things like that to keep dark? Don't you think they could bring charges of corruption against you or me?

"It's not exactly the courageous course—I admit that. But self-respect, my goodness! What for? And where are you going to get it in times like these? Perhaps they're wearing character in the old-fashioned provincial towns, though I'm not too sure of it. You can see, can't you, what goes for respectability in this world around us? You've got to realize at last that we are in the midst of a revolution. Have you ever heard of people keeping their character unsoiled in a revolution? Just read a bit about Talleyrand and Fouché and that lot. A little slip won't do you any harm. As things are, we are simply pushing our own interests, the whole lot of us."

Opportunism is not the right word for this attitude. It was not due only to the desire to be on the side of the stronger and never to be in the minority. There is more than that behind it —a materialism that no longer takes anything seriously except immediate personal welfare, and a readiness to sacrifice for the sake of that ever sublimer thing—honor, conscience, and high tradition. It is always the highest rank of society that is responsible for the pursuit of that path. But to sit "in the seat of the scornful," in the Psalmist's words, is not only the privilege of a degenerate clique of aristocrats. They all sat in the seat of the scornful, all the party chiefs of the Weimar Republic, with their skeptical party and trade union secretaries, and alongside them the "syndics" of great industrial enterprises, the banking magnates and Junkers and officers, the men of learning and the artists, the pillars of tradition just as surely as the firebrands of revolution.

What happened in Germany can occur in other lands. The

Umbruch or "ploughing up," as the new German jargon so well calls it, is no new invention of the Nazis. It began as long ago as 1914. It is the crumbling of the spiritual basis of our civilization. In Germany the organized workers and the army were the two classes with the most definite standards and criteria. No wonder that in the crisis of the "ploughing up" both sought shelter in their machinery, each in its own fashion. But flight into the machine is flight into a collectivity. There is no question of individual moral responsibility within a collectivity, but only the question whether the requirements of the collectivity are being met. Moral decisions are confined to the sphere of the individual personality. The liberation from considerations of moral responsibility comes, therefore, to be regarded, by all who thus take refuge in their day-to-day tasks, as a typical deliverance, a relief and a step forward. Hence the feeling of superiority in the radical, rationalistic experts which has such a powerful attraction for all who live in spiritual surrogates.

The attractive power of any kind of radicalism is based especially on activity. The men of tradition, continuity, and balance seem to uphold a sort of quietism. At a dinner I happened to find myself sitting next to von Papen and opposite *Freiherr* von Hammerstein-Equord, the former Commander-in-Chief, and joined with them in a conversation concerning the prospects of the German Revolution. This took place shortly before the retirement of Hammerstein, who was an advocate of moderation and peaceful development.

"Don't interfere. Let it run its course!" said von Hammerstein. "Any sort of interference is only one more short-circuiting. This sort of thing must be left to run itself out."

"So long as it isn't then too late," I objected.

The General shrugged his shoulders. I gained the impression of a resignation that went deeper than his words when he said: "Cures cannot be forced. I regard all this as a fever which must run its course. It may lead to complete recovery, but it is also possible that it may have a fatal issue."

No further interference with events! Let matters develop organically! Don't ask questions, but keep at work! Go ahead with the allotted practical tasks, and don't fuss! Such were the regular answers to any questions about Germany's real aims, or any doubts expressed concerning the rightness of our policy as a whole. It was not difficult to see that these replies concealed misgivings. As time went on, there was deeper and deeper resignation or cynicism in the tone in which people uttered such phrases as: "Why get excited? Better join in the game! You won't change things! Neither you nor I can!" All the jargon of cynicism, self-mockery, disgust, and shameless self-exposure does not date simply from the National Socialist *Umbruch,* the self-styled Nazi "renascence."

Could these leading Nazis be other than what they were? I should not like to see any legends, good or bad, grow round them; otherwise, some thirty years hence, their memory might give birth to new errors, perhaps in a distant land in the other hemisphere.

Therefore I should like to answer one question. What is the eternal stain on them which we do not find on the revolutionaries of other revolutions, even if in their day they shed as much or even more blood, if they wrought no less destruction than the world is witnessing today?

Did these Nazis lack loftiness of spirit, faith, ideals? What were the means of seduction possessed by these revolutionaries, which had wrought such a change for the worse?

2

"WHAT FELLOWS THEY ARE!"

WHEN I MET an old acquaintance in Zurich two years before the war (the shadows of the coming catastrophe were already obscuring the safe, comfortable, self-assured solidity of Swiss life) the first thing he said to me was: "What fellows they are!" The words betrayed reluctant admiration and a touch of pride in all the Nazi vigor, and a trace of envy.

"You know how much against the Nazis I was," said my friend. "But we must be fair. Those fellows have put in some very hard work. Their success didn't just fall into their laps. Sheer nonsense to say that! They stuck to their jobs all day and all night. Yes, they did, and they're doing so more than ever now!"

At that time people abroad still turned up their noses at the Nazis, and were more inclined to ridicule their blunders than to fear their energy. People talked of the poor harvest prospects in Germany, the deterioration of the food situation there, and the increasing figures of floating debt. I must admit that I was not entirely uninfluenced by this trend of thought. When about that time I published parts of the German edition of *The Revolution of Nihilism,* I was told: "But all this is very pessimistic! It's enough to make us despair of the future." I had, indeed, some doubt myself whether the pessimism of my diagnosis was not excessive. After all, these Nazis were "little men." They understood nothing. I had been in close touch with them. Ignoramuses. Sometimes they seemed just like children. How could anything they took in hand have permanence?

"Crazy fellows!" said my acquaintance. "But the most amazing thing is that they haven't done for themselves. Anyone else would have been finished long ago if he'd committed a fraction of their crimes. How did they get away with it? I don't know. It's a fact that the Germans are quite satisfied with them. Naturally they grumble, as they always do. But don't imagine there's any real opposition in Germany, among the masses or in any section of society. Everyone admits that those fellows are moving, at least. They are getting something done. So people condone their corruption. Let them fill their pockets, they say. Politics is a dirty game. No one gets particularly excited, either, at the way they carry on with their women, and take nice houses for themselves, and run about in fine cars, and buy up jewelry and antiques. Why shouldn't they have their pickings if they do what they're doing? That's what the man in the street thinks. If they all lived like monks, he'd think them uncanny. As it is, they show their kinship with the 'little man.' He admits he would do just the same if he were at the top. I see you're associating with émigrés. Don't get it into your head there are many people in Germany who want to see that feeble milk and water Weimar crowd back again, just because their record was a bit cleaner. Maybe it was, but they did nothing but talk. Those of the old bosses who had any guts, had no brains; and the men with ideas were just literary chaps without any spunk in them."

I was violently excited by what he said. I forgot my part, and delivered an indignant lecture. But he was not impressed. It seemed funny to him. He stared at me with a merry twinkle in his eyes.

"Man alive, what's riling you?" he broke in at last. "Fundamentally I agree with you. But what can we do to alter things? Decency, book learning, and character—all these are only trimmings for happier days. In the revolution and gangster drama now being performed on the world's stage there's only one thing that counts, and that's will power. You've got to be a regular bull. Not merely because it's the only way to impress the mob, but because it's the only way to carry on in this filthy course. Good taste is a hindrance. A good bringing up is a misfortune. Too much knowledge makes for impotence. Good taste is a thing those fellows certainly haven't got. It's pathetic to see how they try to acquire it, try to introduce a bit of style into their scratch furniture, collect dud antiques, and so on. But, frankly, is there anything strange in that? Haven't the revolutionaries of all times done just the same?

"No, old man, those fellows have made a damned good job of it, they've done capitally. They've not merely kept their end up, they've made things hum as well. Germany is running at full speed, I can tell you. Hell, they're a clever lot. You really can't help admiring them. How did they pull it off? There weren't any fairy godmothers round their cradles. I'll tell you how they managed it. They've got wills of their own. The rule of intellect is over, even in Germany. Today the big man is the man of will power, and not the man of knowledge. Yes, it sounds silly, but it's none the less true."

I referred to the threatening outlook—it all seemed to be making ultimately for war.

"Don't talk rubbish," replied my friend. "This man Hitler is quite right. What does it matter if there are two or three million fewer nonentities in the world? What is war? Just one of the many phases of the big revolution we're in, up to our necks. Away with all these nonentities, these little Meiers and Lehmanns! Make a clean sweep of them and rejuvenate the world! History and life will justify us.

"I know," he went on, cutting short my attempt to speak. "I know what you're going to say. Germany will go to the dogs in the process. It's possible. Even, perhaps, probable. But what does Germany, or France, or England matter in this revolution? Germany's future is at stake, you will say. Sounds quite a good argument for a while. But in reality it's quite other things that are at stake. Our funny mode of life, for instance. Let's do some ventilating work! Make an end to this eternal material progress—water closets, bathrooms, refrigerators, contraceptives free for all! Splendid! an earthly paradise! In England every man will have his own golf clubs as well; in Germany there'll be a six months' free holiday trip for all. I don't know what the Americans will want. In France they've evidently got all they want already, they're full up and contented. The clock is standing still now. People start revolutions nowadays in the same frame of mind as they do their crossword puzzles; yes, they're big revolutionaries in their bars. No spirit about it. My dear man, let's have done with all this bunkum of progress, material civilization, paradise on earth. I can tell you what's the mission of these little Nazis at whom we turn up our noses—you and I and all the other people with well-groomed fingernails, we people who won't eat fish with our knives or wipe our mouths with the table-cloth, as your illustrious *Gauleiter* Forster does. I tell you what they're after—they mean really to revolutionize Germany. This nation of super-discipline, super-orderliness, organization run mad, must be so shaken out of its security that it will become at last the battering-ram of the world revolution. I believe they've done it. They've got the world in motion again. Yes, they have sown the storm. They've got the revolution inside them that those respectable trade union secretaries and hair-splitting Marxists only talked about occasionally in their sleep."

This was characteristic of the general tone in Germany, as I gathered from news reaching me from time to time, and it showed me the profound demoralization going on, especially in the most prominent and most intelligent circles. We must realize it and appreciate the fact. My acquaintance was right, of course, in his contention that corruption in such times of revolution is of no great account and does not particularly excite the masses. Such things only cause a stir in comparatively normal times. It is ridiculous to make a fuss about them. Can we not find equal corruption in the heroes of the French Revolution—those men whose names are held in high honor by all friends of progress, enlightenment, and human liberty?

Were they not just as cruel, just as brutal, just as indifferent to the worth of human life? Were they not just as ready to shed human blood?

3

THE FIGHT FOR THE REQUISITES
OF POWER

MY COLLEAGUE, PRESIDENT of the Chamber of Agriculture for East Prussia, was astonished at my news when he came to see me at Danzig. "What!" he said. "You have given up even your party office of Regional Peasant Leader? Don't you know that you will entirely destroy your foothold in the party? How will you keep any hold over power? You have not even the police; your rival, Greiser, has got them. Why, you have no real power at all."

When I said it should be possible to rule even without the factors of material power, he went on, "Don't take it so lightly. In the party there's only one way of maintaining your position. You must so build it up that, if you fall, a wall of the party edifice falls with you. Just look at my *Gauleiter,* Koch—he has worked it! Don't you suppose that Hitler would have been glad to send him to the devil long ago, if it had not been too costly a business for him? Koch, the intimate friend of Gregor Strasser! But he holds some trump cards. The man has got power into his hands. Hitler knows that if he were to take Koch by the scruff of his neck a whole bastion of the party would fly into the air, and many other honorable party members would go up with it. I have been longer in the party than you, and I know the tricks. A man must be feared by his party friends, and then he can hold on."

The big men among the Nazi leaders all had a very robust idea of what they called power. They did not content themselves with political power. Its only value lay in the access it provided to the requisites of actual power. What requisites? Army, navy, and air force above all. Police and administration. Real power is provided also by a leader's own party formation, though here there are great differences in the reality. The sections of the Storm Troops, or S.A., are a factor in power. Still more so are the S.S. sections. But power is conferred also by the masses on those who control the organization that dominates masses and public opinion.

Long before the party came into power in the State there existed among the chief leaders a sort of division of power agreed on in advance. On this division depended Hitler's life and the future of the whole German revolution. No one must be permitted to control too large a share of the factors of power. Hitler could rule only if he could maintain an equilibrium of forces. There must be no concentration of power, no monopoly of power, in anyone's hands. Naturally each of the chief leaders was trying to get that very thing. Each of them considered that nothing could make his own position impregnable but a concentration of the means of power which was stronger than any possible combination against it. Each was constantly on the watch to defend himself. The party's struggle for power over the nation was accompanied at all times by a struggle within the party between the rival chiefs for the greatest share of the requisites of power.

Roehm, with his Storm Troops, controlled the revolutionary masses of the German people. But he wanted also to gain control of the armed forces of the State. With those he counted on becoming the real dictator of Germany and having Hitler on a lead.

Goering claimed not only control of the principal state of the Reich, Prussia, by means of which he counted on being indirectly the real controller of the whole of the German administration; he also demanded supreme command of the air force and at least the Prussian police, with all its secret ramifications. If Goering secured this, he would have under his command a power at least equal to Roehm's, and an absolute predominance if Roehm failed to get the army into his hands. It was therefore to his interest to maintain the independence of the army. His ready support of the wishes of the generals and championing of the professional officers against Roehm's claim to leadership was a very shrewd act of self-defense against what might have been decisive power in the hands of a rival.

High aims like these were out of reach of other party chiefs. Gregor Strasser, Hitler's dangerous rival in the party, was out to gain control of the whole of the party formations, the organs of public administration, and those of social and economic life, particularly the trade unions, which he proposed to form into a great and comprehensive force of Workers' Guards of the revolution. This brought him into conflict with Roehm's similar ambitions for the S.A. Through his control of the economic system, Strasser considered that he would be able to control the whole life of the nation. His breach with Hitler rendered him powerless, and thereafter Hitler succeeded in blocking any similar ambitions on the part of others. Hitler made a division of offices, and gave Hess control of the party, and Ley control of the Labor Front formed out of the trade unions; economic control at that time could not be placed in any single person's hands. If Roehm, Goering, and Strasser had succeeded in their designs, there would have come into existence a genuine triumvirate, in which decisions would have been enforced by the union of any two of the three power-groups.

But there were other chiefs. Himmler was trying to get entire control of the police. After an obstinate struggle, Goering had to cede to him control of the Prussian police. This meant that Himmler was partly under the authority of Goering as Prussian Premier. However, he still had his S.S., the actual revolutionary and, at the same time, counter-revolutionary nucleus organization. The S.S. was as superior to the S.A. as modern cadres specially trained to carry out a coup d'état are to old-style revolutionary mass troops. Here again Himmler was under superior control. He and his S.S. were subordinate to Roehm. When Roehm was shot, Himmler became independent commander of the S.S. under Hitler. Thus it had been in Himmler's interest, in the interest of his pursuit of power, to range himself against his own supreme commander in the massacre of men of the S.A. on June 30, 1934. Later Himmler succeeded also in shaking off Goering's control of the Prussian police.

There was yet another chief, an intellectual—Goebbels, a figure strangely out of place among the robust pretenders to power. His ideas generally went far beyond those of his comrades in the struggle. He kept hold of his position as *Gauleiter* of Berlin, which gave him ample power to go on with. But in his view real power belonged to the controller of public and party opinion. Since every revolution is not only a material struggle but still more a conflict of ideas, the command over men's minds and morale was at least as important as the command of troops. The intellectual command, moreover, was not to be confined to the masses. Its influence must extend to the whole of the leaders, including even the Fuehrer. Goebbels did not dream of restricting himself to the direction of broadcasting and the newspapers. He meant above all to be Hitler's source of information, the regulator of all relations between leaders, the intermediary, the officially appointed Intriguer-General.

Then there were the lesser magnates—Frick, who was out to control the public administration; Darré, with his peasants; and above all, the "Counts of the *Gaue*," the *Gauleiter* or regional bosses, each with his own allotted sector of territorial power. Each of these lesser magnates tried to improve his position and increase his power by gaining important offices in the various formations and spheres of power. A *Gauleiter* would try, perhaps, to get a big post in the S.S. from Himmler, and at the same time to acquire another post in the Labor Front. Through this principle of personal union of offices, each leader was able to extend his sphere of influence, and to secure support in the struggle against his rivals from the great sources of power. He "fortified his position."

This partition of power was an extraordinary phenomenon. There has been nothing quite like it in any other revolution. Was it a sign of internal weakness? Was it a sort of pluralistic administration? Did it mean that Hitler, the only one who commanded no concrete source of power, was fundamentally in a weak position and the plaything of his magnates?

It was not a pluralistic order. It was only a transition, a means to the gradual winning of that exclusive position of authority for making final decisions on all questions, which Hitler sought and has achieved. It was a technical tool with which he succeeded in getting even the *Wehrmacht* and the bureaucracy completely under his control.

It is certainly a mark of Hitler's supreme ability that he has not only maintained his position in face of the real elements of power but has continually imposed his will on them. Hitler lets matters take their course, but at important points he gives them a push, with the utmost accuracy of aim. Roehm did not get the supreme command he wanted of the new *Wehrmacht,* the German military forces in process of creation. Even without Roehm's threat to make Hitler his prisoner and compel him to rule for him, Hitler knew that the combined command over the *Wehrmacht* and the revolutionary Storm Troops would have meant Roehm's actual dictatorship. He cut down Roehm, and so brought over the army to his side; at the same time he was rid of a dangerous pretender to the dictatorship. Goering, in his turn, was allowed to create the *Luftwaffe,* the air force. Hitler did not prevent him from developing it also as a special arm for and against coups d'état.

He could not prevent him from making the air force a sort of universal weapon with pronounced political aims. But Goering was made to give up his police. His office of Prime Minister of Prussia was made purely decorative. Hitler seized every opportunity of restricting the "private armies" of his paladins, and of so distributing the requisites of power that he always remained the deciding factor, always controlled the turn of the scales.

But will this unstable balance, which Hitler has succeeded so far in exploiting, continue indefinitely? At any moment groupings of power might come into existence which would force Hitler to take desperate steps—groupings which would make his effective leadership impossible. The struggle behind the front goes on unceasingly. At times it is a life-and-death struggle.

"He always carries his revolver now, when he goes to his office in the Brown House," said Darré to me in 1932, that critical year of struggle. "We may get a bullet in our hides any moment." At that time the issue was between the groups loyal to Hitler and those who regarded Gregor Strasser as the coming man. The opposing groups were fighting so furiously that they were continually on the verge of bloodshed. Similar violent hostilities were frequent between Nazi magnates. The tension was not as extreme as in 1934 when Hitler resolved to have several thousand party comrades shot. But again and again struggles for power were fought out behind the scenes.

One day in the autumn of 1934 a man with the gold medal of the party came to see me—a member of the S.A. who had escaped from the June massacre. His hatred of the S.S., who had been constituted the firing parties at that mass execution, had not been diminished by Hitler's Reichstag speech after the massacre. This man—incidentally, he had high legal qualifications—was aware of my dislike of Artur Greiser, who later succeeded me as President of Danzig. Greiser was an officer holding a high command in the S.S. My visitor considered, therefore, that it would be a fit and proper thing to kill Greiser as an act of vengeance against the S.S., and imagined that this could be "wangled" with my assistance. It seemed to him to be only natural that I should regard my rival with the same sort of hatred that he felt. If the result was my own "bumping off," so much the better—one reactionary the fewer.

Similar suggestions had been made to me before. The naïveté of these confidential proposals, this advice on the way to "build up one's position," showed how deep-rooted was the idea of a permanent struggle for power among the old party comrades, how much it was regarded as a matter of course. In East Prussia there was latent civil war for two years between rival groups of the party. Beatings to death, assaults, and shootings occurred every few days, not against Communists or reactionaries, but among the party comrades themselves. National Socialism grew up amid internal quarrels. Fratricide lurked at all times behind the door. Such quarrels would have been the ruin of any other party or organization. Yet the Nazi party held together. How entirely the inner clique of leaders must have been dependent on one another! Will the permanent struggle for power end one day in a struggle of all the groups against one another, ending finally in a last gruesome self-annihilation?

4

THE POULTRY FARMER

THE MOST STARTLING grotesques are beyond invention. Gentle rabbits, brainless fowls, inquisitive ducks—that world of innocence and pensive peace was the original basis of the existence of Herr Heinrich Himmler, poultry farmer, head of the Gestapo, and Commanding Officer of the S.S., Hitler's corps of "Black Guards."

This man, to get the right impression of him, should have been seen before he began wearing fine uniforms of black and silver—when he still went about in the plain clothes of the civilian. For without the support of venerability and significance which constitute a brilliant uniform in Germany, Himmler was revealed as the man he really is: the very type of ordinariness. A man barely of medium height, with a face that is no face. Eyes? Has he any? Whether or no, he could not look anyone in the face. He has a sleepy look. An ill-conditioned fellow. Probably with damp hands. One would have summed him up as a dirty little bit of vermin.

One day at a peasants' meeting an insignificant-looking, disgruntled individual suddenly jumped up to the platform. He wanted to speak, but he was prevented. He was pushed down. But he was persistent, and soon was back again on the platform. There came shouts from the hall:

"The man does not belong here! Throw him out! What does the fellow want? How did he get in?"

The proceedings were resumed. After a time he appeared at the back of the hall. I watched him. He was nervously smoking cigarette after cigarette, throwing each one away after a few puffs. He could not stand still for a second. He swayed from the knees. He kept shrugging his shoulders. I looked more closely at him. The man was almost on springs with suppressed passion. His hands shook. His body was tense. There was more to this man than there seemed to be at first.

Suddenly he was back on the platform, and speaking. The agricultural meeting had just closed. Before the peasants making for the door could protest, he was in the midst of tirades about the distress of the peasantry, about the crimes of the Weimar Republic, about Jews and jobbers. He spoke of the salvation of agriculture that could come only from National Socialism.

That was Heinrich Himmler, at a farmers' meeting years before the Nazi seizure of power. Himmler, the most extreme and bloodthirsty of all the revolutionaries of the nihilist revolution, the most remarkable of the Nazi demigods, was then serving as a sideline as the party's agrarian expert. Whether he was much interested in agriculture, I do not know. But he was interested in the revolution. This "gentle Heinrich," who in the Nazi farm, if one had only known it, was fox and wolf and jackal in one, was as seedy-looking and ill-proportioned an individual as Hitler himself. But he did not have what unquestionably distinguished Hitler, the hypnotist's power of suggestion. Whence, then, did the man draw the strength that has enabled him to acquire and retain the immense power he has accumulated in the course of time? How is it that this man, outwardly a vulgar nobody, is nevertheless the greatest revolutionary, after Hitler, of the party?

We met three or four times, in private intercourse on social occasions, and officially. I can give only a few traits of his character. It would be mistaken to describe him as a pawn or as just the figurehead above the ex-naval lieutenant Heydrich, head of the police of the Reich (later, "protector" of Bohemia and Moravia until his assassination in the spring of 1942). He knows his job. He has a mastery of the science of terrorism, of the coup d'état, of conspiracy and of the means of defeating it. His cruelty is not a matter of feeling or passion; it is a carefully contrived, logically developed discipline in the service of the ruling power. He spent years preparing for his work. He studied the literature and technique of revolution, and the methods of criminality. He became an expert in every branch of subversive activity. He instructed Hitler in this discipline. He won him over to a modern and realistic technique of the coup d'état and of the exercise of political power. Goebbels belongs to a widespread type of revolutionary; he is the intellec-

tual revolutionary, mentally alert, inventive in destructive
ideas, and a master of inflammatory speech. Himmler is the
practical, working revolutionary. Instead of speaking, he or-
ganizes revolutionary cadres, forms terrorist groups, uses for
political purposes the methods of the world of international
crime—extortion, maltreatment, theft, murder.

The way this man worked himself up step by step is a
notable passage in the history of criminality. He practiced a
continual deception of those around him, ingratiating as an
agent in a small way, until he had built up for himself an
all-powerful organization and had concentrated in his hands
the most dangerous apparatus of power. He made subtle use
of the fact that he was generally looked down upon and regarded as incompetent. While many National Socialists, to
say nothing of the middle-class Nationalists, contented themselves with the externals of power, Himmler, with his acquired knowledge, assured himself of the reality of power.

"We do not rule with the military, but with the man with
the warrant card," Himmler used to say. He took his own
political ideas from the tactics of gang leaders and the theory
of the modern coup d'état. "The modern State," he said, "is
controlled by the same technique by means of which it is conquered." If he was asked how power can be won in a modern
State, a mass democracy, he pointed to Trotsky. "A State is
not to be conquered by mass revolts nor by military coups,
but by specially drilled, highly trained revolutionary nucleus
groups, which in a surprise assault occupy all the key positions
in the State and in industry."

"The methods developed by the criminal world," he said,
"are the appropriate methods for combating crime. The tactics of the revolution offer the best tactical means of combating revolution." The paradoxical thing about this man is
that although he appears to be at all times in a feverishly
revolutionary frame of mind, he became the Cerberus of the
revolution, its jailer. Though he is in spirit the extremest of

nihilists, his ideas are concerned at all times with the problem of the canalization of the revolution.

In an earlier work I published a few extracts from a talk during which Himmler gave me the benefit of his radically skeptical views as to the value of science. His interest in the things of the mind and of art is confined to the question of their usefulness or perilousness as means of influencing the masses. Nevertheless he was, next after Goebbels, by far the most intellectually active of the Nazi leaders. In talking among colleagues he used clear-cut, surprising phrases, which revealed a keen intelligence and intensive study. On one occasion I spent half a day with him on the estate of a mutual acquaintance, Herr *Obergruppenführer* Lorenz, a sort of general of the S.S., who has since come a good deal into public notice, and is rather a striking personality. Like myself, he was a Prussian cadet, and then an officer. An elegant, good-looking man, he had married a rich and very ambitious woman, and had become a sort of amateur farmer. He farmed his property on the "biological" method of Rudolf Steiner, the anthroposophist, and the result was that the financial return from his farming grew steadily more meager. Lorenz, who later filled a high office in Hamburg, and played a certain part in the background, assumed the appearance of an innocent bon vivant, fond of his joke and of wine and women.

During this visit Himmler, Lorenz, and Artur Greiser shut themselves up for a considerable part of the day in a special conference. I took no part in the conference, but learned later what it was about, both through Himmler and later from the rather talkative Greiser. I give here a summary of the discussion, which seems to me to be of importance because Himmler was on a tour of inspection of the whole of Germany and the subjects mentioned at Danzig were brought up everywhere else.

It was the late autumn of 1933, and the discussion was concerned with the serious situation of Germany and Nazism at that time. Himmler declared that the party must arm itself against an attempt at a military putsch and a counter-revolution under von Papen. It must also be prepared against any rising of the Storm Troopers, who were dissatisfied with Hitler's policy and wanted to see their second, Socialist revolution. The possibility must also be reckoned with of attempts at a general strike on the part of the industrial population. Other Powers, particularly France, Poland, and Czechoslovakia, were trying to upset the internal order in Germany through subversive activities. They found dangerous auxiliaries among the numbers of politically discontented persons in Germany, and there were also dangers of Communist action. At any moment a preventive war might be launched against Germany. But the worst peril of all was the threatened decay of the party. When power had been attained there was not only no unity in regard to future policy but no united group of leaders. The party included a sort of sample collection of all political outlooks in Germany, from crass reactionaries to doctrinaire pacifists and the extremist Left-wing Socialists.

The splitting up of the party into various camps, involving the collapse of the whole German revolution, continued Himmler, was inevitable if stern measures were not adopted. Thus an impressive terroristic act was indispensable. Every branch of the opposition must be intimidated and kept in permanent fear. Many other measures, however, were also needed, and it was these that he had come to discuss. All these questions must be considered in the light of the possibility that war might break out at any time. Consequently they were of the utmost urgency. At any moment Adolf Hitler might be the victim of an assassin. He, Himmler, was earnestly occupied at all times with the protection of the Fuehrer from assassins and conspirators, but he could not guarantee effective protection. It was necessary to create an atmosphere of terror, and not only among the masses and among Marxists and Catholics, but above all among the middle-class Nation-

alists, the so-called allies in the national revolution, the officers, officials, industrial leaders, and Junkers.

We must all be prepared for harsh measures, said Himmler.
He had no use for mealy-mouthed, soft-hearted individuals.
The most useless of all were the ideologues, and unfortunately
the party was full of them. There were lots of them among
the old party comrades. These men were always ranting about
their views and their convictions, and claiming the right of
the "old guard" to criticize. There would have to be a sharp
pruning of them. The training and selection of the S.S. was
one of the principal tasks in the safeguarding of the future.
He would not have in the S.S. a single party comrade, of
however long standing, who gave reason for the slightest
suspicion that he regarded himself as entitled to offer his personal criticism. There must be blind obedience in the S.S.

Himmler described the methods by which he proposed to
create the "atmosphere of terror." To begin with, all existing
groups of so-called leaders must be got rid of, and all classes,
not merely the industrial workers, made leaderless. These
groups included officers, officials, industrialists, Junkers, and
also ministers of religion, teachers, and high school professors.
The scale of treatment was to win them over, apply pressure,
destroy. He recommended the first method. The best means
of winning persons over was corruption and the exploiting of
human weaknesses—alcohol, gambling, debts, women, boys.
Ambition, envy, greed were useful auxiliaries. The first thing
was to know all about these people. Index cards must be
accumulated and dossiers collected. All this must be scien-
tifically done. No amateurishness! It was not a matter for
petty informers. They might, indeed, spoil everything. Bureaus
for the combating of corruption, such as had been set up in
many parts of the country, were nonsense. On the contrary—
let the swamp flora grow merrily! Keep registers! Keep
silence—and then, at the critical moment, send a friendly invitation to the man: Look here, we know all about you. Will

you do what we want with a good will, or shall we leave it to the public prosecutor?

Himmler called that the noiseless revolution. It was far more effective, he said, than shouting and menaces and cocky speeches. "Get them all into the cadres of the S.S., these barons and young aristocrats!" he said. "Once they are in, we shall have them under control. They will belong to me, and woe to them if they do not obey. Don't be afraid of their spoiling our cadres. We shall tame them, not they us. I know the Stahlhelm and the German Nationalists have given the word to get into the party, gain influence, work up to the leading posts, and corrupt the National Socialists. They will have the surprise of their lives. One year will be enough for me to make such a change in them all that they will no longer remember what they used to think and believe. We will give them successful careers. They'll eat into the army for me. They'll permeate and win over the officials. Get them all in, the young sons of the old nobility! Each of the youngsters will drag not only his old papa but a lot of old uncles into our zone of influence.

"Only, no mistaken jealousy! The big jobs are not all reserved for old party comrades. The old *Pg's* (*Parteigenossen* —party comrades) can wait. We are sure of them. But the correct officials, the men who are proud of their immaculacy, we must have them. Just note down each little peccadillo, money irregularities, other men's wives, tampering with documents, French leave, whatever it may be. Everybody has his hidden record."

Himmler was a typical representative of the lower middle class, with its envy and hatred of the more fortunate classes; and he despised the past ruling groups. But instead of the sanguinary conflicts of earlier revolutions he considered it better to take the path of corruption. It was less expensive and less dangerous. He went on to make a sharp attack on Roehm, leader of the Storm Troopers, as a frivolous, out-of-date ama-

THE POULTRY FARMER 29

teur revolutionist. Roehm imagined, he said, that he had organized the revolutionary masses in his Storm Troops. All Roehm had really done, said Himmler, was to create an ex-service men's association in which the revolutionary spirit had degenerated into beer drinking and boasting. He, Himmler, cared no more for revolutionary emotion than for heroic feelings in the troops on the battlefield. He valued the efficiency and adaptability of special troops of a nucleus organization, men who had undergone practical training, more than all the revolutionary feelings hatched out by idle intellectuals. Roehm, with a mass of Philistines stuck into brown shirts, whom he regarded as the advance guard of the revolution, was trying to attain ends of which he, Himmler, was assured without any noise or any mass play-acting. To get the Reichswehr under his control required entirely different maneuvers from the setting in motion of the masses.

The true purpose of the S.S. was just what Himmler had stated. It was to be the nucleus organization, working with precision and drilled for special objects, of the permanent coup d'état. Protection from counter-revolution was to be secured by the same cadres with which, if the need arose, a coup d'état would be led. The revolution of dynamism is nothing but a permanent coup d'état.

As for the admission of members of the old aristocracy to the S.S., Himmler largely succeeded, and with the result he anticipated. The young men of so-called good social position did not gain the influence over the S.S. of which they dreamed; it was they themselves whose backbone was broken. They became diligent students of nihilism. They were soon the best and most rabid of the officers in Himmler's coup d'état forces.

A few months later I had the doubtful honor of an official visit from Himmler during a new tour of inspection. His motor car was driven by young Prince Dohna-Schlobitten, a scion of one of the oldest Prussian families. He was a simple

S.S. man, and came in his uniform. Over our beer in the
evening at my house, in an incautious moment, I asked the
prince what had brought him into the party. He stammered
a few enthusiastic words about Germany's future greatness. It
was evident that his reasons were of a different nature. His
properties were on the verge of bankruptcy. He had to obtain influence among the new rulers if he was not to lose
everything. It was the specter of the expropriation and settlement of their estates that drove many Junkers into the arms
of the Nazis. But there were yet other grounds. Their capitulation was hidden from their own eyes, and their self-respect
preserved, by the slogan which Himmler himself cunningly
promoted: "Into the party cadres, in order to gain influence
and ultimately control."

Only those who had the opportunity of witnessing this
whole process from within are competent to form any judgment of this subtle contest, this competition in cunning, this
tricking of the tricksters, this whole witches' sabbath of craftiness and despair and self-delusion.

Himmler was a friend of Darré, who succeeded him as the
party's agrarian expert. Darré held very high rank in the S.S.
Both men were interested in the racial improvement of the
German people. Darré kept a sort of stud-book of the S.S.,
with precise genealogical tables for every member. The S.S.
was to be not only the revolutionary or counter-revolutionary
nucleus organization but also the racial élite of the German
people. Here the new nobility was to grow up. A new nobility
of blood, not of patent or of business success.

This was a curious fancy in Himmler, the cold revolutionary and policeman, but very characteristic of the German
revolution, in which radical rationalism is coupled with a
biological mysticism. It is easy to understand a radical revolutionary who has chosen the wildest and most unscrupulous
and brutal elements from all classes to form a Praetorian
Guard for the revolution. One can understand an Al Capone

being promoted to be the guardian of a State and its supreme
policeman. Many a landowner has turned his most dangerous
poacher into the most efficient of keepers. But an Al Capone
who proposes to make his people "racially efficient," and to
convert his gang into the racial élite of his people, is a grotesque, unique in history.

In Germany even the Al Capones turn philosopher. Himmler feels himself to be the savior of the human race. Why have
the great peoples of history perished? he argues. Because they
no longer had a master class left among them. A nobility of
blood gave place to a nobility of trade and wealth. When the
ruling classes have become nothing more than a millionaire
mob, the nation's historic doom is sealed. But why should that
degeneration not be arrested? An aristocracy can be trained.
A cruel, conscienceless, physically highly trained élite, maintained by the harshest discipline—to create something of that
sort is to preserve a nation from decay. Revolution means the
rise of new leader groups. The meaning of the great new
revolution is nothing else than the endowment of the world
with a new master race. In the revolutions of the past the new
leader groups were thrown up by chance. The masters of the
historic revolutions were chance leaders. That is why no successful revolution ever lasted long. Those leaders were unable
to maintain their success. Together with the supposed achievements of their revolutions, they sank back into obscurity.

A revolution can win through only if it brings into power
a master class that understands how to use power, an enduring, self-renewing class, transmitting its rules of leadership
and its discipline from generation to generation. It must be
rooted in the land. It must make itself responsible for its
families, and must have the prospect of long-continued success.
It must be prolific. The best thing is to settle it, as Darré
proposes, in special nobles' estates, in entailed properties on
conquered soil. As guardians of the frontiers, in an imperiled
situation under the nose of a foreign nation, their superior

strength as lords of all around them must be continually in evidence. So will they be made a class of masters of the State and at the same time a source of the racial renovation of the world.

Such is Himmler's argument. Like Darré, he is a biological revolutionary. "Have you realized," he said in one of our talks, "that we are witnessing a vast process of biological division of the human race? Man is undergoing a biological mutation. In future there will be two species of man." I did not encourage him to pursue the subject. I had heard much the same thing from Hitler. But, preposterous though it may sound, it is just this that is seductive in Nazism. It has the ring of a childish, low-brow version of ideas which so many people have already had, intellectuals of all sorts of schools, men both of the Right and the Left.

The sense of belonging to a new species of humanity has been implanted by Himmler and Darré and Hitler in the rising revolutionary élite, which acts on the strength of that sense. Himmler, once a breeder of small livestock, now marshal of the Gestapo, no longer breeds rabbits and geese; he breeds men. And out of the great ferment of the world revolution he imagines that he is breeding the new man.

5

THE ETERNAL PAGAN

"REVOLUTIONS THAT EXHAUST themselves in the cities are not events of secular importance. Only when the peasantry are on the move does a nation enter a new epoch."

It was Darré who dished up that portentous generalization for us. Darré, whose talent for organization had enabled him to create the Nazi party Bureau for Agrarian Affairs (*Agrarpolitischer Apparat*), became the *whipper-in of the peasants.*

There is a measure of truth in that statement of his. Even the Marxist Socialists had grasped the fact, if somewhat late. They tried to revolutionize the peasants. But entirely in accordance with their system of ideas. They tried to draw the rural population into the class war. They played off the agricultural employees and workers against the landowners. They tried to set the landed peasantry into opposition to the larger owners. They squeezed the farmer's life into the Procrustes' bed of their economic doctrine. What resulted was anything but a revolutionizing of the peasantry.

The peasant farmer, together with the agricultural laborer and many of the large landowners, belongs, on the Continent of Europe, to a pre-capitalist order. He is not to be impressed by economic slogans, in spite of the proverbial acquisitiveness of the peasant. Marxism failed to realize this. But Nazism grasped the fact. It was Darré who interpreted the problem of the peasant to Hitler in a way he could follow. The revolutionizing of the peasant then meant winning him over to National Socialism. It was considered that Nazism would never enter into power without the support of the peasants. But that would not be achieved merely by promising economic advantages. The peasant is by nature suspicious. He will place no faith in benefactors who set out to make him presents without demanding something in return. National Socialism attacked him from another angle.

Scratch the peasant's regular routine of life, with its incrustations of relics of ancient traditions, and everywhere there are revealed hidden vestiges of immemorial mythology and a paganism that governs, not his actual thoughts, but his subconscious reactions. From weather lore to the no longer intelligible customs and ancient magic rites to which he clings, he lives in a world that contains many elements of the ages before the coming of rationalism. His conception of property, his immersion in the life of the homestead, his conceptions of work and remuneration are influenced by elements to which the political agitator from the cities is as complete a stranger as the white colonial is to the primitive savage.

The world of the primitive man cannot be set in motion by rational propaganda, but only by rousing his subconscious self. That is just what Nazism did. It appealed to certain primitive instincts of the peasantry. It lured them into listening to the earthbound voices that recalled memories of an age long before civilization and Christianity.

I observed the process of revolutionary subversion among the German peasantry from very close at hand. We farmers, far from realizing what was in the wind, listened to Darré's argument that what was wanted was the liberation of the peasant from the clutches of sterile economic rationalism. The American farmer, he explained, treats his profession as an economic occupation like any other. He easily gives it up, he is not rooted in his profession. He is indifferent to the requirements of the soil; he lives only by the ruthless exploitation of the fertility of his fields. That may do well enough for two or three decades; then he abandons his farm—it is becoming a desert. He is compelled to live in this way by the economic laws of profits and prices. So long as he remains subject to these laws, his life is passed in progressive self-destruction. He ruins his private existence, and he also ruins the irreplaceable soil. There is no stopping the process of turning vast regions of once fruitful soil, of which the fertility was maintained or increased through thousands of years, into barren wasteland. The process is only accelerated by the use of artificial fertilizers. Mankind is marching toward crises of unimaginable dimensions.

Darré worked on these ideas, right in themselves, ideas which have long filled many thinking agriculturists with concern for the future. But he used them to spin the threads of political seduction with quite other objectives. How, he asked, can this suicidal agrarian policy be stopped? By continually tightened rationalization of the farms, by the subtlest calculation, by struggling for every fraction of a pfennig that can be added to the profit on working? Or by a Liberal agrarian policy, allowing the economic law of competition to wreak bankruptcy on the farms until the farmer has been found who produces at the minimum prime cost?

"No," replied Darré, "that is not the way at all. The peasant farmer must not only be freed from the Liberal system; it must be recognized that he does not follow an economic occupation in the ordinary sense. His purpose is not to make money but to support a family. Agriculture follows economic laws of its own. It cannot be confined within the modern capitalist commercial system. It does not even belong to the pre-capitalist commercial system. It must be given the conditions it needs. It can breathe and live only in an independent economic province. That sort of thing cannot be achieved through politicians who regard as impossible everything that lies outside current ideas. Even the so-called agrarian parties, the Conservative German Nationalists with their Hugenberg, the *Reichslandbund* or National Land Union with Count Kalkreuth at its head, even these groups think only in capitalist terms, in categories of Liberal economics, and are therefore unfitted to offer any real guarantee of the farmer's vital rights. Only the revolutionary movement of National Socialism has the strength to recover for agriculture its proper place as the highest, the leading class. Higher even than its occupation of feeding the nation is its mission to serve as the source of the renewal of the blood of the nation. The towns die out. They depend for existence on a permanent influx from the country. Without that source of life in the families on the land, the Western nations would perish, just as the peoples of the Mediterranean were desiccated and burned up in their city colonies."

Darré hammered ideas of this sort into us. We were convinced that they were right, and we found ready listeners in our professional colleagues. The peasant is more or less con-

MILLS COLLEGE
LIBRARY

scious of belonging to a different way of life than the townsman's. Others may rail at him as a stupid peasant because
they cannot follow his slow and alien logic, but like anyone
else he feels his own way of life to be normal, and judges the
townsman's life by it. Nazi propaganda worked on the agri-
culturist's self-esteem. It did not address him as a backward
semi-savage. It did not talk to him with ill-concealed pity and
condescension, "as if he were a sick horse"; it set out, on the
contrary, to increase his self-assurance. It overcame his inferiority complexes, cultivated for centuries. Suddenly everybody of importance set himself down as a peasant, or of a
peasant family. Thus the peasant grew ready to rebel against
ideas and views which up to then he had felt to be unnatural
but with which he had put up as an inescapable burden
against which rebellion was of no more use than against bad
weather or cattle plagues or any other blow of fate.

In this way, in a few years of acute agricultural crisis the
German peasant, until then a patient and generally unpoliti-
cal, indeed unhistoried class, was won for a revolution not
concerned at all with the restoration of the peasant to his old
rights, as the most ancient class in human society, but with
a revolution aiming at something entirely different.

The paradoxical result was achieved, here as elsewhere, of
tempting the peasant with the opposite of what was really
afoot. Darré showed him a Promised Land of tradition, tempting him with the restoration of his independent status, with
liberation from urban control. He was promised security of
tenure and recognition of the peculiar nature of his calling.
The peasant's customs, his proverbs, his way of thought, his
old faith, even his superstitions were acclaimed. By bringing all these things into the foreground and making him conscious of them, by continually talking about them, by making
festivals of them, and by erecting them into a preposterous
substitute for religion, they were robbed of their value, torn
from their roots; and the peasant, like other classes, was de-

livered into the hands of skepticism, unscrupulousness, and finally nihilism. He was unsettled and revolutionized, the even tenor of his life was upset, and the very things that were ostensibly to have been preserved and fostered were destroyed. Instead of a separate economic province for agriculture there was built up an all-powerful machine that turned the German peasantry into a single vast, all-comprehending collectivity. In this there remained no vestige of the things that had filled the peasant's life. Under the grotesque make-believe of a struggle for freedom, the peasantry were delivered up by Nazism to a new servitude, a new serfdom. In place of dependence on the changing conditions of a market alleged to be manipulated by smart city dealers and Jew speculators, there came total dependence on the State.

It took the peasants a long time to discover the deception. I am not sure that the bulk of them yet see clearly the perilous condition to which they have been reduced. Good prices have concealed for years the fact of the collectivization of agriculture. Agriculture is today a branch of the public service. The peasant is a civil servant, and one who is tied to his post.

Was this a deliberate, cunning piece of deception, or has it all come inevitably, against the intentions of those responsible? I am inclined to believe that both the one and the other are true. Darré is a shrewd organizer, with a passion for organization. It was his ambition to organize agriculture on a military model. His directing staff was a copy of the army General Staff. But his first ideas undoubtedly ran in the direction of a peasantry with an independent status. He belonged originally to the revolutionary Conservatives, whose conservative ideas are always at issue with their modern methods of organization. The result is that they carry into practice not the ideas but only the methods of organization. The saving of the peasantry—that was the ideological deception. The machinery was the reality. All that remained of the grandiose enterprise of peasant liberation was a very efficient subjection of the peasantry to the public authorities. Bolshevism has achieved nothing approaching it.

That was not all. At the first agricultural exhibition after the Nazi seizure of power Darré allowed himself to be acclaimed as the great liberator of the peasants. But in addition to this, although less openly, Darré took the credit for the spiritual liberation of the peasantry from their most dangerous oppressor—Christianity.

Cautiously, but with steady purpose, Darré took up the struggle against Christianity. He succeeded very gradually, but very effectively, in shattering the Christian traditions among the German peasantry. He steered clear of the coarseness and brutality of Julius Streicher. He was craftier even than Hitler. He showed the more positive sides of an un-Christian belief in the forces of nature, the gods of fertility, of life and death, of race. From old and forgotten customs and sagas and folk tales he deduced a sort of half subconscious, half vigorously alive primeval faith. This he claimed to be far superior to the Jewish-Christian religious conceptions, and to give the peasant the thing he sought in his many hours of lonely work, the answer to the riddles of life, an answer in face of which there is neither sin nor salvation. Subtly and effectively this new faith was instilled drop by drop into the peasant through every conceivable channel—magazines, exhibitions, recreations. This propaganda is worth studying. It is of the same order as Goebbels' mass propaganda, but in my opinion much subtler and more dangerous.

Why did Darré want to wean the peasants from their Christian faith? There is only one answer—to revolutionize them. The peasant was to become the battering-ram of the great world revolution. He had to be set in motion, and he had first to be made spiritually detached. He had to become ready for great adventures. He had to be divorced in spirit from his slow, shackled life, in order to be prepared to take part in the modern form of the barbarian invasions, in vast conquering migrations which would mark the main lines of a new age.

Darré's struggle against the Christian peasants for a new pagan peasantry is more than a fad. It is the kernel of his agrarian policy. Outsiders used to wonder at it, and to laugh at the continual inclusion in the agricultural periodicals, alongside serious articles, of these articles on pagan beliefs, plant worship, and so on, with veiled attacks on Christianity. But they were there for a purpose, and they were of more importance than the technical education of the peasant.

There is, however, an inconsistency between this romantic revolutionizing and the super-rational collectivizing of the peasant, subjecting him to the machinery of a vast organization. Such inconsistencies belong to the fundamental facts of our harassed existence. Men like Darré, for all their air of rationalism and of magnificent planning, do not act rationally. They act instinctively, like all revolutionaries, even when they preach the gospel of economic and social planning. They become dominated by a revolutionary temperament that urges them to the destruction of everything in the old order they meet with. It does not matter in itself what interpretation they offer of the fact, but it is certainly of interest to a later period. Here is what Darré himself had to say to his closer intimates about the "greatest peasant revolution of all times."

"There can never again be any turning back. Humanity must make an end, once for all, of this degenerate Christian epoch of faintheartedness and spiritlessness. Man must be strong. Man must be entirely rooted in this world. Dominance, harshness is our duty!"

Darré is no orator. He speaks haltingly, lifelessly. He is rather better as a writer, but still wooden and uninspired. There is nothing in his speeches or writings that would suggest that he is one of the real driving forces among the leaders of this nihilistic revolution. He told us once that we should grow old and gray in this struggle. We were destined to grow prematurely old. We were using ourselves up like a candle burning at both ends. But he did not complain of it. It was the mission of our generation to start on its course the greatest movement of all times. Man had to be saved as a biological creature, as nature's highest breed. He did not know where we were going. Even the Fuehrer did not know. There lay his greatness—in spite of this he dared everything at every point and staked his whole existence. He would win. That was our course, and it was all we knew, and all we really needed to know at present. Perhaps the National Socialists would be remembered through all ages as the greatest destroyers in the history of the world. All reserves must be thrown into this struggle. The last reserves were the peasants. That would mean the destruction of the last remains of a primitive society, with the whole of its unbroken strength and power of regeneration. This was extremely perilous. He was just as well aware of it as the Fuehrer. It might exhaust the German nation, perhaps the whole civilized world, exhaust it utterly. But the venture must be made. Power must so be released. The power that would rejuvenate the world.

Christianity, Darré went on to say, was the mortally dangerous doctrine of a suicidal race. It sealed the death of the great civilizations, the death of races and of free men. The struggle against Christianity could be brought to a victorious conclusion only by the unbroken strength of the peasants, who had never been completely Christianized. Not the atheistic, frivolous proletarian of the great cities was called to lead the struggle; if he did, it would end in a superstition even more pernicious and destructive than Christianity. Only the peasant, with his faith in the powers of nature, could really liberate the world from the nightmare of Christianity. The peasant, who witnessed daily the practical demonstration of the value of race. The peasant, who was familiar with the conception of breeding. The peasant, who knew that life knows nothing of the conception of equality but only of quality and of organic structure.

Darré then gave us his ideas of a new constitution for the peasantry. He showed the tasks of the landowner who, he said, was in no way out of date but had important duties of education and example. The normal farm for the free peasant should be of the size that could be cultivated with a team of four horses. He condemned small holdings as demoralizing. He put forward his idea of the "nursery farms," on which the best racial élite should be settled as a new aristocracy. He showed the necessity of improving the human race by systematic breeding. He explained the gigantic task of the compilation of a stud-book of the whole German people, in which each family should be registered with the chief traits of its heredity. Systematic breeding on the basis of the best blood lineage would effect, in the course of generations of selection, the elimination of the meaner components of the German nation. But this elimination by breeding must be confined as an esoteric doctrine to the German race, and not extended to the other races, the Slavs and the Mediterranean peoples.

Men must be liberated, said Darré in conclusion, from the falsified outlook on life for which Christianity was responsible, before the great ideas of a systematic perfection of humanity could be comprehended. The struggle for human liberation was not concerned with material alleviations of the burdens of life or the spread of so-called technical advances, which liberalistic and socialistic doctrinaires praised as human progress. With all this comfort men were going to ruin just as certainly as in the close atmosphere of Christianity. For that reason National Socialism was the enemy of both "Jewish" Christianity and Jewish liberalistic-socialistic doctrinairism. Only we, the revolutionary peasants, could preserve the meaning and the mission of life. Life would sink if it ceased to rise. "The raising of life is the meaning of the revolution."

At its climaxes this Nazi revolution was always half a

Wagner opera. The other half was cunning conspiracy. Yet these Parsifal-Young Siegfried tirades were the expression of genuine feeling. We were then under the influence of suggestion—the suggestion that we were witnessing the beginning of a great world epoch. I could see the impression made on my professional colleagues, on farmers all over Germany. They were influenced, not by the actual content of the appeal to them, but by a fanatical will. I must admit that I, too, was under the influence of its suggestive force.

This Darré was a fanatic, a revolutionary, in spite of his cold-blooded nature. So began the drilling of the peasants, who plunged head over heels into the new adventure.

6

THE LITTLE MONSTER

GOEBBELS, THE "DOCTOR," was not very popular in the party. Forster, who was well informed about internal party matters and about the party magnates, was not the only one to warn me, with a gesture of contempt, not to have too much to do with the man. He was dangerous. A useful man, Forster said, but not a genuine National Socialist. From other quarters in the party, too, I heard nothing but disapproving remarks about Goebbels. The simple party comrades had very soon got the feeling that he somehow did not fit in properly with the National Socialist style. The initiated probably had more solid grounds for disowning this dialectician among the German revolutionaries as an alien element.

The first time I heard him in public I had the same feeling. "He belongs," I said to myself, "to another school of revolutionism." He belonged to the big city, the asphalt streets, the proletarian quarter; this talk was all logic-chopping, pure culture of intellectual extremism, ready to assume any color, red or blue or pink. The subject of Goebbels' speech on this occasion was as popular as could be; it had the strange title, "Political photo-mounting." Political phantasmagoria, I kept thinking, as the little man with the limp and the excessively big head and the sonorous voice delivered a malevolent, over-smart, fundamentally empty and even unexciting review of current political figures and problems. "The secret representative of Communism in the party," said a prominent party member to me later in Berlin. Goebbels understood the technique of subversion and incitement. Did he understand anything else?

Later I saw this Mephistophelean little *Spottgeburt aus Dreck und Feuer,* this "vile abortion of filth and fire," in Faust's words, at close quarters, and I had a few conversations with him which told me enough about him. He was one of those morbid intellectuals, torn by ambition and hunger for power, who saw in a revolution the great opportunity of getting real power into their hands. If radical intellectuals like Lenin and Trotsky could bring down and build up realms, and perhaps rule the world, then it could be done still better with the German nation at one's back. Left unsatisfied by all other "adventures of the spirit," this unsuccessful writer threw himself into the waves of a revolution like Stavrogin in Dostoevski's *The Possessed.* He would have been at bottom the familiar type of revolutionary, if he had not been the pre-eminent example of the utter lack of any doctrine, any ideological mission, in the German nihilistic revolution.

"These people have no future; that is why they cling so much to the present." I noted these words of Goebbels' in a talk I had with him. I no longer remember the connection in which they were spoken. Perhaps he was referring to the democracies; perhaps only to the men of the middle class which he so hated, clinging to their little jobs or offices because they had a vague but justified feeling that their day was over. But perhaps the phrase still better fits the "Doctor"

himself, the eagerness with which he threw his arms round
the present, enjoying everything except the one prize which,
with all his tactical maneuvers, he had not yet been able to
win, the possession of real power.

The "Doctor"—he was a man with a certain literary and
historical education—was aware, with the morbid gift of an-
ticipation of the radical intellectual, of the direction which
this whole Nazi movement was taking. The great division of
epochs had come. It mattered nothing whether a man proceeded from Bolshevism or Facism; the only thing that mattered was whether he was for subversion or conservation.
There is only a single party of revolutionaries, as there is only
a single party of reactionary conservation. If one has grasped
this mystery, one knows one's real friends and enemies. One
also knows the right weapons with which to achieve victory.
Only the stupid fool who does not trust himself to accept
real life, full life in all its cruelty, to enjoy, to rule, is not on
the side of the revolution. But what is the meaning today of
being on the side of the revolution? Can a Liberal be on that
side, an advocate of reasonable, moderate progress? Is the
class-conscious worker, fighting for wage increases, on the
side of the revolution? Are all the petty phrasemakers on that
side, the men who plume themselves on being in thought and
feeling "on the side of human liberty," those hysterical individuals, eaten up with envy, who are eager for a fundamental
reformation of the world and for the introduction of universal
State planning, but at home cannot even manage their wife
and their spoiled child? All these cocks crowing on their
dunghills to announce the European revolution and continually fighting for freedom and the future at imaginary barricades? All those crazy utopians and planners, to say nothing
of the goody-goody humanitarians who prostitute themselves
for a world of eternal peace? The motley army of Philistines,
the "rebel" Bohemians—are all these on the side of the real,
the great revolution?

Revolution today is a launching into the unknown, is the brutal destruction of the things of yesterday out of a cruel lust for annihilation. It no longer wants equality, but the noble, gay inequality of the creative life. It is not fraternity, but the intoxicating struggle for power, the eternally dangerous gamble for success, for high place, for dominance: the steeling struggle for existence, the nobly brutal struggle of the jungle, life for life, in which the victory is to the strong and the strong is the lord of the jungle. He alone is free. For liberty, too, is not for the masses, but only for the sons of the gods—for the truly free spirits, the pioneers of a new human race that has liberated itself from the chains of a millennial servitude to the moral doctrines that are the enemies of life.

Such is revolution today as Goebbels sees it. It is a great adventure. Nothing but that. And it no longer holds promises of blessings for humanity. Anyone who still has aspirations has not yet given himself up entirely to this delirious movement, he is only half a revolutionary. Such are the dreams of this ill-grained little Doctor, who was credited in Geneva with the "Latin spirit." He looks upon himself as a man of the Renaissance, and in reality he has the cold cruelty and the studied falseness of those earlier writers, beyond good and evil, who were the first to betray the spirit in order to sun themselves in the radiance of brutal power.

I will not repeat what I have already written on other occasions about Goebbels. How, for instance, he has remained, when all is said, a little stinking insect. How he crawls in false friendship to all those from whom he can suck power, and how he is coldly contemptuous and brutal wherever he feels that he is the stronger. To know what he is in reality and always will be, and to see him in the light thrown upon him by his many adventures and the scandalous stories of him, is not enough for an assessment of his character and his significance. It is necessary to know how this cripple regards himself, what he thinks he sees in his mirror.

War, to this physically weak person who has never had anything to do with soldiering, is a necessary but essentially outmoded and ridiculous thing. He is no more a militarist than a patriot. Hitler, whom he utterly hates because, though profoundly inferior to him in intellect, he is nevertheless at the head of the revolution, where Goebbels really ought to be—Hitler, with his passion for all things military, is absurd. To go on dreaming today of battles and victories in the old style, and to have the ambition to be "the greatest warlord of all times," is a ridiculous folly. There will be no more world wars, but only world revolutions. A war, it is true, is inevitable as the beginning of the last phase of a revolution. Hitler, as the revolutionary of a first or second phase, is really used up already. He belongs to the older generation, whereas he, Goebbels, may count himself as belonging to the younger, triumphant generation.

Nations may seem to be battling for world domination. But the future war will turn at a critical point into open revolution. Suddenly it will no longer be nations that are in conflict, but classes and groupings. The masses of all lands will rise against their directing classes. At that point, when the war has become meaningless, the Doctor's chance will come. Not until this chaos has arrived will the summons come to the shaper of the new—the modern Caesar.

The new Caesar will have no resemblance to the old. He will have the stamp of an entirely new type of ruler. We can have only a dim notion of his quality. And there is no need to try to visualize it more clearly until it is revealed in his active presence.

All this will sound fantastic and absurd. But recent years have shown how much that is fantastic has become audacious reality. It will be asked how I know it all. I have it at call in various statements which, when put together, become a mirror that reflects the carefully concealed truth, the jealously preserved secret. Hitler and his friends were well aware that the

"Doctor" was in reality their enemy, pursuing ends and aims of which they knew nothing. Goebbels is and always has been surrounded by mistrust and deep dissimulation. It was this mistrust that accounted for his being set down as a Bolshevist in disguise, though he cares no more for Socialism and Communism than for patriotism and nationalism. Germany? The testing ground for revolution. Socialism? Nothing but a means to an end—a means to revolution, but never the goal of one. Long before the party's arrival in power Goebbels had written the famous article in which he pointed out the kinship between National Socialism and Bolshevism. At times he spoke enthusiastically in favor of a peaceful permeation of Bolshevism by Nazism and a German-Russian symbiosis. But to his confidants he always showed how clearly he realized that Communism is at all times simply a path leading to a new system of private property and private capital, and that the classless society is bound to lead to a new class formation with a new grading of incomes. The whole revolutionary process in our Western civilization remains always a simple rotation with no more result than the changing of places. Thus he also spoke of a "symbiosis of élites," in other words, of the Nazi and Bolshevik party leaders. But his own thoughts were concerned with breaking out of the circle of the old process in our civilization into a new course in the void.

Sometimes he played with the idea (and it was certainly not just an idle speculation) that it might become necessary to let the rising radicalism work itself out and run its course. He said he knew his Berlin workers very well. The moment might come when Nazism must seek new and firmer ground. Perhaps before some great crisis. It might be that the only safe course then would be to throw over the helm and enter into the closest collaboration with Communism both in home and foreign policy. If there came, for instance, a conflict with the army, the closest cooperation with the Communist workers in the Reich and with Bolshevism in Russia would produce

revolution and war simultaneously, in face of which the whole
lot of the generals would shut up like a pocketknife.

That was a few months before June 30, 1934. I do not
know how true it is that Goebbels had advised Hitler to resist
the army, or whether he conspired against Hitler and the
army for a time, perhaps with Roehm, and what it was that
then induced him to side once more with Hitler.

Knowing nothing about the truth of these things, I had
repeatedly tried to win Goebbels over to a moderate foreign
policy. I was used to having to deal with a robust type of
Nazi, and, assuming that this intellectual would be more likely
to appreciate the motives of my own policy, I overcame my
repugnance to this reptile. But Goebbels did not fall in with
my ideas. He insisted that there was no possibility of war,
"unless we ourselves want it." With reference to Britain and
France he said: "Those people have grown too comfortable
to cut down their high standard of living, even for a few
years, in order to maintain their position for the future."

He seemed to be particularly satisfied at the growing political tension and confusion, and advised me not to worry about
temporary difficulties. "We have to get used to working with
high-tension current." Later, when I proposed to call on him,
he refused to receive me. Instead I had an informative talk
with one of his adjutants, an ex-police officer still suffering
severely from wounds received in the last war. This officer
was unaffected by criticism of Goebbels and was completely
devoted to him; he regarded him as not only the cleverest
but the noblest and most helpful of men, a true philanthropist,
and a good comrade who treated him with the greatest consideration at times when his war wound afflicted him.

The "Doctor," he said, was the most brilliant man conceivable. It was a pity that the Fuehrer did not provide him
with the field of activity that was really his due. So far as
this officer could judge, Dr. Goebbels had entirely new ideas
which might be described as a revolutionary strategy. In a

future war, for instance, the supreme command might not lie in the hands of the military. Such a war would no longer consist only of armed conflicts; these would have to conform very closely to a general plan drawn up not by any means from purely military considerations.

As a former officer, such ideas had naturally been thoroughly alarming to him at first. Not to attack, for instance, when from a military standpoint the attack should be made, but to wait for the right political and psychological moment, had seemed to be really an astonishing idea. How was the right moment to be determined? But in the end he had seen the point of it all. The "Doctor" had the idea of waging war in the way a revolution or a coup d'état is carried out. The military would not come into action until the last moment—for a sort of spring cleaning when everything was already cut and dry. Before that the enemy must be politically disintegrated. He must be crippled by divisions. When that had been done, the rest was merely a sort of pursuit of a beaten enemy.

Wars today, he continued, are no longer carried on with vast masses of troops, but with highly trained, totally mechanized special troops. But unfortunately there was a disinclination to employ these in the right way. They were used on the old military lines—"pincers" movement, outflanking, encirclement, Cannae! That was a mistake. The generals always rejected revolutionary ideas at first. But the day would come when they would have to accept them. The day would come when, for instance, the wide spaces for operations, of which the military were so fond, would no longer be had, and a confined space strategy would have to be worked out—when there was simply no field of operations in which to fight.

"The Doctor," said his adjutant, "thinks that in future wars there will be no fighting lines, but there will also be no deep fighting zones as in 1918. The war will be really total, that is to say, universal; it will be everywhere. Feeling in the enemy country will be worked on in advance. Disunity will be sown among the ruling classes. An opposition group will be won over. Perhaps it will be possible to start putsches, to stage a notable change of government, to engineer unrest and strikes. Suddenly countless detachments of specially trained troops land from the air. They do not attack the enemy, but try to avoid him. The aim of the strategic plan is no longer, as in past wars, the destruction of the enemy forces; the aim in the modern warfare of the future is to seize or destroy at a stroke all the keypoints of political, economic, and social life. Communications will be destroyed, and life brought to a standstill. There will be no struggle between armies. The enemy's forces will have, instead, to attack all over the country in order to recapture the occupied points.

"Can you imagine the confusion!" concluded the adjutant, looking at me in triumph. "The old government has been captured or killed; the whole of the machinery of the State is in the hands of the conqueror or destroyed or put out of action. If the plan has only partial success, the confusion will be so great that the final act then following, the military attack in force from without, is absolutely bound to succeed. Everything has been worked out down to the smallest detail. Every detachment has its special duty, in which it is carefully trained in model operations. Bear in mind the unrest already created in the enemy country, the political dissensions, the revolutionary efforts, the strike movements; assume downcast skies, and then the moment of complete surprise in the midst of peace, or of conditions approximating to peace—that is the 'Doctor's' idea."

That vision is similar, incidentally, to ideas Hitler himself suggested. It has not yet been carried out in its entirety. Some of these ideas have been used, but for the rest the old military plans have continued to be followed. The new potentialities of mechanized arms have been tried out first. But it may be that the new ideas will be applied one day where all these new arms no longer suffice.

At that time I regarded such ideas as the creation of a mad revolutionary. Today I begin to understand the contempt Goebbels plainly showed me in our few meetings. That revolutionary regarded the men who were unable to think as he did, in terms of new continents and of the phases of a world revolution, with all the arrogance of the man with knowledge in the presence of the ignorant. At a moment when the war has been fought to exhaustion or enters a critical phase, he is the man who might succeed in tearing up the home fronts in all nations and whipping up the masses into a great, open, universal revolt. He may try to weld together Nazism and Bolshevism and the proletarians of all countries into a single powerful bloc. It may be that he will then unfurl the flag of the most radical Socialism. It may be he who will lead the final thrust of the revolution, with a wild cry for peace: Proletarians of all countries, fight against your warmongers! The "Doctor" is still waiting for his great opportunity.

7

WINNING THE REVOLUTION

RUDOLF HESS, HITLER'S deputy, once gave me a lecture which revealed those peculiar qualities of his which inspired universal respect for him. Why, it will be asked, was Hess, that rather diffident, embarrassed, shy man, with so little self-reliance that he rarely ventured to open his mouth, intelligent enough to achieve that?

Intelligent was just what he had to be. Hess had the thorny duty of composing quarrels—party crises, conflicts as to competence, rivalries; and clashes between government departments and party organs, military and civil authorities, business

leaders and the party. Not an enviable job. He performed his
duty with tact. He listened—a rare characteristic among the
leaders; most of them only spoke. He listened to both sides.
Frequently, that done, he remained silent. But not infre-
quently he dealt successfully with difficult conflicts. The man
wanted nothing for himself—everyone who had anything to
do with him felt that. He seemed also to be free from the
pushing self-importance of most of the high "Pg's." Hess
inspired confidence.

I first met Hess at Obersalzberg. I found his quiet, friendly,
reserved manner attractive, and felt that he was to be trusted,
so that I frequently went to him with my troubles. I found
him always ready to be helpful. I spoke to him on every
question of importance concerning Danzig. The Danzig
"Pg's" complained one after another, and my colleagues in
the Government in a body, of my democratic, pacifist, pro-
Jewish policy. I had reason in turn for complaints of excesses
on the part of Storm Troop leaders and of the whole policy
of Herr Forster, the *Gauleiter*. It was on one of these occasions
that the silent Hess came out of his shell and gave me that
rebuke.

"Listen," he said, "you were, of course, perfectly right. But
need you have told Forster that he knew nothing about industry?"

I replied that what I had said was that if the *Gauleiter*
insisted on certain measures he understood nothing about
industry.

"We need not dispute about the precise words. In any case
you stressed your superior knowledge, and that is not pleasant.
Why need you have shown this man your superiority? Could
you not have made things clear to him?"

I contended that I had done that to the very best of my
ability.

"Then you did not tackle him the right way. Forster is
well meaning. We are not theoreticians. If you get hold of

the right arguments, he will give in to you. We are always ready to listen to reason. But riding the high horse and flaunting your better education won't do among comrades. Think of the burden all these *Gauleiter* have to bear. They have to face the whole pressure of the party. They have to face the masses, with their hopes and claims. They are the men who have to justify to the masses the harsh and sometimes unintelligible steps taken by the party. Don't make the man's job still more difficult. Of course he may be wrong. Then you must put him right—in the proper way. But how do you know, after all, that your economic ideas are right? What do you mean by 'knowing something about industry'? The ablest experts have been wrong, and many more of them will be. The whole lot of them, all the professors and bank directors and Ministers of Finance and of Economic Affairs, have known nothing about industry. Least of all the men actually engaged in industry. We may find in a year's time that Forster saw things more accurately than you, because you have not realized what he knows very well, that we are in the midst of a revolution which is making hay of all the rules of experience."

I contended that in this particular case the issue was over a simple matter that had nothing to do with controversial economic theories.

Hess ignored my remark. "Do you suppose," he continued, "that I do not see sometimes that Herr Hitler is mistaken about something? But I hold my tongue. By and by I come back to the subject and put things right. As a rule Hitler notes the correction. Sometimes I fail to convince him. Then we have to put up with it." He had found, he continued, that "education" at times like the present did more to falsify than clarify the vision. "These men are all what is called uneducated, but they are energetic. They have a devotion to their duties that nobody can exceed. The result is that they get infinitely more done than the respectable politicians of the past, even if they sometimes make mistakes. Their mistakes can be made good. But there is no getting rid of the indolence of the old political parties and officials—except with the jackboot."

Personally Hess was a man of integrity. He has an attractive, quiet wife, who manifestly is without ambition. The gossip about him is nonsense. Certainly he was no speaker. There was a certain woodenness, a lack of harmony about him. Occasional spasmodic movements showed that behind his calm exterior there was not the inner peace and harmony it suggested. It would, indeed, have been impossible for anyone to achieve that who lived for years in the closest association with the hysterical Hitler. Hess's intellect was certainly in no way outstanding. But there is no reason for looking down on him. What was surprising was to find in that environment a man who was particularly awkward in expressing his views and often failed in the attempt to do so, so that he might easily seem to an occasional visitor to be less intelligent than he really was.

He was not what is called "inhibited"; he was rather a man whose personality never entirely developed. He belonged to the type of the many Germans who never reach complete maturity, and who thus retain an element of the puerile. This gives their character a peculiar stamp. Youthful exuberance and fanaticism, and incapacity to think things out, are among their characteristics. The present generation of Germans, to which many of us older ones also belong, have lived through too many violent contrasts for their character to remain uninfluenced. Hence also this strange and disastrous mixture of doctrinairism and realism.

Hess had curious fancies; he was inclined to mysticism, and interested in food reform and in new ideas of healing. But these peculiarities afford no ground for doubting his sanity. His good will and good faith may be questioned by those who know him only from his public acts—his support of the anti-Semitic legislation, his praise of the murderers of the Austrian Chancellor, Dollfuss, and his justification of the concentration camps. Those who know more of him are bound to admit that these things are not so simple as they seem. He accepted responsibility or joint responsibility for things of which he did not approve. Like so many others, Hess felt it his duty to stifle personal doubts and even personal repugnance. The good will of such men as Hess was not a mere matter of party, but of love of a Germany of whose greatness they had romantic conceptions. Hess was a fanatical patriot, though an erring and misguided one.

He was no narrow-minded party boss. He protected Conservatives and other non-Nazi nationalists from unintelligent party magnates. He also protected many Socialists. He said to me repeatedly that he was for retaining and incorporating in the new order as much as possible of the old institutions and personalities. His maxim was: Let everyone who does not intrigue against us and treacherously oppose us be permitted to work with us. "We will smooth the path to us for everyone," he said to me. "We will turn away no one who has not proved by his past that he is an enemy of Germany. We want everyone who can do anything and is ready to contribute his share to Germany's future greatness. We have no idea of helping only old party comrades to high office. You may pass on that message from me to all party comrades. Efficiency comes before everything. We cannot permit ourselves to replace experienced and qualified men by ignoramuses. We shall not repeat the mistakes made by Soviet Russia and oust the intelligentsia instead of setting them where they can do good service. Political keypoints, of course, belong only to the party comrade. There is no room for others in those."

Hess had set up a party supervising organization of his own, directly responsible to him—party inspectors who belonged to no particular formations and who watched over every part of the country independently of all authorities. These men were chosen with good judgment. Going quietly and individually to work, they remedied many abuses and encroachments, and administered raps on the knuckles to the petty local dictators.

But Hess is not a man of strong character. He may be capable of a great sacrifice. But simple, straightforward opposition, when he considers that something wrong is being done, is not for him. Any judgment of this must be subject to taking into account the false ideas held of loyalty and obedience and faithfulness to the party. We see then that National Socialism, like the Marxist Socialist parties, has a sort of religious element that demands the sacrifice of the intellect and of individual opinions. He often acted—as he did in my conflict with the party—against his own better judgment. He kept silence. He capitulated to the demands of the party. He remained silent when war came, although he was utterly convinced that the war was wrong. In foreign affairs Hess was pro-English. There can be no doubt of that. He was also at bottom a pacifist and no militarist. He was silent when Ribbentrop concluded the treaty with Russia, instead of attacking her, although Hess regarded the destruction of Bolshevism as one of Germany's main tasks. He had been silent at the many earlier critical moments when Germany had to choose between a moderate policy, with limited but permanent achievements, and a radical policy of conquest.

Finally his long suppressed concern over foreign, and also domestic, developments sought release in a desperate action which in the non-German world must have seemed like the act of a madman: his flight to England.

The closer circumstances of this event are as little known to me as they are to the general public. But from a knowledge of Hess his motives seem clear. It was a last, desperate attempt to reach a peace with England before the Germans had to take the field against Russia.

To speak of a "flight" of Hess, in the sense that he might have been attempting to save his life from persecution by Himmler or other National Socialist radicals, does not penetrate to the heart of the matter. It is possible that there were such threats. The "Egyptian," as he was called in party circles, was not beloved among the radical power politicians of the party.

But his strongest motive was, without doubt, a peace quest. Possibly even with the knowledge of Hitler. No doubt other circles were behind him also, namely circles in the *Wehrmacht,* big industry, and the high bureaucracy whose thought processes for years had followed the direction set by Ludendorff. This was to finish the process of decentralization of the immense land mass that is Russia, which was already begun in the first world war with the detaching of the border states. None of these politicians imagined that this idea would not have the approval of England. For, as they reasoned, was not the national rebirth of Poland and the Baltic States, which was made possible in 1917 by the German victory over Russia, later recognized by England and the United States? The decentralization of Soviet Russia into a series of middle-sized states seemed to these politicians to be equally of interest to Germany and England. And identity of interests is the basis of realistic alliances. So why should not the unusual be attempted and the parallelness of these interests be made clear in the middle of a war?

This mixture of false deductions of realism and cynicism, with naïveté and total blindness in judgment, is characteristic of Hess. But it is characteristic not only of him.

In analyzing the whole course of the regime and its personal and material motives, it became clear to me that Hess had had no possible chance of doing anything other than what he did do. For he, too, was not a Conservative, however he may have imagined that he was—a revolutionary Conservative —but simply a revolutionary. He, too!

To win the peace and not merely the war—that slogan has often been heard. I have heard Hess talk of "winning the revolution." What revolution? The national, German one, the *"Aufbruch"* (national rising) or *"Umbruch"* (national renascence or "ploughing up of the soil"), as it was called? No, Hess meant the great world revolution into which we were born as into our inescapable destiny. He meant the universal revolution, of which Bolshevism, Fascism, the technical revolution, the revolt of the masses, and finally National Socialism are but a phase. A world revolution? Outside the Continent of Europe there are not many who are ready to accept this as their inescapable destiny. What is meant by winning this revolution? Does it mean the victory of Nazism? Does it mean that the revolution is to conquer? Or does it mean the overcoming of the revolution, its end? Such questions are outside the sphere of everyday, practical politics. Fantastic notions, one says to oneself, unpractical stuff.

"Winning the revolution," I repeated absently, looking about the new room in the Wilhelmstrasse in which Hess had been installed as a Minister of the Reich. "But the revolution has been won by the seizure of power."

"That," retorted Hess, "has only given us the right and the opportunity to win it."

Our talk had begun with a discussion of the German-Polish agreement. I had put before Hess my ideas in regard to cooperation between the two nations. He listened patiently to what I had to say. These, he then answered, were only transient difficulties; the right remedies for them would be found. Then he advised me to study the works of Karl Haushofer, the writer on geopolitics. "I notice," he said, "that you are too much concerned with Continental and Central European ideas. This may easily falsify one's conception of the scale of our problems. We must expand our picture of the

world. Up to now the party has not done that, and deliberately
so, in order not to bring confusion into its straightforward
propaganda. But in reality we are not concerned with Poland
or Czechoslovakia, or for Austria's union with Germany or
for the eastward march. Not even France matters greatly. You
must look out to the Far East, to Asia Minor, Africa, South
America, and the United States. Your Polish policy is quite
good. But it gets us no further. The conflicts of interest and
the national problems of the European nations are, after all,
quite uninteresting. It's no use arguing about them; they will
solve themselves in due course. The real issue is over a new
world center. This world revolution is not going to end in a
new League of Nations, but perhaps a new equilibrium of
continents about a center of power."

I had already met with these ideas again and again in
intelligent circles. I was rather surprised to find Hess occupied
with them. "But," he continued, "it is not a question merely
of a revolution in the society of States. We are at the same
time in the midst of an economic and social and a spiritual
and moral revolution. These are inseparable from each other.
It is a single indivisible revolution, perhaps the greatest of all
time, because all other revolutions of which we have knowledge have run their course only in single continents. We cannot even see clear fronts. Probably we shall all change our
front several times in the course of this revolution."

The critical questions of the day in foreign affairs really
interested Hess no more than Hitler. In his eyes they were
merely means of laying the basis of the future great revolutionary moves. These men's thoughts were cast far into the
future. They were occupied with things which the rest of us
did not yet take seriously.

The idea of the world revolution was perhaps the crowning
conception. From it proceeded that policy of continual change
and movement, that new ethic of dynamism. There was no
denying that all the elements of order in the world had begun

to be in flux. Outside Europe, in the East, this happened in the form of the incursion of Western civilization into the last remains of primitive orders, the breaking up of the last remaining tribal systems. But we in Europe were ourselves much more in the tribal condition than we were ready to admit. What were these national ambitions and State civilizations but mechanized forms of tribal cultures? Were we now approaching a great world civilization with a long-continued peace? With first a gigantic Battle of Actium to decide the leadership of the universal peace empire? To decide whether the world empire should be a union of the Socialist, totalitarian worker-republics, with a common State economic system operating on a vast plan and with gigantic cooperative collectives?

Hess made it perfectly plain that he did not consider the "winning of the revolution" to consist in the attainment of a material earthly Paradise of collectivism, with the "ultimate man" of Nietzsche living without God, without tragedy, without struggle, through the unhistoried ages of an undisturbed "petty happiness."

What was the alternative solution? Adventures, master race and slave classes, eternal unrest, eternal war, living dangerously? I am afraid no one knew the answer, and Hess certainly had not discovered it.

Hess used that expression "winning the revolution" in another of our talks. Perhaps I am exaggerating its importance, but it stuck in my memory. I was complaining at that time of excesses on the part of the Storm Troopers. They had boxed the ears of Poles who had failed to salute the swastika flag in the streets. There had been other and worse excesses against Communists and Catholics among the citizens of Danzig. We came to the subject of the concentration camps and other elements of terrorism. Hess rejected my protests. He denied the existence of atrocities on the scale alleged by the whispering propaganda.

"Things are happening of course," he said, "which would have been better avoided. The whole business of the concentration camps is an unpleasant one. Suggest if you can anything else that is equally effective with less cruelty. There must be concentration camps so long as we are passing through this revolution. When we have won, we can let people run about as much as they like and wherever they like. But not until then. It is essential to retain the fear of the concentration camps. If they were just boarding houses, we should be making ourselves ridiculous. Power becomes ridiculous when it is not feared."

Did I suppose, he added, that it was any pleasure to him or to anyone else, to Herr Hitler for instance, to know about the concentration camps and all that was going on in them? It had been difficult for Hitler to make up his mind to employ them. He had asked again and again whether the same measure of security could not be achieved by other means. Always he was told it could not. How could secrets be guarded and treason prevented? We were in too dangerous a situation as a nation. We had to be hard.

I pointed out that the indiscipline and the swaggering of party comrades, as in these cases at Danzig, probably did more harm than the few Marxists and Jewish shopkeepers. Hess replied that he would see to it that there should be an end of the indiscipline.

He repeated: "Do you suppose the business is any pleasure to a single one of us? Every one of us has to be constantly pulling himself together, to prevent becoming soft. Sometimes Hitler seems harder than he need be. But he has to protect himself from his own softness, which is his greatest temptation. We are not out," he concluded, "only to make Germany great, we have to win the revolution. And it can be won only by placing ourselves at the head of it, in order to guide it."

8

THE REVOLUTIONARY IN DISGUISE

THERE ARE MANY people who think that Frick, the Reich Minister of the Interior, is a Nazi nonentity, because, in strong contrast to the habits of the party, he does not push himself into the foreground in order to be seen playing his part. Many in the party look down on him. "That man's just a bureaucrat," they say, "not a revolutionary at all." In reality Frick has carried through revolutionary measures which will probably have tougher life in them than many other of the Nazis' revolutionary actions. The reason is that Frick has his own idea of what is called revolution.

At first I had been no less disappointed in Frick than most of the party members and others who had official or social relations with him. Was not the man the very prototype of a fossilized little provincial official? Dry and matter of fact, without any spirit. He had, it was true, a good presence. He was not lacking in vigor. His gray, close-cropped hair, his austerity of appearance, and his inclination to curtness were noted as queer features by his party friends.

More energy had been expected of him in the party. He had been expected to see that the machinery of government came at once under Nazi control through a revolutionary act, needless to say, and a striking one, like the Reichstag fire. It was expected that in every branch of the administration, including the local administration, the party nominees designated long in advance would be installed as special commissars and sectional dictators. This was intended to render impossible the thing most feared in a struggle for power, the passive resistance of the officials, obstinate obstruction from the administrative staff.

Frick did not fulfil this requirement in the revolutionary

way the impatient activists at the head of the party had envisaged. Everything the man did was much too leisurely for
their taste. He had no go in him, he was just respectable. That
was the verdict passed on him. He had given Hitler the clever
and exceedingly effective idea of the *Reichsstatthalter* or Gov-
ernors of the German States, at a very dangerous moment of
internal crisis; at all events, he had given legislative form to
the idea and carried it into effect. But he provided no legislative means for the occupation of the whole administration by
the party. On the contrary, he set a brake on that development,
and put people off with promises. The result was that he was
frequently attacked. If he had not enjoyed Hitler's special
favor in recognition of earlier achievements, he would have
been thrust out of the inner councils of the party like the engineer Feder, who had had great influence in the early years.

It may be that the continued attacks from the revolutionary
Gauleiter or regional party administrators accounted for his
aloofness. Probably it was because of his desire to escape from
further troublesome discussions that he did not receive me
personally, though I had made an appointment with him. I
had gone to him to learn from the responsible quarter in the
Reich the answers to some practical questions, but instead I
was given by Frick's deputy some indication of the Minister's
interpretation of the National Socialist revolution. These views
seem to me to be worth placing on record.

The *Ministerialrat* received me with apologies. The *Herr
Reichsminister,* he said, had unfortunately been prevented by
a conference from seeing me personally. But the Minister was
glad to give me any help I needed. Before I came to the subject of my visit, however, the *Ministerialrat* mentioned that he
must say at once that the *Herr Reichsminister* did not at all
approve of rigorous interventions in the administration. It was
the *Herr Reichsminister's* unshakable opinion that the only
way to a lasting success of the National Socialist movement
was not through a radical, revolutionary upheaval, but

through gradual absorption or elimination of the elements of the old order.

I replied that I was far from proposing any sort of revolutionary interference with the administration; on the contrary, I wanted to keep the administration intact, but that in consequence of Danzig's difficult situation, with State bankruptcy very near, rigorous measures of economy were necessary, and one of the most urgent of these was a strict retrenchment of the administrative staff. The simplification of the administrative organization and of the conduct of business—these were the only things about which I sought to learn the experience and the plans of the Reich Ministry.

Unfortunately, replied the *Ministerialrat,* the position was not what the party comrades imagined, rightly as they resented the all too inflated staffs and the dilatoriness of procedure. In consequence of the many new tasks and the necessary supervision of the authorities by party organs, the official staffs would swell and, for the present, procedure would be even further complicated, instead of being simplified. This was an inevitable concomitant of every revolutionary development, and could only be changed in the course of time. All we could do was to cut down excesses as far as possible; at the same time, we must bear in mind that measures of economy were always illusory in a period of revolution. Revolutions were times of temporary squandering of resources, human and material, much in the same way as wars.

I replied that I was rather disappointed by these explanations.

The *Ministerialrat* said that he would take the liberty of giving the reasons for the *Herr Reichsminister's* views at greater length. "A revolution," he said, "is not merely an upheaval. All spectacular revolts come to a stop after a short outburst. Revolutions that have permanent results are movements that make their way gradually but steadily. That is the view the *Herr Reichsminister* habitually puts forward when pressed by the *Gauleiter* and *Reichsleiter,* the regional and national lead-ers. In these views he has the full support of the Fuehrer. We are judging revolutions, says Frick, according to the categories of Jewish writers when we imagine that a revolution is won by the storming of a Bastille, by fighting at the barricades, and by the solemn burial of victims of the revolution. Successful revolutions extend through many years, and are not to be identified with memorable episodes. Changes that are to en-dure must be slowly effected.

"The *Herr Reichsminister* generally goes on to remind his hearer that before we came into power he continually warned the Fuehrer against any 'March on Berlin' and any 'Night of the long knives.' If we had carried out a putsch, we should have ended our careers as revolutionaries by now. And his opinion carried the day. The *Herr Reichsminister* also insists that no one among the party comrades can be more thoroughly convinced than he of the correctness of the principle of the identity of party and State. But these are not merely ideas, to be proclaimed like the fundamental rights of a liberal consti-tution. They are the elements of a new reality. If today the organs of the State are removed or their premises occupied—as, for instance, water works, slaughter houses, wireless sta-tions, and electricity works may be occupied in a revolt—it will prevent them from functioning under the existing regime but it will not assure their working under a new one. It is more likely to promote a counter-movement. A great adminis-tration cannot be occupied. The only practicable method is that of displacement, absorption, and penetration. If we are the tenacious revolutionaries we consider ourselves to be, we shall have made the whole problem meaningless in ten years' time. The new structure will be in existence, and we shall have avoided all useless protests."

This conversation furnished me with some further informa-tion as to the views and ideas current in the party, and strengthened me, at least at the time, in my impression that elements of high intelligence had an influence over the general control of affairs. Frick was absolutely against any idea that an enduring new order and Constitution could be created for a people by legislative decrees. The new, he held, can only be allowed to grow; all that can be done is to help to create new realities and then to legalize them, not the other way round.

"We must go to work," said Frick, according to my informant, "the opposite way to that taken by the Weimar Republic. If we start by creating a Constitution and leave till later the creation of the organs for the working of the Constitution, we shall never emerge from the conflict between a pretended condition and an existing one. In practice those laws will come perpetually into conflict with the vulgar but concrete reality. We must first create the new conditions and then give them legislative form. The creation of new State and social conditions is possible only by empirical methods. Those who think they can master developments by theoretical planning end like the German Republic or the French Revolution. They end, that is to say, in the total reverse of their intentions, or in empty phrases."

I must confess that these views of Frick's made me thoroughly enthusiastic, because they liberated me for the time from the oppressive feeling that the developments in Germany were entirely in the hands of extremists. This idea of gradually creating the new form and Constitution of Germany through continual attention to the new problems of the social, economic, and political crisis, seemed to me to be a sound one and conservative in the best sense—straining toward the goal as nature does, not simply following a logical argument like the revolutionary intellectuals. I arrived at the conviction that Frick must be a Conservative in much the same sense as I myself. This conviction was strengthened by the information the *Ministerialrat* gave me about Frick's ideas on the reform of the German *Länder,* the constituent States of the Reich.

I recall one more phrase of Frick's. In a great revolution, he said, what matters is not getting quick results but keeping the revolution at work as long as possible. Not until later did I begin to see that, moderate as he appeared, Frick was really a revolutionary, for the very reason that he did not measure results by a few years. He envisaged developments over far longer periods and with much more fundamental changes. He saw revolution also outside Germany's borders, a revolution only in its initial stage, and one to which limits should not be set prematurely by new elements of order, but which should be allowed to work itself out as long as possible.

Here again he rejected any detailed program for the future. He studied the form of new supernational State amalgamations. But he refused to work out a formal scheme. In spite of his mask of an intelligent political realist, of a mentor urging moderation on the radicals, he was anything but the genuine Conservative who wanted to divert the revolution into a moderate course of evolution. He was the revolutionary who profited by the methods of a conservative policy to assure for the revolution a yet more enduring success.

9

THE BULL

CONCERN FOR THE prosperity and magnificence of the German Empire—that is the essential of Hermann Goering, not the pseudo-asceticism of his mountain hunting-box or the shifty glance of the drug addict. Goering was the hope of all the moderates, the protector of the middle-class nationalists and the sheet anchor of private enterprise. When, in the pomp of the new ruling power, with be-starred, gold-laced uniforms around him and on him, he steps forward and thrusts out his massive belly with tremendous self-assurance, everyone forgets that this is a man of scarcely average height, ill-proportioned, with slanting eyes in his broad face with its fat double chin, and with the high cheekbones that in Germany are regarded as Slav. Hitler's gait is an ecstatic stilt walk or a sort of guilty slinking. Goering steps out in naïve self-assurance, full of the sense of his own importance.

In spite of his fame as a warrior, pomp and self-assurance have not always been the accompaniments of his existence. I remember one of Goering's first speeches in Danzig. It was long before the seizure of power. The famous officer aviator, with the highest Prussian order sticking out below his neck, stuttered and stammered out before his audience a feeble and meaningless jumble that certainly did nothing to convert anybody to National Socialism.

On the platform a few ex-airmen formed a sort of guard of honor. One of them wore a high Finnish order in the shape of a swastika. As Goering came down from the tribune he stopped, struck, in front of this distinguished man, and stared hard at him. He went on a few steps, stopped, turned back to look at the order, strode on to the exit, dripping with the sweat of the orator, and then for the third time looked round covetously at that rare and precious distinction before he disappeared into the speaker's room.

I have never been in close touch with Goering, though there were things that might have made it possible for me to work with him. My first impressions of the man had made him irreparably distasteful to me. When I next saw him, in the palace of the President of the Reichstag, and later, after the seizure of power, when I heard him talking to some of the *Gauleiter* at the Chancellery outside Hitler's door, and boasting to them of his organization of the Reichstag fire, I had lost all desire to try to get his help in my small efforts to set moderate limits to Nazi policy. The words he shouted to the *Gauleiter* with stentorian brazenness, "I have no conscience. My conscience is Adolf Hitler," gave me the first great shock which set me in doubt whether or not to abandon the National Socialist path at once. I have given my account of Goering's part in the Reichstag fire, based on hints thrown out by various leaders, in *The Voice of Destruction*.

Goering's boast that he had no conscience hit the nail on the head. He is the least problematical, perhaps the only uncomplicated, individual among the party comrades who came to the fore. His unscrupulousness is not a product of speculation and reflection. It is a completely naïve lack of the inhibitions which are a matter of course for other people. In many things he has remained a youth who has failed to grow up, with all the irresponsibility and adventurousness of that type. There is certainly no perverse lust at the back of his cruelty and brutality. They are the natural reaction of a human beast of prey.

In saying this I am not expressing a judgment but simply stating a fact. This natural, uncomplicated consciencelessness is, perhaps, less shocking than the reasoned, deliberate brutality and stifling of scruple which a man like Hitler has forced upon himself for the sake of certain dark doctrines, overcoming his natural plebeian sentimentality. Goering's character has been imposed on him by his past as a famous flying officer of the last war, a man who could never settle down to any humdrum occupation in civil life. There are things about him that were certainly the inevitable outcome of his special fighting qualities, which at one time were highly valued. Even when he was harsh and cruel, Goering retained traces of chivalry and a naïve youthfulness, which do not diminish his share in the responsibility for war and revolution, but help to explain some of the sympathy with which he has been regarded by a good many people both in Germany and abroad. His politics were similarly simple and unproblematical. He was no thinker; he left it to others to rack their brains about high policy. This does not mean that he had no interest in home and foreign politics.

In declaring that he had no conscience, in the ordinary moral sense, Goering was certainly speaking the truth. But in the rest of his confession, his declaration that his conscience was Adolf Hitler, he spoke, consciously or unconsciously, an untruth. Goering has certainly a measure of respect for Hitler and devotion to him. But so far as I learned in my experience of the inner processes of the party, Goering has never recognized Hitler as the great and preeminent leader. He regarded him as a necessary interim phase, as the mouthpiece, the colporteur of a coming new age, never as the hero who was to determine Germany's fate for the next thousand years. Not that he was jealous of Hitler—the idea never entered his mind. His opinion of Hitler was far too low and of himself far too high for that. It was the deep differences in the instincts and the conscious aims of these two main figures of the German revolution that inevitably brought them into disagreement.

The true relation between Hitler and Goering was described to me, as so much else, by the *enfant terrible* of the party, Forster. *"Ach!"* he exclaimed to me one day. "Hitler has such trouble over Goering. Hitler is very sad. Goering's style of living is a great vexation to him. We must remain simple, Hitler warns us. We must go on living as in the period of struggle, before we came into power. Goering is a serious drag on the party."

About that time I heard among the initiated in Berlin that Goering had spoken out in the plainest of language about Hitler. "What! That brat of a proletarian—is he to lay down to me what I shall do? We are not playing the ascetic. I have no intention of doing anything else than what suits me. He doesn't understand anyhow. A bit of a show of luxury in life gives food for the imagination. It gives people something else to think about. They have got to have something to look at and talk about."

Goering had a close knowledge of the history of the French Revolution, and showed a considerable knowledge of history in general; and in this matter of revolutionary luxury he was acting not idly but with deliberation. Splendor and luxury are part of every display of power.

As for luxury, his natural instincts and his historic insight pointed for Goering in the same direction. He loved pomp and possessions. And he could enjoy life with all the coarse broadness of his nature. He had none of the twinges of conscience, in doing so, of other men whom National Socialism had raised to eminence. He never gave a thought to the broken promise to return to Spartan simplicity. He took all his luxury as a matter of course. It was not an unfamiliar style of living for him, as it was for Hitler and Hess and Himmler and the rest. In his uniforms and his comic fancy costumes the fat man moved about with astonishing liveliness. He was of a robust type. He had in him something of Danton. His naïve robbing of shopkeepers who had jewelry, antiques, paintings, and other luxury articles to sell was almost disarming in its complete unscrupulousness. In this, too, it was whispered by those in closest touch with him, he had drawn a golden lesson from his studies of history. He quoted the enormities committed, from the Condottieri to Talleyrand and from the Medicean Popes to Napoleon, which had always been approved by the masses, and had been accepted by historians, because they had given rein to the imagination.

Goering had no program. He had no *Weltanschauung*, no philosophy of life. He was not even a revolutionary. He loved power and magnificence. His personal interest in these two things was sufficient motive for his "untameable" patriotism. He was no timid soul or dried-up literary man or lecturer. He was an officer, a famous war hero. But was there any substance in the persistent rumors that he was playing a really notable part, that one day he would be the liquidator of the revolution, and would then give Germany a lasting, well-thought-out order? How did this coarse and brutal sensualist acquire the saintly odor of a liquidator of the revolution? Simply through having enjoyed a better bringing-up than most of the party comrades? Through his readiness to live and let live, and because he was no doctrinaire? Because right up to the time immediately preceding the war he was a protector of Jews? Because he was the absolute contrast to the ecstatic Hitler—natural and uninhibited in all his impulses, his love of drinks and good dishes and doing things and philandering and acquisition and the noble sport of hunting?

There is certainly more behind this rumored function of liquidator than a mere inference from the contrast between those two natures, Hitler's and Goering's. Goering is more than the mere corrupt profiteer that a one-sided press calls him. This man is a primitive force. He is the Bull. He was given that high title, amid howls of approval from the party comrades, at a great meeting in the Sports Palace in Berlin by no other than the Fuehrer's Deputy, Rudolf Hess. He is the bull who can lift with his horns things that are too heavy for anyone else. He has little real understanding of the great majority of the tasks he tackles. He frankly admits it. But with his ruthlessness he beats to the ground all the opposition which, in perhaps most cases, is no more than red tape. He acts as the battering-ram for the experts behind him. He enables them to overcome interested or prejudiced opposition and to cut through the snares of passive resistance. If he takes up a problem he settles it. For better or worse. Often for worse rather than better. But it is not always his fault that commissions are entrusted to him with the result of irreparable destruction in Germany's economic or political fabric. Sometimes he achieves wonders. His forest administration and his hunting regulations, for example, are in some sense masterpieces.

He liked to assume an air of simple respectability, but he could never free it from a suggestion of trickery and malice. He was fond of addressing intelligent people in the style in which officers used to address recruits in the time of William II—with a genial gruffness, and with a downrightness that

ignored difficulties of the most serious nature. He never really
rose above the level of the cadet or the young officer. "Airmen
never tell untruths! Understand that! Get out!" That was his
short way with a Gestapo official, for instance, who had been
so indiscreet as to make an ex-airman the object of his professional interest. On this occasion Goering took a former comrade under his protection, and in thousands of other cases he
similarly helped to mitigate hardships. But in still more cases
he "showed no mercy," and lifted men of the *Systemzeit* out
of their posts and livelihood into a concentration camp.

Goering was the first to copy Mussolini's vast audience
chamber. It was a long march from his door to his desk. At
that time he still received visitors in the Prussian Prime Minister's room.

"Tell me," he said, when he received me to profit by my experiences with our Polish policy. "What sort of a man is this
Pilsudski? Is he really going off his head? Moltke goes about
declaring that the man has gradually become a complete im-
becile. What do you think?"

I replied that I could supply the most conclusive evidence
that Pilsudski still had a very lively intelligence, and I gave
details of my visit to the Polish Marshal.

"So!" said Goering. "That puts quite a different complexion
on it. Now tell me, can we get anything done with those people? Are they fellows you can work with? They have some
thoroughly able men, of course. That fellow Beck seems a
smart chap. With men like that you can get a move on. Well,
fire away! Unluckily I've damned little time."

I tried to compress my impressions and opinions about
Poland into a few brief sentences.

"*So, na!* You seem to be really bewitched by the fellows.
Must say I like them best of all those Slavs. Better than the
Czechs anyhow! So you think they'll show a bit of sense, and
agree to let their little country be shifted just a bit to the east!
Good, good! I'm just off hunting, and can take the opportunity

to sound them. Now, tell me a bit more about the principal men. Can't we manage a bit of personal influence somewhere. Confederation style perhaps, eh?" He made a graphic movement of his fingers, suggesting the handing over of money.

I tried to make it plain that it seemed to me to be very doubtful whether any existing Polish territory would be voluntarily given up, at all events in the present early stage of incipient rapprochement. I suggested that I must have given an entirely mistaken impression by something I had said.

"Well, what's doing, what's doing, my boy?" said Goering with sudden impatience. "You've just been telling me a long story of how the Poles might be ready to work with us against Russia. Well, the first condition for that is surely to clear up our reciprocal differences. Or do you seriously propose to leave the Poles in possession of everything they have occupied? Any idea of that sort is entirely out of the question."

I replied that I felt that the existing very delicate situation needed to be gradually improved as the condition precedent to any further action.

"Rot," he shouted, cutting me short. "We have no time to lose. With us or against. They've got to make up their minds, and quickly."

Goering was keenly interested in the Polish question, and not only on account of the splendid hunting at Bielowicz. I do not know what were his reasons, but he was probably trying to reserve foreign politics as his sphere, in addition to so much else. He obviously regarded it as his domain because he had been entrusted occasionally by Hitler with foreign missions. For a time there was a sort of universal tussle in Berlin among the prominent leaders as to who could bring Poland into the German camp. Goering had probably been trying to prove to Hitler that he was the only one who would really do it. Goebbels had had no particular success when he went to Warsaw.

I gave some indications of my idea of a Central European

policy of federation, but he pounced on me. "A bit behind
with what's been going on in the world, eh? Partitioning of
Europe? What's your scheme? Western Powers, Central Powers, Eastern Powers? You ought to have been hawking your
ideas, my dear sir, fifty years ago. Today it's a bit late.

"Well," he went on after a short pause, "we're to play the
Great Elector for a bit—sit on the fence—with Poland or
against her, with or against—eh? Or is it just the opposite
you're after?"

As the interview came to an end, he asked me about Danzig
and about his old friend Forster. "There is something we can
do there," he said. "Only don't be obstinately bound to a single
course. Adaptability, adaptability! You're not so old as to have
become slow-going already. Anyhow I shall keep my eyes open.
And don't make difficulties. They tell me you're at loggerheads with Forster. Chuck it. He is stronger than you. You
had a good start. Don't begin losing ground!"

That sort of fisticuffs politics was new to me then. This
conversation strengthened me in definitely writing off Goering
as an asset in our accounts. He was not, after all, what rumor
had called him, the representative of the monarchists in Hitler's camp—so I concluded, perhaps prematurely. He had, I
inferred, no principles of any sort. He was against everything
that is commonly regarded as broadly Conservative. He was,
of course, equally against Marxism, whether Socialist or Communist. Yet the rumors that Goering was the one hope for a
reasonable solution would not be silenced. He intended, it was
said, to plunge Hitler into the abyss at one of the next turns
in the road. Were these rumors deliberately spread in order to
inspire the anti-Nazis with confidence and make them talk,
and so to discover the real opponents of the regime and their
views? Goering was capable of a maneuver of that sort. He
was ready to take on anything, and was not above putting
people on the wrong track.

I think there is more in the rumors than merely the machinations of an eminent *agent provocateur*. It may be that Goering too lacked only the courage to break away at the critical moment, just as the old generals lacked it. He was not as bellicose as he affected to be: he had played a part in good earnest in the last war, and had no need of further laurels. He had also grown rich and powerful. Like the other *arrivés* of the party, he had more to lose than gain from war. He began to dislike taking risks, especially in dealing with powerful elements in the party. He was not always spoken well of by the "Counts of the *Gaue*." His lordly style irritated them. The more Hitler's star rose, the more difficult and dangerous it became to attempt anything against the Fuehrer. The extent to which Goering began to grow easy-going and disinclined to move was revealed to me by a little episode involving a well-known big industrialist who had urged Goering to intervene on behalf of industry. Goering promised to do so, but did not, and finally, after waiting a long time, the industrialist asked why this was.

"*Ach!*" said Goering. "You know, I have been on very bad terms with Hitler lately. Now I have just shown him my new works. He expressed his satisfaction to me so overwhelmingly. How could I spoil his good mood and spoil my good standing with him once more?"

He had lost his confidence. The old independence was gone. Goering, like others, had slid down imperceptibly rung by rung, while Hitler had been steadily going up. Perhaps Hitler also knew something about him. Battles were continually being fought out behind the scenes. Meanwhile Himmler had grown in importance and improved his standing. Ribbentrop was in favor. New demigods were coming into the foreground. Hitler was surrounding himself with military men. Even the most eminent of the old party comrades, formerly his closest intimates, seldom saw the Fuehrer in his aureole. They were no longer his equals; he was no longer merely *primus inter pares*. They were all far below him, and Hermann Goering with them. The members of Hitler's private General Staff, those officers, smooth as eels, ingratiating, but entirely out of reach of any sort of influence, had almost entirely ousted the old "strong men" of the "victorious movement." Hitler had betrayed his supporters a second time. Today the *Wehrmacht*, the armed force of the Reich, is his party. He had chosen once more between party and *Wehrmacht*. He had decided once for all in favor of the military. Goering was becoming suspect. Perhaps the day would come when he would no longer be indispensable. No one heard of him any more.

So it seemed. Is not this process under way, perhaps already completed? Did Goering perhaps hang together with Hess? Did the two of them, perhaps, make a belated and unsuccessful attempt to prevent the wheel of ill-fortune from turning further? Did they fight for the party against the military, did they speak out for Germany against the infatuated Fuehrer, who was leading the nation into the abyss? Did Goering try prematurely to obstruct Hitler amid his succession of conquests? The liquidator of the revolution is now in the background.

Shortly before I finally left Poland in the summer of 1938 and went to France, I was given this account of Goering's plans: "Let Adolf commit himself. He will take over sole responsibility. He will have to act without the men who have done everything for him. A sort of general strike of the demigods. Then, take a firm line. Detain the Fuehrer in safe custody. Then make a public proclamation: 'All must take their orders from me. Germany is in great danger. The Fuehrer is showing signs of a grave malady. Any resistance will be ruthlessly stamped out.' And then slowly right-about turn. Germany becomes once more a monarchy!"

It was for that coup d'état, and not merely for war, that Goering had built up his air force. He had been made to give up his corps of sharpshooters and his formations of bodyguards. But against that loss he had so built up his air force that it could destroy the strongest opposition the moment it showed itself, by means of lightning blows. Its corps of officers is said to be blindly loyal to Goering. It has its special formations, its flame-throwers, its tanks, its artillery. Coups d'état are made today with the air force. Goering had the monopoly of the implement of the coup d'état. Where and when he would carry it out, whether at Berchtesgaden, in the field, in Berlin, or in Munich, was immaterial. But one day he would do it!

What a flight of the imagination! Was the wish once more the father to these thoughts? Certainly the plan had a snag: Hitler could always find men to do what others, more conscientious, more scrupulous, declined to do. That was the flaw in the reckoning. Thousands were waiting, distorted by ambition, for "their" hour, when they would at last be brought from obscurity into the limelight, to begin their great career.

One thing is certain—that Goering did not expand the air force simply to fight Germany's battles, but had the clear consciousness that he held in his hand a force which in its lightning speed of concentration was superior to any other combination of military forces in the arena of Germany herself. I have no knowledge of his military ideas. There were whisperings of gigantic plans. Goering, too, occupied himself with a new tactic of surprise and mass attack from the air. For him the air arm became the universal arm. It was no longer one among others. In any case it was entitled to supremacy. He had the ambition to make his General Staff the rallying point of the most modern tactical ideas. He spoke of air infantry, air artillery, air tank corps, and air pioneer corps—at a time when all these things sounded like tales from the Arabian Nights. There was talk of three-dimensional and four-dimensional war. All strategical problems had become soluble—the conquest of Britain, of Africa, of Russia, of Asia. He talked of how, the next time England tried to obstruct Germany, he would send thirty thousand aircraft over London and convert it into a heap of ruins. Boastings of that sort were, of course, not to be taken seriously. At bottom he was an Anglophile. He saw no reason why Britain and Germany need fight. "Only don't madden England prematurely!" he often said. He blamed Hitler for blurting out in advance much too often everything he proposed to do. He cursed the tomfoolery of *Mein Kampf*. "He does nothing but make difficulties for us," he said once. "I'm constantly being asked, 'But it says this and the other thing in *Mein Kampf*. Haven't we got to carry that out?' What answer can I give to that?"

His ideas on foreign policy were like all his ideas—primitive. But they were thoroughly concrete. His whole foreign policy led to one single idea—first work our way vigorously ahead, and be armed against all possible combinations. Equally primitive was his Socialism. It was a sort of modern patriarchalism —the genial, paternal lord and master: the people have to be managed like a horse, a woman, and a recruit. First take a tight hold on the bit, and give a good blow of the whip every now and then. Then, when everything has gone all right, give 'em a bit of sweetstuff. "It's footling, all this fear of the masses! The people want to be led. What they need is a strong hand. What they don't want is to be asked and appealed to."

In his primitive love of possessions, he was against all the measures embraced in the term socialization. "Don't come at me with your silly Socialist phrases," he would shout at party comrades who talked of the end of capitalism. "What is capitalism? Can you tell me?" He protected private enterprise, property, and good incomes, because he himself depended on them. "We are busy here with politics, not with the betterment of the world," he would say. He recognized no economic laws. He considered that we can do what we like with economics. "You can stick your head through a wall," he used to say, "if your skull is hard enough." He used *bons mots* of that sort. "Airmen can do anything," he said. His reputed pro-Semitism was connected with his love of property. That made him look upon the clever Jewish businessmen as natural allies. In any case, he had not the slightest interest in the Jewish question. He regarded it as a stupid invention of Hitler's, but he fell in with the business because there was nothing to be gained by getting excited about it.

"Have you ever read biographies of great men?" he once said to an acquaintance of mine. "Mark you this: corruption is what they call the little slips—if a man's caught, for instance, getting hold of a fur coat for his wife at less than the marked price. The big bugs get honorariums."

He had a very direct character, with immense confidence in the possibility of getting anything whatever done provided it was attacked with sufficient energy. This man secured and enjoyed to the full everything he coveted, even if it was playing with toys in a sort of belated boyhood, as with the little model railway on the floor of one of his palaces. Add to his greed for splendor his pleasure in power, and his vanity, the pleasure in sport and also a good dose of sentimentality, and we have the picture of a man able like Danton to appeal to the imagination of the masses. Like Danton, he will be dragged one day by the Robespierre of our time to the executioner—to be followed by the new Robespierre before long.

Can Goering escape that fate? Can he forestall Hitler? Is it not already too late for that? He lulled himself too long into the belief that he was the strongest man in Germany. He could have been the master of Germany at any time. He was perfectly sure of it. "The revolution will be ended by *me!*" But he did not move. And now the bull has lost his horns.

10

WITCHES' SABBATH IN AMERICA

"AMERICA? YOU MUST be mad! America will never again play any part in Europe. America can no longer do anything but bluff."

Gauleiter Koch had come to see me at Danzig. We were sitting at lunch and arguing over international politics.

I reminded him that what he was saying about America was just what had been said in the last war—and the upshot had been very different.

"It will never happen again," replied Koch. "I am an old revolutionary, and I can sniff it right away over here."

"I don't understand what you meant by that," I said.

"Oh, a witches' sabbath is on the way! Pity we can't be there in the midst of it. Do you suppose," he continued, "that there is any more solid a world over there, across the big ditch, than among us here? America has always had it over us as the land of unlimited possibilities. In politics too, indeed in politics especially. Do you suppose that revolutions are the special privilege of this blood-stained old continent of ours? Because, perhaps, outside the Civil War they have had no serious bust-ups? Just wait!"

I contended that the economic and social tension in the United States, widespread as it was, was far from being acute enough to lead to a revolution.

"Who was talking," interrupted Koch, "about that? Though that element may be quite useful. There are the many national groups, for instance. Not even the world war got rid of them. And, slowly but surely, the geographical differences are making themselves felt. But the main thing is that the bond that united all these people, so different from one another, has given way. There is no longer in America, any more than in

Europe, anything left in which men believe. Not even 'prosperity.' Do you suppose they still believe in their political ideals? Perhaps the politically minded and the literary people do. But there's no longer any life in the old ideals. They are just empty phrases, useful for muddling people's heads in peacetime. Let any really great upheaval come in that continent, and we shall see that they are no better off over there than we are. I tell you, I can see such explosions coming as have never before been known in the world. In revolutions as in other things, America will thoroughly earn her reputation as the land of unlimited possibilities."

"Strikes," I replied, "I can imagine those, and on a gigantic scale, perhaps even local revolts. But a revolution? Why should a revolution break out in America? I once heard Hitler say that America is not yet finished. She has not yet achieved stable equilibrium, and this fact, he said, affords opportunities for working politically upon America. There may be some truth in that. Perhaps it means that there will be some difficulties to overcome before America takes permanent shape. But that does not imply any real revolution on the French or Russian model."

Koch cut me short again. "Don't speechify. Equilibrium or no equilibrium, Hitler has no more idea than you of what the actual ground for an American revolution will be. Hitler is not a real revolutionary. It's not in his bones. But I will tell you how I see it. Those Yankees are not simply shrewd businessmen. They have all sorts of wild ideas in their heads. Children, I tell you, letting their fancy run! There's no end to the fantastic things they will do. Have you heard how these sober businessmen will suddenly run wild after lunch in their clubs, like kids, making hobby-horses of their chairs and playing every conceivable silly trick? Or if a celebrity of the moment puts in an appearance, what a rumpus there is! You've seen it in the illustrateds. They're just children. Grand, that country with its rough simplicity! Well, just think for yourself what happens when bright ideas and solid worth and furious energy come together. I can tell you—the unexpected. Something utterly idiotic, perhaps. Or it may be something immense. In any case, a huge explosion."

"What do you mean?"

"Why, for example, a sudden emergence of some mighty nonsense of a doctrine, and everybody falls for it, and it becomes an absolute epidemic. Nobody can get away from it or escape the infection. Didn't they invent after the war that comic idea of Prohibition, an utterly preposterous thing, and an interference with private life, with the liberty of the individual, that is in absolutely grotesque conflict with the so-called democratic ideals? Well, is not that full of promise for the future? There may be invented there, perhaps, a socialism so effective and so radical that the Bolsheviks will go pale with envy. With all the efficiency that distinguishes these Americans, they will suddenly tackle the job of making their country really an earthly paradise. Perhaps they will invent a sort of Atlantic epoch, a new age of earthly blessedness. An enforced and regulated blessedness, of course, with an apportioned share of each and every element of blessedness. We may see people coming to the fore who have made up their minds that only the U.S.A. can manage the thing the morbid old European continent has never achieved."

"Have you ever been to the United States?"

"No," said Koch, "but an old revoluzi like me can feel all that in his bones. In such a country the absurdest things are bound suddenly to become reality. Adventurousness and efficiency cannot fail to bring something clever into being. America, the land of children and gunmen. Life there is primitive and yet fantastic."

"Irresponsible rubbish!" I said. "America seen through crude movies and cheap thrillers. That's no basis for serious consideration of future relations between Germany and the United States."

"Children and gunmen," Koch repeated. "Children are always chucking their toys away and forgetting them. Just so will those people throw away their democracy and demand something new. Perhaps they will be sick of their future State as quickly as they were of Prohibition. But that is not the point. What matters is not what they do but the fact that something does get done. Something vast, new, magnificent. I'm quite sure that something is coming there in the face of which we old European revolutionaries will want to go away and hide ourselves. Think of all the splendid material over there for top-hole revolutionaries, those bootleggers and kidnappers and all the pretty fellows of the Wild West. Those people simply don't know what to do with their power; they are overwhelmed by their wealth."

All this, I repeated, was cinema stuff and not reality. America was the land probably of the most industrious, the healthiest, and the most efficient people under the sun. If they had preserved an element of childishness, so much the better for their future.

"Just wait," Koch went on. "Once the old cow bells stop tinkling, the whole herd will stray into the wilderness. It may be that in America they will make their revolution with all their native care and efficiency, like any other serious job. An impresario of the revolution will stage the greatest event of the sort in all history, as if he were organizing a conducted tour. But it is also possible that the American dictator may emerge with an entirely stupid slogan. What is there that will not go down with the masses in America? We simply haven't the imagination to conceive the absurdities that will pass muster. He will be sure to begin with the women and have his first great successes among them."

I knew that Koch was fond of clothing his ideas in ironic, extravagant language. I asked him to tell me what he really meant. He declared that he meant what he had said. "I'm positive there's going to be the maddest of witches' sabbaths.

The Americans have all those characteristics of ours which up to now have made us the disturbers of the world. But they have a country with almost inexhaustible resources. Our schemes soon run up against the narrow limits of our potential. Over there radicalism can sweep away literally into infinity. Up to now America has still remained an old-world country, only re-upholstered a bit. The real world has still to come into existence. Depend upon it, it will come."

"Well—when do you think this revolution will become inevitable?"

"Who can say in advance? Perhaps after an American-Japanese war, perhaps after some other world-shaking event. It will want the impact of some violent external occurrence. Don't you suppose the wise men of Washington and Wall Street are well aware of that? That's just why they will keep out of war at all costs—especially a European war. They won't dream of coming in. Because even if they won it, as in 1918, they would have next what I am thinking of when I talk of their going absolutely mad—the folly of Prohibition a thousand times outclassed; in short, a witches' sabbath.

"Besides," he went on, "we have the means of giving it a helping hand, if America should show any inclination to intervene again. It may need only a spark for the thing to go off. All the elements of genuine pre-revolutionary feelings are present already. There is the willingness to be led politically by the nose. Busy writers are seeing to the creation of the great confusion of ideas that precedes every great revolution. And once the mess is universal, with strikes, sabotage, and political fighting, the time will have come for an American dictator to obtain legal possession of the power of the State and to make illegal profit out of it."

"Do you think Hitler has any idea of bringing about a revolution in America, as Ludendorff helped the Russians to Bolshevism?"

"Why not? Why not, if America begins meddling in our

affairs? But why need it come to that? We ought to fraternize, not fight. When those old cliques in Wall Street, who haven't the slightest inkling of the volcano they are sitting on, when they're shot up out of their offices and a radical America has at last come, just think what we could do in concert with it! We should turn the world upside down. Conquer America? What rubbish! Via Kamchatka, I suppose, when we have got nicely settled in Vladivostok? We've got to try for America's friendship. That's how I see it. But not the way you imagine. No, unfortunately it won't come that way. And after a war comes the great isolation."

"What do you mean by isolation?"

"Well, can't you imagine? There will remain two or three great coalitions of Powers. Each will shut itself off from the rest. None will want to have anything to do with the others. A new great partition of the world will come. World trade? Exchange of the benefits of civilization? Nobody will venture any longer to travel from one realm to another. There will be no traffic, no exchange. Each group will hug its treasures to itself, will monopolize its inventions, its discoveries. Pretty prospect, eh? But the only logical one. Once war comes again, the universal fear will be so great that the continents that emerge from it will retire into isolation, each of them behind its impenetrable Chinese wall."

"Do you think a war worth while?"

"Worth while? Why should it be? It is only necessary. A weird time is coming. The seas will empty of traffic. There will be no freedom of the seas. Each of the few giant empires will proclaim that parts of the seas, or whole oceans, belong to its sphere. Foreign ships will no longer be permitted to sail them. Territorial waters will reach out thousands of miles from the coast. Wireless communication, air traffic, everything of that sort will be broken off. In the midst of the inventions that have united the world, the continents will be cut apart and will live in voluntary isolation."

"A beautiful dream! Do you fancy the prospect?"

"Fancy it? Why, of course. Because, as I said, it's necessary. For it's only in isolation that we shall fully develop our potentialities. And then we shall see which will be the real top-dog among the great realms. World civilization will end. There will be a new *Kultur*. There will come the great historic epoch of the isolated civilizations."

"What a horrible, artificial world you prophesy!"

"Think of our universal plant, which we were trying to breed. Is not that also artificial? Is it not our task to recreate creation, so far as man is concerned, so that we may find it good?"

11

RAW MATERIAL

GERMANY'S FOOD SITUATION was going to be revolutionized by that universal plant which had been evolved in Germany. Koch, with his love of hoaxing the credulous, spread this rumor. The new sweet lupin was already a sort of revolution on a small scale for the lighter soil of East Prussia. Now, however, said Koch, under Nazi leadership marvels of plant-breeding were to come—not only potato plants that yielded both potatoes and tomatoes, but above all the universal or standardized plant, hybridized from rye, which yielded grain and edible tubers, and was also a textile plant that would take the place of flax. For very light soils there would shortly be a perennial rye, developed from couch-grass; once it had been put in the ground it would need no further attention. Other new plants, which would throw the products of Luther Burbank, the great American naturalist, into the shade, were to be expected very soon.

Koch is a witty man. He has humor, and belongs to the few old Nazis who have even been able to laugh at themselves and at Nazism. He saw very clearly the weaknesses of the artificial planning and the substitute mongering which the Nazis were carrying to fantastic lengths. "What do you say, Doctor?" he asked me once, when he was in an expansive mood. "Do you think the whole bag of tricks is worth while? Why do we go on with this German revolution if the good times are coming very soon and we'll all be stuffed full of good things? Wonderful, when you no longer need to plant your rye and can just stroll through the fields with your walking-stick to see how the bumper crops are getting on! But I've forgotten all about what will happen to our workers. Nobody will need to work any more. The machinery will do it all for us, and attend to itself in the bargain. Great heavens, what shall we do with all the time? You can't just play football all day long. And then no more matrimonial quarrels, because it will be free love everywhere and marriage will be done away with! What shall we have left to do?"

I must admit that although Koch was one of the wildest of the Nazis, I liked him in a way. It was impossible not to feel a certain respect for men of his type. Koch had been a subordinate railway official, and had never had more than the minimum of elementary schooling. But he had picked up an extraordinary amount of knowledge; he was a man of quick comprehension, he had immense energy and endurance, and he was a great organizer. A furious worker. He could manage for weeks on end with very little sleep. Nothing could tire him. In spite of his tremendous exertions he found time to read, to write articles, and to take in ample supplies of alcohol. Koch may well serve as the type of the best of the *Gauleiter* and old party members. These men were all full of ideas and suggestions and initiative. They had indeed, as Hitler said, an "untameable will." No one can deny their industry and devotion to duty. It is an absurd underestimate of the political achievements of these men to attribute them to luck or to mere intrigues of party wire-pullers. No party organization in Ger-

many demanded such hard work from its officials as did the
Nazi party. Before the so-called taking over of power—the
great "wangle" with Papen—Koch had led a life not altogether
destitute of the extremest privations and sacrifices. We have to
make due allowance for this sort of thing if we are to understand what happened. Where there was such devotion and
initiative, it was fair to assume that there were great moral
forces.

Koch was one of the sincere Socialists in the movement. He
was a follower of Gregor Strasser, like most of the North
German bosses. "Of course the world will become socialistic,"
he said to me once when I went to see him at Königsberg.
"Capitalism has done for itself. Do you suppose that Hitler
can stop at this reactionary beginning? My dear man, many
things have to happen yet. Your Junker cousins, we shall kill
the lot of them," he added, laughing. "We shall sweep them
all away. Peasants must take over; we are settling them on the
land. The things the slack Sozis (Socialists) never carried
out, we shall put through. Away with the Junkers and the
captains of industry! Do you suppose we were just talking
through our hats about nationalizing the banks and abolishing the stock exchange and all that? Everything in due time,
step by step; don't let them go nursing false hopes. The
gentlemen mustn't imagine that now, with our arrival in
power, the revolution is over. It's only beginning. And if that
whimpering instrument Hitler doesn't squeak out our tune,
we shall get another fiddle to play on. Or do you think, because we are being so gentle with the fine folk, that we are
afraid to touch them, like the old Sozis? Hugenberg's turn is
coming all right. All in their proper turn—don't shove! But
why should we slaughter them, as the Bolsheviks did? They
are useful, good raw material. We'll soon make something
out of them."

Koch, a little, stocky man with bright eyes, but otherwise
in no way striking, a regular specimen of the lower middle

class in spite of his uniform and decorations, was a revolutionary from top to toe. He had revolutionism in his blood, whereas the respectable party secretaries of the earlier Socialist parties had had it at best in their mouths or their pens. His idea was that the course must be through State capitalism to true Socialism. His patriotism as a German was subordinated to his Socialism: Socialism could be achieved only in wide territories.

"You can't have a socialistic system in Germany, a neo-capitalist one in France, and a patriarchal one in Poland," he said to me. "Either all Europe is run socialistically, or it's no go. We must conquer Europe so that it may become socialistic. Do you understand, my dear man, why I'm so strongly in favor of an alliance with Russia? Adolf doesn't like it. He runs after his phantom of power—and he'll have the whole world jumping on him. Adolf has no liking for us Socialists. All he cares for is his fame. He wants to go down in history as the great man. Some day millions are reverently to make the pilgrimage to the mausoleum of the greatest German of all times. In his foretaste of these touching occurrences he already weeps secret tears of pity for himself. Have you ever heard Hitler sob? Grand, I tell you. He'll do us yet out of all the reward for our pains."

Like many old party members, Koch was no militarist. He hated the old officers, just as he loathed the big landowners and industrialists. He gave them all the trouble he could, and made no secret of his repugnance to them. "Ask yourself," he said to me, "how far Germany can get by herself. Is there anything to be gained by resoling the old Nationalist boot? Of course, we've got to have a strong army. A revolution without power will fizzle out and get no further than a revolt."

Koch was absolutely against all political and military plans that aimed at the restoration of Germany's old frontiers of 1914, and at the creation of a great Central European realm.

"All that," he said to me when we were discussing the policy toward Poland, "may be useful preliminary work, but you must realize that it gets nothing lasting achieved. Just consider—how can a great free order of many nations be created out of the world of ideas of nationalism? Any such suggestion stultifies itself. The foundation must be built with other material. What other foundation than Socialism is possible? You needn't look askance at me like that—as though I were a Marxist pacifist. But what Adolf is after won't work. Can you rule peoples permanently with the knout? You have got to find something that will hold them together."

Koch was at bottom nothing more than an outcome of the old German Socialism. He had thrown away the pseudo-scientific crutches of Marxist doctrine, and he believed that with the aid of the national impulses of National Socialism a Socialist Germany in a Socialist European federation was a possibility. He was not the only *Gauleiter* to hold this belief. In any case, he had no faith in a lighthearted policy of conquest. For the rest, he abandoned no national claims; and he condemned the insulting of everything German, which had been common in certain circles among the Socialists, as one of the greatest follies of the Weimar period. He was full of the idea of harmonizing the Socialist with the nationalist outlook, and he thought that it would be possible in a Socialist national and international order to reconcile most of the national claims.

He seldom spoke of such things, as he had so many enemies who would at once have used what he said against him and passed it on to Hitler. All these Nazi leaders, great and small alike, practiced mimicry, just like the great mass of the oppressed people, and tried to conceal their own views beneath phrases in Hitler's style. Whether Koch's views have changed since, I do not know. At that time he regarded it as senseless to risk wars for Germany's national greatness. Wars were probably necessary, but only in order to compel the capitalist democracies to recognize the new Socialist community of Europe. France and the small States on the west must be revolutionized and brought in by war if they could not be without it; Britain must be thrust out of Europe. Beyond this he had only one aim, German association with Russia. If that could not be effected by fair means, it must be attempted by foul, through war. "But why a war," he added, "when everything is already prepared as if by nature for the closest alliance?"

"Russia!" said Koch enthusiastically, after a Königsberg fair to which he had invited me—"Now, leave aside for once all the usual prejudices and tell me, is it not a grand, tremendous country? And the people! Magnificent raw material, eh? You can make something of them. Why always be casting eyes at that feeble West, which, after all, only spits at us? Russia, my friend, that is the world of the future. Germans and Russians, let us weld together our miserable existences. I tell you, it will bring the biggest boom in the world, the most tremendous that has ever been known."

Koch was not a Prussian. He came from a West German family. He made the acquaintance of all the problems of Germany's eastern policy only when he became a *Gauleiter*.

"I've worn my tongue to rags," he confessed to me, "trying to persuade Hitler. You've no idea what battles there are at times in the *Gauleiter* conferences. Really, Adolf is a funny sort of revolutionary. He lives in the past. He is blind to the future. Do you think he has vision? He is a revolutionary facing backward. What he would like best is to be Charlemagne, but not converting the Saxon king Widukind to Christianity but being converted by him to the old Teuton faith. What does Adolf really want? Just see him swimming in the ocean of his phrases, old man! That sort of thing won't get our revolution anywhere!

"We are the raw material," he continued, "for a new creation. Anyone who does not feel that he must be put in the

melting pot like old iron is no revolutionary. Adolf is crying
out for raw material. Why? Will it help? The best raw
material is lying unused. Which, you ask? I'm telling you—
the raw material Man! Isn't he being squandered? Worse
than coal and oil. Well, what are we to use him for? As a
sacrifice to Wotan, for the glory of his prophet Adolf?"

He was a real idealist, that fellow Koch. So were many
others like him. Misguided idealists.

12

THE GENUINE NAZI

QUITE DIFFERENT WAS Forster, Hitler's Benjamin,
rumor said his pet. They called him "Bubi" (Little Boy) Forster at Danzig. Cautious women members of the party spread
the story that Hitler had brought him up, that Forster was
Hitler's foster-child. Everyone knew that he was on the best
of terms with Hitler.

The gossip may be dismissed. I am personally acquainted
with Forster's parents. They made it unnecessary for him to
be brought up by anyone else. Honest, likeable, highly respectable Franconians are those parents. Not a trace of pre-
tentiousness; decent lower middle-class people, the mother a
sterling, kind-hearted woman. The father was a prison inspec-
tor at Ingolstadt, in Bavaria. I have eaten *Weisswürste,* Bavarian sausages, at the parents' home.

This fellow Forster is typical of the young generation, the
youngsters who have broken out of the paradise of solid,
healthy lower middle-class respectability into the life of adventure. They had tales to tell of the inflation years, of post-
war experiences, of hardship in their young lives. How these
young fellows were made into revolutionaries is a chapter by
itself. In any case, this young man was a revolutionary,

though a revolutionary of a particular type. He is the genuine Nazi, of the sort Hitler wants. His glowing enthusiasm is not the Socialist's but the nationalist's; and the nationalist's whose dreams are of the simple people. He is a German above all. His voice trembles when he speaks the word *"deutsch."* He is of the type which the outside world takes to be characteristically Nazi—the German fanatic. A *Herrenmensch,* one of the "master-race," aristocrat of a new world, proudly conscious of his great mission. Like Hitler, he used to go through the streets with a riding-whip in his hand. He had never been on a real horse.

One thing must be said for Forster. Even if he is no aristocrat, and his manners are *bayerisch-bäurisch rüd,* those of a rough Bavarian boor, this young man has worked, he has been one of those who can show stiff determination, who can organize and maintain a harsh discipline. A young man out of the ordinary. Greiser, later President of Danzig, had allowed the region to go to rack and ruin. Forster was sent there by Hitler, and soon got things humming. He kept his end up with savage energy. The petty local party magnates trembled in front of him. Intrigues helped them not at all. Young as he was, only in the twenties, he mastered all the old comrades, however indignantly they might harp on their services to the party. He dismissed men and appointed others. He settled disputes, ruled with a rod of iron, and forged ahead. It was he who set the party in Danzig on its feet. No question about it, this young man had the "untameable will."

Beyond that he had nothing. He came to Danzig without so much as a cigar in his case. No education, no fortune, no profession. He was a shop assistant for a short time. The rest of his life was propaganda, politics, and faith in Germany and in the Fuehrer. He was crafty, tricky, brutal, but also, in his way, sincere and devoted. He did not have a very quick comprehension, but he was able to grapple with difficult problems. He was a magnificent speaker. His articles were distinguished by lucidity and energy of style. An extraordinary young man, who with his energy and industry and talent for organization would have done well in any ordinary career, if there had been any chance at that time of business success in Germany.

Forster, who today owns many houses and a substantial fortune in Danzig, was a fanatic who would have given away all he had gained, if it had been necessary for the sake of the movement and the Fuehrer. He was one of the members of the party who believed, or were determined to believe, every word Hitler spoke.

"Oh," he exclaimed once to me, "our grand movement! I feel happy only when I can be making speeches, telling the people what our movement is, taking them out of themselves and their petty everyday cares, and showing them Hitler's great aims. If I am disheartened and despairing, if I am dead beat through the eternal party quarrels, and I go to a meeting and speak to these simple, good-hearted, honest people, then I am refreshed again; then all doubts leave me."

He honestly meant every word of it. He preached the virtues of the simple folk, who must not be betrayed. "Go to the people," he said to me; "learn what a glorious feeling it is to have to do with simple folk."

What a grotesque contradiction! This man, who was busy seducing the masses into the new political servitude of the totalitarian State, talked in sentimental tones, like Rousseau and the Russian philanthropists, of the grandeur of the simple folk. Was it hypocrisy? Certainly not. He undoubtedly believed that he "loved the people," that he learned from them and was serving them. He was also constantly pointing out how necessary it is in taking any political action really to convince the people, and how indispensable it is for every politician to adjust his action to the wishes of the people. No politician, he would say, can continue in the long run to rule against the people and against the popular will. He therefore

indignantly rejected any suggestion that National Socialism
was ruling dictatorially. He firmly believed that only National
Socialism could create the conditions which would assure to
the simple folk a natural and happy life.

Thus there is in National Socialism a sort of Rousseauesque
longing for the simple and primitive in life. It is the revolutionary impulse to throw off the burden of civilization and
return to a primitive state, the idealized state of simple, strong
life. The National Socialists were able, with German sentimentality, to set apart in the midst of this tremendous revolution of destruction a small place for the idyllic, and here to
carry into reality the dreams of the age of puberty. Like Hitler, these genuine National Socialists of Forster's type fled
into solitude, rested in the bosom of nature, with the daily
arrival of orderlies and an impressive post; there they cultivated intimate intercourse with the charms of the unspoiled
wilds, while enjoying every domestic comfort.

Both Adolf Hitler and his young disciple Forster longed
to escape from the artificiality of civilized life. Forster built
himself a little house in the midst of the forest, near the sea,
far from any other habitation. It was with sincere, naïve
pleasure that Forster painted to me his enthusiasm at being
able to enjoy, far from the city, the idyll of a life in union
with nature. He preached the return to the primitive to all
his intimates, and they copied him, even if the rustle of the
forest was as meaningless to them as the noise of the motor
traffic in the city streets. But there was more behind it than
the mere desire for unending days in the country. I once
asked Forster what he meant by the primitive, and he replied
with a fantasy that was far removed from the things that are
usually associated with Nazism.

The Fuehrer, said Forster, had become a politician much
against the grain. It had been a painful wrench to him to give
up his profession as a heaven-inspired artist. He had made
the sacrifice deliberately, for Germany's sake. The world had

thus, perhaps, lost one of the greatest artistic geniuses of all times. But Hitler would not reveal his unique mission until later. He permitted glimpses of it only to a few. When the time came, however, Hitler would bring the world a new religion. God, or whatever we preferred to call it, life or the universal spirit, spoke to him in solitude. He drew his great power from intercourse with the eternal divine nature. The blessed consciousness of eternal life in union with the great universal life, and in membership of an immortal people—that was the message he would impart to the world when the time came. Hitler would be the first to achieve what Christianity was meant to have been, a joyous message that liberated men from the things that burdened their life. We should no longer have any fear of death, and should lose the fear of a so-called bad conscience. Hitler would restore men to the self-confident divinity with which nature had endowed them. They would be able to trust their instincts, would no longer be citizens of two worlds, but would be rooted in the single, eternal life of this world. "Sometimes," added Forster with romantic enthusiasm, "I hear those voices of which Hitler speaks. Then I feel strong, and know that we shall conquer and live for ever."

These romantic ideas of world redemption form an undertone in Nazi life which should not be missed. It gives the movement something of the irrational powers which other revolutions have drawn from the enthusiasm for their doctrines. Nobody among the Nazis had any serious belief in Wotan or any other of the Teuton divinities. Their creed was a simple pantheism, brightened with sentiment. It did not greatly differ from the spirit spread by the Marxist cultural associations, imagining themselves to be specially favored free spirits; they did not dream that the ideas they took to be new and enfranchising were very old and rather hackneyed.

"No," said Forster to me once, "if all that National Socialism meant was the creation of a great new Germany, we might go and bury ourselves. It is a new world epoch that we are creating, an entirely new, great civilization. Oh, if you would but realize Hitler's greatness!" he added, in a burst of ecstatic enthusiasm. Then he walked to and fro, with long, stiff strides, and sermonized in tense, strained tones, with ungainly gestures. "Hitler," he said enthusiastically, "will redeem the world. He will one day receive divine honor as the savior of the peoples. If National Socialism had not come, the human race would have died out. Literally. Or don't you believe it? Don't you see that it is going to ruin with its civilization?"

I will not reproduce the whole vision Forster described for me. He saw not only a single people threatened today, as in past ages, with national extinction, but that same fate threatening all the peoples of the world. A materialist civilization and a false morality were driving humanity step by step to self-destruction. Things that ought to be mere conveniences of existence had come to dominate life. Man had imprisoned himself in a labyrinth of his own making. Only truly strong and free men could still remove the curse of the mechanized civilization and of false morality. Such fanciful ideas of the inescapable death of the civilized peoples through their materialist civilization and their political forms of life were popular in Germany even before Spengler. Nazism regards its use of them as the basis of a practical policy as its greatest achievement.

"Hitler," Forster boasted, "is snatching the world back from the path to death. The glorification of the weak and morbid is Judaism, is Christianity. That is why we hate both. We talk of the Jew, but we mean the Christian as well. Jew and Christian are one and the same thing, don't forget that. The time is coming when we shall destroy the Christians, just as today we are persecuting the Jews. Christianity is the mortal sin against the healthy life."

In such utterances Forster was the primitive mouthpiece of

Hitler. It is worth while to take these trivial utterances seriously, for they express what Hitler was planning. What is important is not their naïve formulation but the fact that the sublime thoughts of philosophic spirits and serious students of life's problems, dragged down to the service of the meanest intellects, were here becoming the arsenal of the nihilistic revolution. Thoughts dragged down to feed the universal revolution—and not originally through the Nazis.

Forster saw judgment already pronounced on the great world democracies. Tried and found wanting! England, he constantly assured me, was dying out. It was really a pity to see that race vanishing. But in a hundred years' time, he considered, Britain would be reduced to the level of a smaller Sweden and Norway. There again Forster was merely repeating Hitler's opinion. France? She was anemic, comfort-loving, pacifist. A nation of regular fellaheen. America, on the other hand, would become entirely primitive one day. It might be that she would throw off her hothouse city culture and go back to the land, to the life of the peasant. That would mean America's real emergence as a nation. But it could be achieved only through a National Socialist leader. Sooner or later America would get one.

His only real anxiety was about the Slavs. He had an absolute hatred of them, although as a Bavarian he had not the inheritance of the Prussian-Polish antipathy. He could not speak of the Slavs without abuse. He had not the slightest knowledge of their culture and history, and he did not want to know anything about it; he wanted to keep all his primitive, carefully tended hatred. To the Danzigers, who were by no means anti-Polish at bottom, he called this "fortifying the national consciousness." His hatred was due to the fact that all the Slav nations were just what the Germans wanted to be. A prolific peasantry, bound to the soil, firmly rooted in the soil, unspoiled, and, taken all in all, the future great nation of Europe, in relation to which Germany would stand in fifty years' time where France stood today in relation to Germany.

The only race, it was held, with which Germany would have to fight a life and death struggle for predominance in Europe, and for her rank as a world-nation, was the Slav race. Forster shared this idea. Consequently he regarded my ideas of arriving at an understanding or an alliance with Poland as an atrocity. The moment he noticed that my search for an understanding was sincere and not merely tactical, he became my opponent. He did not shrink from declaring to me in public that I had been bought by Poland, and owned an estate in Pomerellen that had been presented to me.

At the outset of our Polish policy he told me that there can be no accommodation with one's mortal enemy. Hitler's policy, he said, did not aim at denying the Poles the right to exist. The simplest thing would be to transport the Poles and the Czechs to some other region, and settle them there; in Siberia, for instance. They were a relic from the Middle Ages that had most unfortunately lived on, and there was no longer any justification for their existence. For the rest, the Slavs must be split up into many small States, and prevented from becoming a great political unit. That, in his opinion, was the only way to exorcise the Slav peril. Germany had to make good all the errors of her history. Today the last, irrevocable opportunity had come for making good as a nation our omissions of the past. These omissions, in his view, lay not only in territorial matters. We had, of course, to become the great united realm which it had been our mission to create in the Middle Ages. Our frontiers must embrace Austria, Bohemia, parts of Poland, Hungary, parts of Croatia down to the Adriatic; we must gain Denmark, Holland, Belgium, parts of France, Alsace-Lorraine, and Switzerland. But that great unified German realm could exist only as the nucleus of a still greater one, in which Bismarck's realm of allied countries would be repeated on a greater scale—the realm of the European nations, around Germany as its center.

At that time these were fancies to which one listened with impatience. They could be made reality only by the hard blows of a war—this Forster admitted in the circle of his intimates. But he forbade the disturbing of the mass of party members with such prospects. If the world were reasonable, he said, it would leave Hitler a free hand. He wanted to do the best, even for the people whom at present he was handling harshly and cruelly. "Hitler has got to be hard," he said once to me; "if you only knew how he has to force himself to be hard, and what a tender and sensitive heart he has!" But probably Germany would be unable to achieve her destiny without war, without great sacrifices. No nation received its greatness as a free gift.

Why it should be Germany that was called to reset the dislocated world was a question with which Forster dealt in his purely political speeches. "We have to have a faith," he used to say; "without faith there can be no victory. Why is the German called? Destiny has given him knowledge. He has passed through the greatest privations; always he has come away empty from the great decisions of history. He has never come into his own. Alien powers have dominated him. Alien spiritual powers and alien political powers." Germany had never had a form of her own. Even in the Middle Ages, when she administered the Holy Roman Empire, she was guided by alien ideals. She not only had always to defend her frontiers, as the country placed geographically in the center; she not only had one territory after another taken from her; as in the fairytale of Hans in Luck, her well-earned possessions had been talked out of her hands by one rogue after another. Her original heritage had been exchanged again and again at a loss. The final exchange had been for democracy by the grace of France. Now Germany had thrown that away as Hans dropped his whetstone. She was free now to face her destiny anew. In her freedom she would finish all the tasks the rest of the world had hitherto attacked in vain. Work and bread for all, and no more hunger, destitution, or unemployment. Reconciliation of classes, reconciliation of nations under a just order. Freedom from superstition, and ability to enjoy this life in all its grandeur with a good conscience. Thus, democracy is the sum total of all that is wrong and noxious. It is unnecessary to consider what democracy is and what it might be. What is wanted is not an impartial valuation but a symbol. Democracy is the deception practiced on the productive classes by a class of conspirators controlling and exploiting them. The term "democracy" is used as other revolutionaries use the term "capitalism." There is no need to know any more about it.

Democratic impartiality is the worst vice of the age. Impartiality is weakness of will. It is a duty to be onesided, to set out big, simple, easily comprehended symbols. To paint things in black and white. All the intermediate shades cripple the will. To understand and forgive is the extreme perversion of the will to live. Life does not forgive. Be deliberately primitive, deliberately unjust, deliberately impulsive! Don't be shackled by reason! The reasonable is always the enemy of life. No longer reflect, only react. It is impossible to get anything done unless one is onesided. Those who know too much no longer get anywhere. They no longer have even a sound judgment. Consequently, fight against the intellect, and especially against the intellectuals. We no longer have to know, but to believe.

That was the sum total of the teaching of Forster and that ilk. The main thing seems to me to be their determination to have faith. They shout their faith, they force themselves into it. They shut their eyes and ears, to hear nothing but their raving confession of faith. "We believe in Germany! Why do we believe? Because we are determined to believe!" Behind declarations of that sort lurks doubt. Did not Forster have to indulge in this "deep talk" (a sort of ersatz religion) so constantly in order—as he admitted—to become sure of himself again, to be able to believe again? "Shout when you feel weak," he said once to a doubting party comrade. "If you are not quite sure of your case, then shout at your opponent. When in doubt, shout."

13

SIEGFRIED AND HAGEN IN THE PARTY

FORSTER AND KOCH represented, roughly speaking, the two types among the high Nazis, one socialistic, the other nationalistic. They were enemies, at loggerheads with each other.

Once when I asked Forster what was the chance of a political alliance with Bolshevik Russia, and mentioned Koch's ideas, the young man fairly raved. That, he said, was just the treason that crept into the ranks of the party. That was the danger of which Hitler was constantly warning his men. National Socialism would never be conquered if it could keep its ranks pure. But Hitler sensed already, and in his tragic hours of solitude it filled him with sorrow, that the day would come when treason would grow in the very ranks of the party, destroying National Socialism or, what was worse, leading it into the camp of its mortal enemies.

Yes, he continued, in tones of theatrical pathos, Hitler was very lonely. No one understood him. He had hours of the blackest apprehension. Never was he greater than when he tore himself away from these trials, to be once more the hard, great Leader. National Socialism could come to grief, like all that was noble; one day perhaps, like Siegfried, it would bleed to death from the treachery of a malevolent Hagen. But from the downfall of the movement, from the vast struggles that would precede it, from the Twilight of the Gods that must descend upon the whole world, there would nevertheless arise in the end a rejuvenated world, and so the sacrifice of the movement would not have been in vain. "Koch had better look out," he added threateningly, breaking off his tirade. "Hitler watches that sort of thing for a very long time, but once he moves he is pitiless. Hitler knows exactly where his enemies in the party are."

It was a fact that Hitler for a long time was on the point of putting Koch out of the way, in order to make an end once for all of Socialist tendencies among the *Gauleiter*. Forster, as he himself later admitted to me in confidence, was even designated as Koch's successor. I did not learn why the deposition did not take place. Hitler, who had no illusions about the character of his movement and of the men in his confidence, was compelled to carry his enemies with him in his own ranks; he could no more get rid of them than of his past.

The first time I heard Forster talk in this Nibelungen-Ring style, I set it down to his youthful sentimentalism. But Forster was a sort of feebler edition of Hitler's sentimentalism; he copied, uncritically and rather innocently, Hitler's secret fears and his emotional outbreaks. Hitler's foreboding that he would not live to complete his "life's work," his certainty that there would come a vast treasonable volte-face on the part of his own collaborators and the destruction of everything that had been achieved, must constantly have oppressed the Fuehrer. The way Forster reproduced Hitler's forebodings revealed, for all its rhetoric, a deep sense of a coming and inevitable catastrophe. The eternal doom of the German people lay in wait, Hitler felt, for him too.

"Hitler knows his destiny," declaimed Forster on another occasion. "He will fall in combat with Bolshevism. He knows that he will be conquered in the struggle with the greatest of our enemies. But he will in no way be deterred by that knowledge. He will always do whatever is necessary. Like the old

Teuton heroes, he will go out to battle even when it means his certain overthrow. Germany and the whole world must first pass once more through a long period of the deepest darkness. A horrible machine age will come throughout the world. But that will not be the end. Only then will the real struggle for freedom begin. And only then will the greatness of Hitler and the meaning of our struggle be understood."

This sentimental, tasteless rhetoric cannot disguise the fact that Hitler's foreboding of an inevitable catastrophe is something real, perhaps something of great importance. His own friends would one day stab him mortally in the back—that was a complaint that frequently recurred. And it would be just before the last and greatest victory, at the moment of supreme tension. Once more Hagen would slay Siegfried. Once more Hermann the Liberator would be murdered by his own kinsmen. The eternal destiny of the German nation must be fulfilled yet again, for the last time. The German nation would destroy itself. It would throw away this victory like the others. "Red Front and Reaction" are, after all, not merely memories of the vain putsch of 1923; they are the threatening signs of the future.

Siegfried and Hagen in the party—they are Forster and Koch. But those two figures will face each other in continually changing forms. Strange how Hitler gave himself away to his intimates in other ways too. How he would blab his secret weakness and foreboding, perhaps not even unintentionally. Once more it was Forster who drew my attention to Sulla, from the period of the hundred years of Rome's delirium, who by means of proscription decimated the old families, and who began to settle his soldiers on the latifundia as a new and genuine peasantry. Hitler secretly compared himself with this wild destroyer who imagined that he had once more set up a permanent order. Hitler found this figure attractive. He found in it his own reflection. Was it no more than a sign of his lack of historical education, or was it the expression of a deeper knowledge of the limits to his mission? Hitler was most attracted, if I can place faith in Forster's report, by the end of Sulla's life; when he regarded his mission as ended, Sulla voluntarily relinquished power.

In my astonishment I replied to Forster on this occasion by asking whether he realized that Sulla was not a figure that could be chosen as a desirable exemplar. But Forster disagreed. He said I did not understand. "Ah," he went on, "just as Sulla did, Hitler will abdicate one day, and will retire entirely from public life. Others will then take up the visible task. He, however, will embark on a new and yet greater mission."

I will not repeat what I have told earlier of Hitler's ideas of a possible "Third Punic War." These are romantic and yet very pertinent ideas, of having perhaps to break off his mission, because Great Britain's world empire can be destroyed only in a third assault. In his seclusion he will then pursue two aims. He will complete his religious mission and will proclaim the new religion. And from his "little Elba" he will also make a return in state to power and reappear at the head of the Reich, after his successors have failed to cope with their difficult problems.

Play acting, cunning political scheming, romantic dreaming, real pessimism and genuine forebodings of an early end—all these things seethe in Hitler's intimate talks to his closest confidants. But the deep divergence of views in his party remains, a constant threat to its existence. One day it will break out, and destroy again all that has been attained. The patriots, the German nationalists, will stand on one side, asking each other how Germany can yet be saved. The Socialists, the utopians, the radical planners will stand on the other side, determined to carry their great radical world revolution to completion, heedless of Germany's future. The party will split and be delivered over to its two mortal enemies of the past, "Red Front and Reaction," as the Horst Wessel song has it, that song with no cheerful melody suggestive of strength and victory, but slow and dragging like a funeral march, melancholy and full of forebodings.

Forster, like Hitler, tears himself away from pessimism and foreboding by means of his fanatical faith in the German people and their mission. He is convinced that the German people are called to bring true Socialism into the world in the greatest revolution of all time. For, declares Forster in these homilies, only Hitler understands what Socialism is in truth, and why it is a national Socialism, not the utopian, rationalistic Socialism that seeks realization through the dictatorship of the proletariat. Hitler's Socialism does not upset the natural order of mankind, but perfects it. It means the perfection of the nation unto eternal life.

Nations no longer have to perish, as in ancient times—they are the eternal pillars of humanity. The nation is the true earthly god; it is the immortal man. In the nation the individual man, too, is immortal, and he is so only in the nation. This immortality is no chimera, like the Christian belief. He who lives in his nation dies not. So to weld the nation together that it is a single great being with one heart, that is Hitler's true mission, and one which such men as Koch will never understand. It is a new creation, it is the perfecting of creation. Just as the individual bee no longer lives a life of its own, but is only a cell in the hive-community (*der Bien* as the German bee-keeper calls it, to indicate that that collectivity has an animal existence of its own), so the individual human existence no longer has any reality, the individual exists only as part of that great biological creature the nation, which alone has personality in the mental and spiritual sense. This is true for the German nation, and equally so for other nations. Not, of course, for all, and especially not for the Jews, who are the "non-folk," the eternal antithesis of a natural nation. Hitler will introduce the evangel of this belief into other nations besides Germany.

With all the frenzy of his semi-education, Forster saw in Bolshevism the incarnation of the unnatural, the bestial. An artificial order, instituted against the nature of things, and one which must lead men to destruction. For Forster Bolshevism and liberalistic democracy were one and the same thing. The only difference between the two was that one was the initial and the other the final stage of development. For him, as a faithful disciple of his master, there could be no compromise with either.

Forster only half understood all this. All that his simple audiences grasped was the mystical ecstasy, and they were seized with a vague enthusiasm. They felt the emergence from his speeches of a world of light and a world of darkness. The two faced each other in mortal combat. Valhalla and the dark world of Alberich, the realm of the "Aryans" and the world of the Jews.

"What a pure soul!" said an acquaintance enthusiastically to me after one of those speeches. He was a diplomat.

Actually the masses believed, as one man expressed it: "This man is a dreamer, but he is doing something for the difficulties of the small people. It's impossible to understand a word of his Socialism and his fine poetical similes, but it's nice listening to that sort of talk. It is exciting and beautiful. That man means what he says; he is not on the side of the fine folk; he makes common cause with the poorest of the workers; he faces up to the rich people and tells them they have got to pay. Forster is not just an official. The man is genuine."

Hitler knew why he stuck to his Benjamin. Forster was for him the embodiment of the fanatically credulous youth, no longer content to have a good time and enjoy life, but hard and combative—the new youth.

14

UNDERLINGS OF THE REVOLUTION

IN ADDITION TO the "big noises," the demigods of the party, there are the underlings of the revolution. I do not mean the *Amtswalter,* the hundreds of thousands of party comrades given jobs as petty officials. I mean such figures as Ley the Swiller, Funk the Fleshy Financier, Streicher the Jew man, and fat Baldur, men who had no contribution of their own to make to the ideas of the party, but who carried out vast set tasks and had immense explosive energy. What strange contradictions they all showed in themselves! That dissolute schoolmaster Streicher, for instance—in addition to his criminal Jew campaign he took an interest in nudism and felt himself to be a prophet of a new science of natural healing. The dirty dog had yet other fads. He fought for the purity of "Aryan" blood from admixture with the "poisonous" Jewish element. He founded a Paracelsus Institute, with that great physician and philosopher of the Reformation period as its patron—an institute for purely "Aryan" medicine, liberated from the tradition of Arabic and Jewish physicians. "Aryan" blood must not be poisoned, moreover, with chemicals. Compulsory inoculation must be abolished. All these methods of treatment drawn from a system of medicine resting on a Jewish basis served only the continuous poisoning of the great white master race.

Then that fat and jolly ex-financial journalist Funk. For a time he played a part as a guest artist in Goebbels' propaganda machine. A man of no originality, a sybarite, a man whose jovial exterior cloaks the subtle malice of his methods.

And that perpetually drink-sodden, miserable-looking Dr. Ley. The first time I saw him was at nine o'clock one morning. He came in in his dressing-gown, straight out of bed, and, with his throat still rattling with phlegm from the potations of the night before, drank off half a bottle of brandy on an empty stomach.

Next, the huge, wobbling, eternally juvenile Baldur von Schirach, a man stuffed up with conceit, whose gift of gab got him the post of Governor of Vienna, the originator of the characteristic exaggerated rigidity of the Hitler Youth, which is nothing more than over-compensated slackness. A man who is sham through and through like every one of his verses. The bellwether of the arrogant youths who, like the schoolboy in *Faust*, think they can afford to despise their old teachers and are really selling themselves to the devil.

Then the fellow Rust—Minister of Culture is his job—a spinner of empty phrases. And many others who, in their narrow or wider circles, play the petty dictator.

In one thing they are all alike—in their mediocrity. They have retained all the instincts and the ways of petty middle-class insolvents. Herr von Schirach is nothing more than a militarized scoutmaster. They are sham revolutionaries. Their instincts are for dropping back into the comforts of Philistin-ism. They are men who really do not know what to do with the power they have acquired. They compromise the power they possess. They are living witnesses to the fact that in this age of mechanization any brainless ass can play the great man if he has command of an organization.

But in one respect these men are not merely routineers with an organization, but routineers of the great revolution. They all have a kink. They are all abnormal, and have been more or less failures in ordinary life. They are not on good terms with the existing order. They are enemies not only of the Weimar democracy; they have broken away from the world of respec-tability. They are themselves what their master calls the Jews (stealing and misinterpreting Mommsen's phrase)—a "ferment of decomposition." Instinctively they long for the pleasant se-curity of a life of respectability. But their whole career, their very character, is incompatible with respectability. Thus their existence is an oscillation between opposites. They feel the continual temptation of a respectable middle-class life, a temptation that has already overcome large numbers of the revolutionary proletariat. They remain partly in each camp, they are semi-revolutionaries, they remain routineers.

"The things that Marxism failed to achieve, we shall bring to the working people. Justice and an existence worthy of human beings. We shall not permit bosses to come out on top. Genuine leaders of the people are being trained here"—so I heard Ley thunder in the little hall of a "leaders' school" in a Berlin suburb, which the Socialist trade unions had built for the training of their leaders. With thorough naïveté he said: "We are the standard-bearers of the great struggle for the liberation of humanity. The high-spirited effort of the worker to win equality of rights with the middle class was defeated by the materialism and the selfishness of the intellectuals who were his false leaders. It has been left to us to assure the worker his place in our commonweal. No class rule from below, also none from above, but the true classless society of the eternal people, which no longer recognizes parties or special interests but only duties and rights in relation to the people as a whole."

People of the lower middle class were his audience. The recollection of the years of loss and disappointment, of the fortunes destroyed by inflation and taxation, of the things they regarded as fraud and robbery, fermented wildly in these impoverished people who had known better days, these people for whom the Weimar Republic had meant not splendor and advancement but humiliation and privation.

The masses of the workers were no longer the pillars of the revolution. Karl Marx's vision was wrong. It was the proletarianized and radicalized lower middle class that had set up the dictatorship which was to create the classless society. All the people with small independent livelihoods, the small men with savings, the small property owners, the artisans, the craftsmen who had worked for themselves, the people with small independent incomes, the pensioners, all these people who were now delivered over, robbed of their protection, to the insecurity and the hardships of the struggle for existence, had become the pillars of the revolution. At the same time the people who were still called the proletariat in speeches and manifestos were protected at least from the worst misfortunes, and had acquired the old safeguards and advantages which the middle class used to enjoy. Could not all the factory girls have their bad teeth turned into shining false sets by the sickness insurance funds? Did they not all receive assistance at childbirth and premiums as nursing mothers, while the independent craftsmen of the past and the peasant had neither doctor nor dentist, neither medicine nor trips to the seaside for wife and child? Was not vengeance now coming for the fact that a new privileged class had begun to grow, while classes formerly prosperous had sunk into distress and insecurity and anxiety? The revolutionary spark was no longer fired in the prospering classes of the industrial workers, but in these new classes of the disinherited and humiliated.

"We owe it to the war, we owe it to the wretched, humiliating peace, that we have gained knowledge through our need and our cares," shouted Dr. Ley in tones of fury. "On our shoulders has been laid the burden of the struggle for freedom and justice. Now it is our turn! Now we will show what we can do."

"Ours will be the future Reich," boasted the plump youth leader Schirach. "You will live in it, not the old and decrepit. Consequently it is your task to build it. A new mankind is growing up with us." And in the market place at Lübeck, amid an excited crowd of women members of the party from poor but respectable homes in every town of the province, the portly Rust drivelled about the greatness of the future culture of Germany. All these routineers of the revolution forced themselves to feel as revolutionaries. They shouted their aspirations, and in the perspiring ecstasy of their orations they believed in the radical upheaval of the world.

One of Funk's colleagues on the Berlin bourse is known as the "foghorn." He has earned his nickname by his deep, booming voice. Like foghorns the speeches of all these sham revolutionaries boomed through the halls and open places of Germany. How is it possible that so much insincere rhetoric could have so much success? Where were the great, inspiring ideas which in the past had lent nobility to revolutions even amid their worst excesses? Whence came the great power of seduction that worked so wildly on these maddened lower middle classes?

It was the seduction of liberation! Young and old, men and women were suddenly lifted out of their narrow conceptions, out of the pettiness and limitations of their aspirations. A great world, a world of great appetites and passions, was spread before their eyes. This Nazism made them dizzy with the unprecedented opportunities it revealed to them. Satisfaction of ambition, undreamed-of pleasures and freedoms, the strangest and most intoxicating of prospects opened before them. Chances grew up in front of them like magic flowers in enchanted meadows. They had only to wish. The blue flower of romance that had satisfied the wishful dreams of earlier generations through the pleasures of the imagination had become a fruit of paradise—a position, a job that carried a pension, at an unheard of salary, a post of command.

"Youth, thou art free! Youth, thou art the guarantor of the future! Thy life is free from now on! Obedience to the Leader, nobody else! I release thee from the compulsion which narrow-minded parents and petty schoolmasters imposed on thee." Such was the Nazi message shouted by the youth leader.

Young and old tore down the barriers of a narrow and meager existence, failing to see, amid the revolutionizing of their private lives, the new iron ring that was closing round them.

II

REVOLUTIONARIES AGAINST
THE GRAIN

1

THE NEW TALLEYRAND

WHO WAS SCHACHT? What sort of a part did he play? People who claim to know him well see in him the actual evil spirit of Germany, the man in the background who is really answerable for all her ills. They describe him as insanely ambitious and a complete cynic.

In the case of a man like Hjalmar Schacht, president of the Reichsbank and economic dictator of the Third Reich during the rearmament phase, "ambition" explains nothing. There is a mystery about this *Zauberer,* as he is called, this "sorcerer." No one will deny that he is a man of immense ability. But no one will be able to overlook the unscrupulousness of his methods. It need cause no surprise to find him a despiser not only of the *misera plebs* but of the respectable middle class with its inherited opinions and prejudices. But was he really the evil and reckless gambler type, who is ready to sacrifice all else to his personal aggrandizement?

In any case, he was a man apart, unique, solitary, without followers or any coterie of partisans. Schacht had no friends, only enemies. That seems to me to be something in his favor. He had to regard as enemies not only the Nazis but the middle-class nationalists and the remains of the first German democracy, the parties and cliques who proposed, when Hitler fell, to begin again where they had had to leave off in 1932-33.

Schacht concealed his own opinions beneath a cloud of cynical dicta, of which not one deserves to be regarded as anything but the particular subtlety considered by him at the moment to be suited to his particular purpose. Many of these *bons mots* are thoroughly malicious, and they plainly reveal a pleasure in mystification.

"We can get rid of Hitler at any time," he said abroad shortly before the war, to the perplexity of hearers who were beginning to regard Hitler as a great man. A rather naïve acquaintance urged Schacht to take over the leadership of the opposition in Germany as "the only man who can liquidate the Nazi regime." "Really," he replied, "that's quite an interesting prospect!"

To others he confessed: "Every time I come away from Hitler I feel nerved and alert. I have courage once more. Amazing how the Fuehrer can dissipate one's fears and reveal all sorts of fresh opportunities!" Or he would say to foreign friends: "Germany cannot fight for a single month. War? Out of the question! Impossible!"

I do not know Schacht well enough to venture on an opinion as to the extent to which his cynicism is the fruit of his personal career, or just a welcome expedient with which he can protect himself from awkward questions, taking refuge in a cloud of enigmas and contradictions. Enigmas and contradictions are a weapon of which he makes continual use. But at the outset of my political activities I had a conversation with him which seems to me to throw some light on his actual views and the background of his decisions.

I was attracted by two of Schacht's personal tastes—his fondness in the past for unpretentious holidaying with a bicycle, and his love of flowers and gardens. When I went to see him at the Reichsbank I found his room filled with beautifully arranged flowers. On his desk was a peculiar eggplant, the botanical name of which I have never discovered in spite of my own interest in gardening. I meant to ask him about it, but he put the question out of my head by mentioning that he was just going into the country for a few days; we spoke about farming matters, and he told me he had had two motoring accidents, from both of which, to the disappointment of his enemies, he had emerged unscathed.

"Tell me," he said, turning to politics, "how is it that you, a

Prussian Conservative, have managed to embark on a pro-Polish policy, and with such success? What I like about your policy is its pleasantly unorthodox character."

I made a few remarks about my line of political thought.

"Enviably optimistic," said Schacht. "Will the Poles enter into your ideas? Is it all just a flash in the pan?"

I said it was too soon to say; it depended largely on whether any substantial result was produced by the new Polish policy. He asked for details, and I mentioned the possibilities of fairly close political and economic cooperation with Poland, and gave my reasons for attaching so much importance to collaboration with Poland, of all countries.

"I am more interested in our progress in the southeasterly direction," replied Schacht. "But I am perfectly ready to support your efforts if there are substantial chances back of them. It makes no difference to me whether I give financial assistance to industry in the form of unemployment relief or of long-term credits for Poland." He felt doubtful, however, whether political differences could be overcome by such simple economic means. "Poland will be only too glad to let her industrial system be modernized at our expense, but I doubt if she'll let us draw political advantages of any value from the process."

I tried to explain that the economic enterprises which I felt to be desirable could not be undertaken on such simple lines. I gave a few instances of the possible means of intensifying the economic relations between the two countries. But Schacht said he was skeptical of all such ideas, and of any policy of economic penetration of the old type. "That sort of thing is no longer possible on a private-enterprise basis; new methods are needed, and they can only be gradually developed." This brought us to the subject of the general political and economic situation.

I had a definite impression at the time that Schacht was at bottom an advocate of moderation in every field. He spoke of

the great process of healing that was needed, a process that
could not be completed without allowing certain feverish
symptoms to work themselves out. He saw the dangers that
were inseparable from this process of healing. He realized the
risk we were taking, but we had, he considered, no alternative.
"We must beware," he said gravely, "of getting into a situation from which we no longer have any means of escape, so
that we are driven into a course in which we are no longer
master of our movements. Thus it is essential to see that we
retain freedom of action in every situation. We must avoid
both material and personal commitments. If we are drawn into
a course out of which we can no longer escape, we might be
forced to go with open eyes to our destruction, with no means
of doing anything to save ourselves."

In all this, and it seems to me a fact worth noting, Schacht
revealed no trace of the cynical gambler he is generally reputed
to be. He recognized the limits of the possible, both economic
and political. In those years that meant a good deal. The crisis
in his personal career, which ended with his resignation as
president of the Reichsbank, obviously resulted from his endeavor to act in accordance with those maxims, and at least to
avoid so far as he was concerned any course that threatened to
get beyond control.

In our talk he also expressed the gravest doubt of any possibility of achieving a satisfactory solution on the basis of the
good will of those concerned. "Most men have to be saved by
force." This, he added, applied equally to individuals and to
nations. "But my radius of action," he said, "is very restricted
at present. You must not expect too much from the new policy,
or too rapid results. Great setbacks are inevitable. We must be
prepared for them. No one who intends to pursue a reasonable
policy ought to squander his resources at the very outset, as is
being done in Germany. The bulk of the resources should be
held in reserve. That, at any rate, is my opinion, and I shall
not depart from it."

Schacht said he had not only to wrest Germany free from the last financial fetters of the Treaty of Versailles and from her foreign indebtedness but to prepare a new and solid basis for the economic life of the country. All this could not be done by a few tricks. The Nazis had fallen into the same error as certain respected economists who expected final salvation from the return to old and tried methods, or else from radically new ones—"they all see things much too simply." In actual practice unemployment demanded altogether different handling from any that was dreamed of by either the old doctrinaires or the young irresponsibles.

"They all seem to be looking to me for salvation by means of some piece of magic or some inspiration of genius. That is not my task at all. The essence of my task, as I see it, is to move step by step to a new but practicable form of national economy in which private initiative and public control are brought into a working synthesis. That sort of thing is not to be achieved as a sort of parlor game, or left to the chance of a happy inspiration. It proceeds only from continual experiment and adjustment, from a mass of specific attempts and practical modifications.

"Don't take too simple a view," he continued, "of the healing of the economic body of Germany. We must allow the utmost possible free play to independent enterprise, and examine with the utmost caution every suggestion for public intervention. I will have nothing to do with Utopias. Besides, I have many other problems, particularly the financing of rearmament. All these things have to be so dovetailed that nothing shall impede anything else; on the contrary, everything should help everything else. So I cannot promise unlimited support for your proposals; all I can do is to help them in so far as they fit in with my main task."

Later I fell out of favor with Schacht through my proposals for the devaluation of the Danzig gulden and the Reichsmark. The idea did not fit in with his plans. I know why today, but at the time I did not. I tried in vain to speak to him on the matter. He would not talk about such subjects. He had no liking for discussion of his own views. So, between utopians and the sterile and the gamblers, and at constant feud with them all, Schacht tried to pave the way to greatness for Germany and for himself.

For he saw in himself the really constructive statesman who would be the liquidator of the Nazi experiment after the ultimate fiasco of the revolutionary phantasmagoria that began in 1932. He worked long and tenaciously to create the opportunities for that change of scene. He was against a military dictatorship, and against a reactionary regime. He had also to safeguard himself from all the other elements that were similarly waiting their opportunity, all the countless groups, obscure or semi-obscure, from Hugenberg to the Weimar Democrats, of which each one had its own plan in readiness for achieving Germany's salvation and its own.

Unfortunately Schacht miscalculated in some important things. He jumped out with immense courage as the car approached the abyss, but even then he did not secure the freedom of action he hoped for. All Germany's industrial resources had been invested for eight years in the instrument of war. There remained nothing to do but to go to war, because disaster could be averted only by opening up vast new regions under German domination.

Friends told me of his pessimistic estimate of the world situation shortly before war broke out. The thing that had been the worst shock to him was the blind unconcern of Great Britain. The Empire's unpreparedness and the unimaginative British leadership had done much to upset his original calculations. He had prepared for a fresh start, intending after his tactical retreat to climb the last step to power. But when he returned from his last journey abroad his one concern was to make sure of his welcome from the powers that be, lest he should find himself after all among those who had backed the wrong horse.

2

THE CROSS-SPIDER

"CROSS-SPIDER" IS what the Germans call the common garden spider. No less a man than Alfred Hugenberg, the last leader of the German Conservatives, or at least of those who thought themselves to be Conservatives, had that nickname. Two or three years before the Nazis came into power it was given to him by the dissenting group of Conservatives because of his political and industrial methods, his vast network of organizations and personal contacts and cross connections, his impenetrable tangle of industrial combines and interlockings of interests. He, the mysterious leader, lurked in the center of this webb, waiting for his prey. The cross, the symbol of the Christian faith, concealed the brutality of the process only from the simple-minded.

This was roughly the interpretation which Hugenberg's Conservative opponents among us country folk placed on the huge posters that showed a great spider in a web spun over unhappy Germany. The split among the German Conservatives was a gloomy omen of the coming surrender to the Nazis. We must not overlook the fact that the subsequent lack of restraint evinced by Conservatives in their dealings with the Nazis originated from the confusion and lack of unity concerning a Conservative policy.

I myself called Hugenberg the grave-digger of the Conservative party. But it would be unjust to term him a reactionary in the ordinary sense of the word. The situation is far more serious, indeed, more tragic. This intelligent politician and great organizer did not mold his ideas and plans in a reactionary spirit, in order to compel the restoration of dis-

carded, out-of-date conditions. He is certainly a patriot. He is
a Christian, as far as one can judge. He is certainly not the
selfish business politician propaganda makes him out to be.
He is personally unassuming. He is not even ambitious, in the
ordinary sense of the word. It was not merely the craftiness of
his tactics, or the means at his disposal as a politician, that became his bane, but his political, or better, perhaps, his philosophical outlook. Hugenberg is secretly convinced that there
can be no more Conservatism in the old and genuine sense. To
desire to be a Conservative in this time of the great universal
world revolution is tantamount to committing suicide.

I did not realize the depth of resigned skepticism underlying this man's political aims until long after I had broken personally with the German Nationalists. This does not imply
that I have so changed my judgment of him as to be ready to
become his apologist. No one can absolve him from responsibility for a share in the catastrophe. What I would say is this:
Hugenberg is not the grave-digger of German Conservatism
because he is a reactionary but because he is a revolutionary. It
is true that he has not the revolutionary temperament; he is a
revolutionary by deliberate choice, prompted by his resigned
skepticism.

The revolution, he argued, could not be stayed. Like so
many other Germans, he held that the only way to save something ancient, eternal, Western, or what ever one may prefer
to call the heritage of our history, was by joining the revolution and using and dominating it. Above all, he was anxious
to avoid slipping back into the position of the lagging, un-
timely accuser and warner, to avoid playing Cicero to Hitler's
Caesar. He did not want to champion the virtues of the older
generation against the vices of the younger one. The new age
and its new Caesar were inevitable. The revolution was bound
to end in the new Caesarism. The only possible aim of anyone
who had been a Conservative up to then was to smooth the

way for this Caesarism—in other words, to go through with the revolution to its logical end.

A German politician is always half a professor of history. Undoubtedly Hugenberg is much more like a grim old schoolmaster than a great industrial organizer. Anyone who has seen the *Geheimrat*, with his bristling hair and thick mustache, delivering a speech in his dry pedagogic tones can have no idea of the way he can chat wittily and fascinate a whole circle of listeners. No one would suspect the existence behind this dry, learned exterior of a profound, keen thinker who threw himself passionately into the problems of the day. He is too bureaucratic to make a really great political figure. But, just as he published lyric poetry in his youth and retained his literary interests all his life, so he never became a politician merely to represent industrial interests. He is a political thinker whose keenness of vision revealed to him the contours of a new age against a dark background. Many of his party associates considered him a pessimist. Few understood the source of his anxieties. His profoundly skeptical view of the future of our civilization was not merely the result of a superficial absorption of ideas from Spengler. He shared Jacob Burckhardt's belief in the inevitability of a new Caesarian age. But while the Swiss was led by his view to a virtual flight from politics, Hugenberg drew the opposite deduction. We must act, was his conclusion. But we can only act effectively along the line of developments, not against it. We must play a part in them if we wish to achieve anything and to save anything.

A skeptical but valiant attitude. Certainly not a reactionary one. But action originating from skepticism will not move mountains. Resignation is not the material from which great leaders are made. It evolves only political tacticians who rely on cunning moves and material means for their success. Resignation can never create the enthusiasm needed for great achievements.

It is worth while to consider Hugenberg's motives. His is

a very pessimistic view of humanity and human progress. Moreover, he foresaw the problems of the age long before other party leaders did. Politicians generally do not take the trouble to study their opponents' political motives. One of the greatest faults of the German political Left has always been the typical intellectual arrogance of the radical intelligentsia, which rejected in advance the ideas of the Right without ever studying them.

I do not believe Hugenberg's political views have ever been set down in literary form. It was not his desire that they should be. They were imparted only by word of mouth to a circle of personal friends. The drawback to this was that the aims and plans of his policy appeared either thoroughly naïve or actually fantastic, according to the intellectual level of his listeners. Perhaps I am interpreting them in too doctrinaire a way, but I believe I am correctly reproducing the essence of them in what follows here.

At a period when the contours of a universal world civilization begin to become distinguishable, it is nonsense to envisage an order of States based on national cultures. Europe has already forfeited her privileged position as the cradle of world civilization. The rise of vast new empires and her own internal disunity are reducing her to insignificance. We are not witnessing a struggle for world hegemony, but the historical epoch we are entering is one which will see the formation of the balance of a few great world Powers. No European nation is capable of becoming really a world Power by its own unaided efforts, and so the task before Europe, which cannot be postponed, must be the formation of a political and economic unity. This cannot be accomplished by pious resolutions, but only by the creation of a nucleus of power.

The coming decades will be characterized by a struggle for the leadership of the European and Northern Asiatic mainland. This will have to be determined between Britain, Germany and Russia. In this issue France can play only a passive

part. The detachment of Britain from the Eurasian continent
can be arranged only by peaceful means. Britain is not directly
interested in the European and North Asian region. The
Channel coast is certainly an essential requirement for Britain's security, but on this question it should be possible to
reach a compromise and make concessions. There should be
no objection to an extension of the British Commonwealth of
Nations to certain West European territories, if British statesmen deem this desirable. If, say, Holland, Belgium, certain
areas of North France flanking the Channel and Atlantic,
Norway, Iceland, and Greenland should opt for the British
Commonwealth, we should have a settlement which would in
no way impair the consolidation of the European continent.
There remains then the decisive struggle between Germany
and Russia for the hegemony of Europe. The issue cannot be
in doubt; there will result a great league of continental European nations and North Asian territories under German leadership. Its member States will not, however, have the same
degree of independence as the States of the British Commonwealth. They will enjoy complete independence in cultural
and internal affairs, but there will be limits to their autonomy
in foreign affairs and on economic questions.

Asia Minor, the Mediterranean, and North Africa will inevitably cause some difficulties. They belong to the European
sphere of power, and consequently a compromise is impossible.
But since France and Italy and their colonial possessions will
enter the new order, a large part of the territories mentioned
will be incorporated in the Eurasian territorial area in any
case. It should be possible to induce Britain to cede her Mediterranean possessions, including Egypt and the Sudan, in exchange for certain territories in the Far East and for the
Anschluss of the Western European States already mentioned.

The result will be the creation of five power-continents or
Great States, which will also constitute the new great economic spheres. National economic orders are just as out of

date as political orders limited to single nations. Attempts at
artificial autarchy may be of service for the duration of the
transition period of struggle for the domination of the continent, but restriction to national internal markets means
suicide. State economic protectionism leads inevitably to
State capitalism and the strangling of economic initiative.
Neither the artificial creation of employment nor currency
policies, neither deflation nor inflation, can bring more than
temporary relief. The only sure way to permanent recovery
lies in the division of the world into great economic units in
which industrial countries will be grouped into an organic
unity with territories forming large but still undeveloped
markets and with the necessary territorial sources of raw material and agricultural produce, leaving only a fraction of their
requirements to be met by international barter.

Today these future great regions exist already as self-contained economic units or are at least in process of becoming
such units. The "self-contained commercial State" is an antiquated notion as applied to a national State even of the dimensions of Poland, France, or Germany. When applied,
however, to the new great regional units it becomes the goal
of the future.

Nowadays such ideas are no longer original forecasts of the
future world. We are accustomed to even more far-reaching
visions. Fifteen or twenty years ago, when Hugenberg was beginning to develop them, they were revolutionary. His conceptions of internal politics and of political means still remain
revolutionary.

The age of Liberal democracies is over. Party groupings of
notables have given place to party machines. The individual
member of Parliament is only an employee of the party. Personal convictions and idealism are serious drawbacks for him.
Men of independent character are unusable. The party machine requires discipline to the extent of blind obedience. The
party is not a community of like-minded individuals but a

machine for control. It demands a dictator with absolute power.

In the long run the existence of rival control machines becomes intolerable; it would mean the ruin of society and the State. Each control machine is out to secure permanent and absolute power over the State. One of the rivals emerges as victor. A single party machine secures dominance; party and State become identical. The dictator over the party becomes dictator over the State. The process is irresistible and logical. Thus all that remains of democracy is the wire-pulling. Public opinion and the emergence of political aims are phenomena that can be produced in any desired form by suitable manipulation.

The political realities must no longer be sought in the ostensible arena of democratic life, but in the work done in the offices of the ruling élite. All that remains possible is an "enlightened despotism," which leaves the masses no real say in political decisions, but compensates them by giving them the feeling that what is done is an expression of their political will. Political power is wielded by the personal élite grouped round the dictator. This élite, like an Order, selects its own members; it does so only after the closest scrutiny, and maintains conformity by the most rigid discipline.

The working masses, and even the lower middle class and the former higher grades of society, will have no further interest in political rights. They can be completely satisfied and diverted from politics by the concession of economic privileges or an improvement of the general standard of life. Wage questions will present no difficulty in the great territorial States of the future. The undeveloped markets will call for an increase in purchasing power, with the object of increasing turnover. A general rise in prosperity will be the natural consequence of the ending of the struggle for the new continents. Many social services now deemed utopian will become possible. Limitations of working hours, leisure periods, holiday trips, and many material alleviations will become attainable to an extent far exceeding the demands of the Socialist leaders.

I need not further pursue this chain of ideas. Their starting point is not to be found in the egoistic attitude to industry of the great industrialist who wants to be "master in his own house" and condemns social services for the workers as humanitarian sentimentality, but in skepticism concerning a political system which the present crises have shown to be unworkable. In Hugenberg's opinion the democratic parliamentary system is an anachronism in the age of the industrial masses. Government can be carried on only by an élite, which must not be elected by the masses but must select its own members. The first claim to membership belongs to the economic leaders, the captains of industry. This body will be responsible only to itself. It cannot be superseded. The Caesar will be chosen from its members, but he will remain only a figurehead representing the élite, and not an omnipotent dictator.

In a State thus undergoing gradual transformation, no classes with special political aims can be permitted to exist. No independent groupings of interests can be permitted. The independence of associations will be curbed by the fact that their representatives will be nominated by the ruling élite. This body will liquidate the system of the class struggle and the struggle between interests by removing the former ambitious leaders of workmen and employees and abolishing the whole institution of syndics and secretaries of associations, replacing all these by office staffs under its own control. Thus the entire problem of the present revolutionary crisis is concentrated on the formation of a personal élite and its seizure and consolidation of power. The essential feature of the present age is simply the struggle between various groups of persons for the right to form the personal élite.

How will victory be won in this struggle? According to Hugenberg, economic means of power constitute the only decisive factor. He believes in the effect of economic dependence. The simplest method of achieving success for a political party lies in the economic corruption of the leaders of the opposing parties. But this is only one of the minor tactical devices. The modern élite will come into existence through a strong network of personal connections. These will be groups of persons whose economic interests are closely interwoven. The interweaving process cannot be accomplished by the creation of a large organization. That method of amalgamation of interests will be replaced by a system of manifold participations in industrial undertakings.

When Hugenberg was serving on the Prussian Settlement Commission for the province of Posen, he acquired an intimate knowledge of the Polish communities in the Prussian State. He observed the way in which the Poles established their political and economic power on the basis of an intangible but strong and elastic network of personal relations between a small group of leaders. This is the principle of personal union, which has a great attraction for Hugenberg.

Perhaps this conception of control over the State by means of an invisible élite in possession of all economic means of power might have been successful if the genuine revolutionary activities connected with the rise of National Socialism had not taken place. But the actual course of events showed that the creation of a dominating élite, and the enforced subjection to it of the masses of the nation, called for other qualifications than those of the amalgamated industrial interests. Hugenberg also recognized this, and here we see the reason for remarkable contradictions in his scheme. He was not merely the leader of an invisible élite wielding industrial power. He was also a monarchist, and a Christian politician, and he wished to uphold the German national traditions.

Mass enthusiasm is one of the requisites of political leadership. Hugenberg tried to arouse it by patriotic memories of the past. He harped on the greatness that had been, while Hitler

harped on the greatness to come. Time has shown which of
them was right.

Hugenberg was completely lacking in the socialistic rhetoric
without which no one can sway the masses. These ideas of
his show how similar the leader of the bourgeois nationalists
was to the leader of the socialistic nationalists, but they also
reveal the glaring contrasts between them. Hugenberg was
not so much Hitler's rival as an incomplete, inconsistent, lagging revolutionary, who was ignorant of the technique of
revolution, who never mastered the art of mass suggestion,
and who had no insight into the motive forces of the great
revolution. He overestimated the effect of economic power,
overlooked its limitations, and completely failed to understand
the real nature of power. His theory of the "economic man"
reveals him as still deeply rooted in the ideas of the nineteenth
century, from which he endeavored to leap into a new age.
Hugenberg was a transition figure. He saw the catastrophe
coming; he also saw the inadequacy of most of the resources
on which the politicians of the time relied. But he remained a
tactician. He lacked intuition and creative power, the conception of great aims and the strength to achieve them.

S., a close friend of Hugenberg and a man I had known a
long time, came to Danzig to see me now and again when I
was President. He also cautiously visited me in exile in Poland,
where I was living with my wife's parents. Once he came just
after the celebration of Hugenberg's seventieth birthday. He
said much of the high intellectual level of the guests he met
on that occasion, and championed Hugenberg as Germany's
only real leader. Not until later, he declared, would it become
generally known what Hugenberg's real intentions had been.
He was the man who could have shown the only real way to
avoid another war. But now war and a vast revolution were
inevitable. When the world had passed through both, men
would remember Hugenberg's ideas, his conception of a balance of power distributed between great independent world

States, and his idea of the leadership of the modern mass democracy by means of an invisible élite.

I was still depressed by my flight and the loss of my estate, and was full of bitterness at the lack of moral courage in all the influential men in the country—the civil servants, the great industrialists, the landowners, and the officers. "Why did Hugenberg stay on?" I asked S. "Wasn't he ashamed to take his seat in this Reichstag, assembled by command, as a member by the grace of Hitler? He would have shown more personal dignity by retiring to his Westphalian estate."

"If you really knew his political outlook," said S., "you would see he couldn't do otherwise. This process has got to go on to its end. It's a necessary phase of clarification. The main line of development, as Hugenberg saw it, is irrevocable. Hitler is preparing the way. It is not our business to obstruct him."

I remarked that he, too, now considered war and continuing revolution inevitable. The end of it all would once more be a broken, vanquished Germany.

"No," said S. "This time the end will not be Germany's defeat. There will not be another Versailles. The central element is not the coming war but the revolution. We have been unable to avoid it, and so we must go through it. We shall all be losers, but if we understand it we shall all be victors as well."

I said I thought it was an easy way out to let matters take their course and to regard that course as inevitable. It was a quietist attitude that would enable anything to be accepted. S. replied that Hugenberg's greatest quality was his refusal to indulge in easy optimism. It was a choice between two evils. "Certainly," he added, "the end of all our thinking today can only be a deep pessimism. Perhaps all that can be done is to keep the masses occupied and diverted, in order to prevent them from destroying themselves. It will be the task of a new social order to make life easier for them. There must be plenty of hygiene, plenty of leisure and recreation, until gradually the inevitable decline of population acts as such a blood-letting in all civilized nations that war becomes inconceivable. Then at last will come the time for re-Christianization. All the world will be in a pessimistic mood again, but from it new and profound forms of Christian piety will arise. Spiritual life will experience a second blossoming. Externally, we shall see maturing a last supreme fulfillment of Western culture. This may last till the end of the present millennium or the beginning of the next. But then new vast convulsions will come, perhaps to pave the way for a new phase in the history of mankind."

There can be no doubt that anyone holding such views can do nothing to provide a desperate nation, entangled in the toils of its doom, with support and political leadership.

3

THE EXECUTOR OF THE WILL

ONE THING HERR von Papen undeniably has—personal courage. To remain at his post for years, the most hated of men, distrusted not only by the party but by many outside it, and expecting at any moment to be secretly or publicly got out of the way—that calls for courage and nerve and great independence. It probably implies also the sense of a mission to be carried out. While his secretaries have been shot at his side, or drowned, or have fled abroad, Papen evades every trap set for him. He remains on top. With his immense wiliness he manages to keep a hand in the game everywhere, and to remain the man who will liquidate Hitler one day, as he brought him from the wings on to the stage. There is good reason for maintaining, however, that it was neither personal ambition nor real loyalty to the Fuehrer of the Third Reich that induced Papen to impose on himself the self-denial which is all that Papen's various missions for Adolf Hitler have amounted to.

Wiliness? it will be asked. Has not this very man been throughout his career a blunderer, committing the worst *faux pas*, unsuccessful chief spy and director of sabotage alike in the United States and in Palestine in the last war? Has he not remained an elegant, superficial racing man? The most ambitious of careerists, ready to take every obstacle at a flying jump in the political steeplechase? It will be said that he has shown horrible lack of character, in continuing to serve a man like Hitler who has had Papen's closest colleagues murdered almost before his eyes. It will perhaps be said, in answer, that after his wild start there was nothing else he could do but remain in the saddle and chance his luck. If he had gone on pension, and retired into inactivity as a private individual living on his estates, he would long ago have fallen victim to the Gestapo.

Von Papen has carried on with ability, in spite of all his *faux pas* and diplomatic failures. With ability, at least, for himself. How did he save his neck in those fateful days at the end of June and the beginning of July 1934 when so universal a hatred flamed up against him? "An eternal shame that he escaped," said my former friend Rettelsky, my successor as *Landesbauernfuehrer* or Peasant Leader for East Prussia. That was the universal feeling at the time. Few were the friends that Papen had gained. But perhaps the *vox populi* of the Nazis told truth. It was the most dangerous enemy of the Nazis who had remained alive.

I was sitting opposite Papen in the Herrenklub. It was during the Weimar regime. We were discussing questions of policy for Eastern Germany. Papen is a man of captivating courtesy. He quickly catches one's point. He makes it easy to discuss things. Not a trace of stiffness or condescension. Even when he contradicts, he is conciliatory. He can listen. He is without pose, unpretentious—in a word, likeable. That was my impression of him at that time. I often saw him and talked with him later, and my impression remained unchanged. One of my visits had reference to the situation of the Catholic

Church. In spite of the Concordat, Nazi policy was then beginning openly to show its hostility to the Christian churches. The initiated party chiefs let it be known in intimate circles that no undertakings would be allowed to stand in the way of the liquidation of the churches; the undertakings would be interpreted as best suited Nazi requirements.

Papen had no intention of giving me any real help. I was struck by the neat way he wriggled out of an inquiry which at the time was awkward for him. He said he would arrange for me to discuss these things with Hitler. It was clear that he did not want to expose himself. He told me that he had repeatedly troubled Hitler about the matter but Hitler would not listen to him. It was interesting to me at the time that he made a point of distinguishing between the Catholic institutions and the Center political party. Cautiously he hinted that he could not accept any identification of the Catholic Center Party with the legitimate interests of the Catholic Church. He advised me to make a rigid distinction in this respect, lest I should be taking the part of political elements which had to disappear once for all from the German scene.

I saw Papen later in other circles. He spoke cautiously the moment he had a number of people with him. But I also came into contact with collaborators of his who at that time, in 1934, were beginning to plot the foundations for a Conservative order and to prepare for the liquidation of the National Socialists. How far these preparations were carried in practice I do not know in any detail; in theory they had made considerable progress. As the majority of the men who took part in these preparations are still living and will probably play a part yet in the liquidation of Nazism, I will confine myself to a summary of their ideas. It gives the needed completion of the picture of von Papen that has so far been shown to the public.

It is grotesque to set this man down as merely a superficial and ardently ambitious careerist. His character is not sufficiently revealed either by his diplomatic past or by his known activities as president of the Herrenklub and as Chancellor of Germany. He helped National Socialism into the saddle in 1933, and is therefore the man on whose shoulders the heaviest responsibility lies for all that has happened since and for what we are now suffering. But it is necessary to consider his motives, and to reconstruct the picture of future political developments which the men round Papen had drawn for themselves at the time.

I discussed the situation with one of his colleagues in the spring of 1934. "One thing," this gentleman said, "you must not forget. It is not sufficient for us to liquidate Hitler. Theoretically we can do that at any time. But we should do it at the risk of losing everything we have gained, and leaving Germany more impotent at home and abroad than ever before. We must not interrupt the process of Germany's recovery. Germany must become free and sovereign in her foreign policy; rearmament equal to any foreign coalition is a sine qua non for any political regime that takes the place of National Socialism. And we must not interrupt the process of economic recovery. Thus you see that we can undertake any liquidation only with caution, and at best in the form of a gradual process. Under no circumstances must there come a new radical breach."

He made use of the phrase then so frequently used—the "continuity of development" that must be preserved. He had to admit, he added, that there had been a grave misjudgment of the character of the National Socialist elements. But that mistake must not be repaired at the expense of making a new and worse one. It was clear that National Socialism was the very thing it had been intended to frustrate: it was virtually the same radical revolution which had been anticipated by the parties of the Left. Whether the further progress of the revolution could be prevented, or there was nothing but to go through with it until the movement could be arrested, depended on a variety of circumstances. The Vice-Chancellor

(Papen) was determined, in any case, to avoid everything that might in any way complicate the situation of the Reich in regard to foreign affairs and to rearmament. He was convinced that it was still possible to influence the movement, and also that at a later stage it would be possible to develop a reasonable political form for the Reich.

So far as Papen's plans are concerned, he was for a restoration of the monarchy, but the important thing is that his conception is not to be confused with superficially similar ideas which were in Brüning's mind. He did not want a modern "popular monarchy," a king of the English pattern, as Hindenburg suspiciously called it, but an order of State and society that went back before the event which all true Conservatives regard as the fall of the Christian State and society —the French Revolution.

Papen was not by any means the superficial, elegant man of the world and aristocrat that he affected to be. He had a political conception which has some title to be described as Conservative in the best sense. In his circle I was made acquainted with the writings of a political thinker who had influenced Papen's practical political aims. This was General von Radowitz, whose writings, dating from the middle of the last century, are still important as the expression of a Christian Conservatism. This Christian Conservatism and the popular Conservatism of such younger politicians as Möller van den Bruck had but one thing in common, which was their opposition to the new absolutism.

They looked for this not where it is popularly looked for, in the institution of the monarchy and in a spirit of reactionary autocracy; they found it in the despotism of an all-embracing and all-powerful administration, and absolutist democracy, which sooner or later, as its logical final phase, would make an end of Parliament.

These two forms of absolutism tended today to unite: such was the fear of the Papen circle. There were two modern

ideas of the State which, they believed, had the same tendency
to set up a despotic administrative system. One was the deifi-
cation of the State and the absolute subordination of the individual to it. That was the solution of Fascism and, as they
added later, of National Socialism. The other was the State
of the common weal, or, as would be said today, the State of
social services. It was the modern form of the "philanthropic"
State, in which the individual was controlled for his good by
the State, down to the smallest details of life. The Bolshevist State, they considered, lay in the line of this conception.
But the old democracies would come inevitably into the same
path. Sooner or later they would be pushed by their radical
elements into an absolutism which continued to call itself a
democracy, but which would show the same marks of absolute
compulsion as Bolshevism on one side and Fascism on the
other.

Is there, then, only the choice between the absolutism of a
personal dictator as the embodiment of an absolute State, and
the absolutism of a new dispensation for the sovereign people
under the dictatorship of the masses? The Papen circle replied: There is a third State that is to be defined first by a ne-
gation, proceeding as a Constitutional State from the historic
conditions. It is not a centralistic State, for centralization is
the first stage on the road to absolutism. It is the State in
which government is reduced to a minimum. Most things
must be left to be directed by those who are concerned. Thus,
they said, we come to the delegation of elements of sovereignty
to autonomous bodies. In this way we counter the hypertrophy
of legislation. But is that not the old and familiar Liberal
State, the *laisser faire* State? No, it is the State which has in-
accurately been called the guild or corporative State, though
the true guilds have nothing to do with the "corporations" of
Fascism. It also has nothing to do with the parliamentary,
representative system.

Anyone who takes the trouble to examine these ideas will

find a well-reasoned political outlook which may be disagreed with but which does not deserve to be lumped together with the National Socialist ideas. This political conception aimed at the exact opposite of the Nazi aims. It was also neither militarist nor expansionist. It demanded full political equality of rights for Germany, but at the same time it affirmed Germany's membership of the Christian society of European States, in recognition of the common spiritual possessions of Western Christendom.

Papen remained ready to carry on his real task even after the shock of the attempt on his life. In this he was playing a crafty game, of which many of his friends did not approve. But the craftiness of his methods must not blind us to the essence of his political conception. He was the first and perhaps the only great adversary of the revolution who remained in its service in order, when the time came, to make an end of it.

"Has the man a talisman?" a foreigner asked me several years after the 1934 purge, when Franz von Papen was still *persona grata* with Hitler. A talisman? Perhaps he has. What, in such situations, is a better talisman than the knowledge of something that might become dangerous to the existence of the all-powerful regime? Strictly speaking, the simple knowledge is not enough in itself; it is often even dangerous to its possessor. Unless it is a document, and this document has been placed in safety somewhere. Has Papen such a document? He has! It is Hindenburg's true will and testament.

Hindenburg's will is said to contain this advice: Get rid of the National Socialists, who have not kept a word of their promises and are plunging Germany into disaster and dishonor. Get rid of Hitler. Reinstate a German Emperor. No war of revenge. Restore the Christian character of the Reich. —And he expresses his deep anxiety in regard to the Christian education of the young and his abhorrence of the fraud of National Socialism, which is poisoning the young and destroying the German people.

A testimony of desperate anxiety and of a wrath which, in its plain, old-fashioned language, might have the most tremendous effect. It is a deadly weapon. But was it the right moment for overthrowing Hitler and restoring the monarchy, in that August of 1934, when Hindenburg died—at the most critical moment in the reorganization of the army? At the peak of the popularity of Hitler and his colleagues? At that moment the weapon was valueless. It was kept for later use. The moment would come when its effect must be deadly. It would come when the masses were in the throes of disillusionment, when they, too, could see what the old Field Marshal had foreseen, the betrayal of Germany and of her future. Papen agreed, in the interest of both sides, of Hitler and also of the Conservatives, not to publish the testament. An ancient formula was smuggled in in its place. Germany was not yet ripe for the restoration.

"Have patience, gentlemen," Papen said to his intimates. "We must outlast this man. The best nerves will win." In that situation the enemy must be beaten with his own weapons. Craft against craft. When the masses are disappointed and all illusions have flown, then is the moment for the counterstroke. Then Antony will bring down the regime with Caesar's testament.

I heard shortly before the war that Papen, who continually endangers his life by his cynical utterances, was still advising his friends to wait yet awhile, and remain at their posts. "For God's sake don't resign," he said urgently to friends who were weakening. "Stay where you are, even if your disgust brings up your gorge. Don't do the fellows the service of resigning. Stay at your posts, gain influence, keep the others out!" It was understood that he would do nothing so long as Hitler was serving Germany's recovery. The dissatisfaction of the masses mattered nothing, but when the patriots began to be rebellious it would be time for action.

"Never balk! Over the obstacle!" That was this diplomat's motto. What a grotesque figure—this elegant man, driven into his career not by ordinary ambition but by this conviction of an inner call to give Germany the only political form that can save her! But why this ghastly mistake with Hitler? Why did he not carry on the government of the country without him, against him?

He saw National Socialism, and probably sees it still, as the ncessary interim phase of a great, slow process of healing, which the Austrian, Hugo von Hofmannsthal, called the Conservative Revolution. We are in the midst of a world revolution—he, too, saw that. His problem was not only how to canalize that revolution but also how to take advantage of it to lift up Germany to the rank that is her due. Just as Hitler was reducing parliamentarism to absurdity by means of its own mechanism, so, by means of Hitler, totalitarian State absolutism and mass democracy must first be utterly compromised, so that the ground might be cleared for a new form of democracy with a monarchical head.

Papen is the executor of the will. He will execute this will of the dying Field Marshal and President of the Reich, who always regarded himself as merely the regent for his king, when the future king can come as bringer of peace, as restorer of justice and freedom.

4

BLOOD NOBILITY AND NEW NOBILITY

IT WAS CERTAINLY not threatened bankruptcy alone, or the fear of losing old family estates and coming down in the world that drove the German aristocracy into the ranks of

the Nazis. This revolution of nihilism works a different form
of seduction on each class. It was natural that a nobility of
blood, a nobility with a past record of service to the State,
with its sense of tradition and blue blood and high caste
and honor and special obligations, should feel some kinship with the Nazi doctrine of the inequality of human
races, of political leadership, and of the rule of a special
élite. The incursion of Nazi ideas into the ranks of the
nobility took place through the younger elements. Those
among the older members who had not sunk into cynicism,
and accepted the status of privileged guests on the "seat of the
scornful," held fast to the principles of the way of life formed
by the Christian ethic. They were still in essentials a Christian
nobility.

I was visited after my resignation, at a time when I was
socially isolated owing to the Nazi boycott, by an East Prussian Junker, Herr von A., a stock breeder. We had long
worked together. As chairman of our breeders' association he
occasionally inspected some of our breeding establishments.
He was a man of refined and cultured tastes. With his extremely fair hair, his incredibly youthful appearance for the
late fifties or early sixties, and his clear blue eyes, he was the
very type of the blood nobility of the purest race. He expressed his regret at my isolation and outlawry. He told me,
laughing, that he had been warned not to visit me. Extraordinary, he remarked, how quickly the political fronts
changed in these disturbed times. On his last visit to me he
had been wild at the Nazis, and would much have preferred
to give a wide berth to me as an arch-Nazi. Now the parts
had been exchanged. I counted with the Nazis as a traitor
and a candidate for death, and meanwhile he had become
persona gratissima at the court of the new rulers. He no longer
intended to become an actual member of the party, but his
two sons, fine youngsters both of them, had not been deterred
from doing so. Both were now enthusiastic members of the

mounted S.S. What could he have done to stop them? He just had to say Yes and Amen.

"You know," he said, "I don't go so far as the skeptics among our older generation in the country, who let their sons go their own way or even approve their joining the party. 'It can't do any harm, and it may help us to hold our bit of land—quite a good division of labor! We will stay with the German Nationalists, and let the youngsters be with the Nazis.' That's their line. But these young fellows have such entirely different ideas from ours. Just listen to what they have to tell you—it will take your breath away—but they are perfectly right in not wanting to remain just ornamental. 'We have a chance once more, Father,' says my youngest boy. 'We can get something to do again, after all, in the life of the nation.'"

Von A. smoked in silence. The teams came back from work. He watched them with interest. "You see," he went on, playing with a little old iron statuette on my desk, "we old *Klutenpedders* (clodhoppers) know something about the rules that govern this comedy of life and growth. We are not quite so easily deceived. What's really left nowadays of your nobility? Is there still anything in it, or must we chuck it all on the scrap-heap? You see, my father was a Liberal—a great man, and a fine farmer in the bargain. 'Boys,' he said to us, 'anyone who sets any store by his nobility proves that he hasn't any.' But, I tell you, the old man put us through a training that stood the test. Amid all the temptations of that disturbed time.

"To get outside the prejudices of rank—that was a great fashion among us for a time. What did it mean? Associating with the rag, tag, and bobtail? Speculating? Marrying a Jewish damsel? Gilding the family tree a bit? Taking a hand in all the frauds of the day? Think of it! When one has grown old as a breeder and spent thirty or forty years weed-

ing out the male beasts, breeding for purity, and playing all
the doubtful tricks with which we stock breeders dabble in
the Lord's own job—well, what sort of a result are we likely
to get if we try the same tricks with men? You will say that
if nobility means anything it means nobility of the blood. A
stock of which one knows that it was capable of this and the
other thing. Readiness for sacrifice, for instance; courage,
endurance, and the like. Anyone who knows us only from the
centers of the gay life and not by our work may turn up his
nose. But we Prussian Junkers, as they call us, have always
had a strong sense that the nobility has a function in the life
of the nation, because it is a select group of the nation, or in
modern language, a true élite.

"But now, just consider our youngsters. They are having a
damned different training from ours. Only think of this post-
war period, the moral laxity, the new ideas. The youngsters
see that their old people are just ridiculous men of straw in
the backwoods. Vigorous young fellows will never be content to be just heirs. But what is there, indeed, for our boys
to inherit? And have they any prospect of becoming anything
on their own account and making their way? The boys want
to live. They want to be leaders. They are full of self-confidence. 'The old people at home, living among the flies from
their dungheap, may have got to the end of their usefulness,
but not we! We shall make our way, we shall work ourselves
to the top. We are not yet behind the times. We shall regain
for the nobility its right of leadership.'

"So our young fellows are all for joining up with the S.S.
New nobility from blood and soil! Who has them, the blood
and the soil? The nobility has got to be modernized. It will
find a new form through National Socialism. We must see
the good and great element in Nazism. Has it not the same
principles of hard training, selection, duty, loyalty, etc., etc.?
'Father,' my boys say, 'you don't understand any longer.

There's no need for you to either. It's our job now. We are not
going to stand aside when a new world is coming into existence.'

"I ask you, what is Father to say to them? They must
accumulate their own experience, the youngsters, and live their
own life. Perhaps in their way they are right. The old privileges are gone. There's no altering that. But how were they
acquired, in the dark womb of prehistory? Was it not in
much the same way as these boys of mine now propose? We
don't want privileges. But we want the right of leadership. If
it can no longer be inherited, then it must be fought for. Are
not the boys right?"

At that time there was little that I could say in reply. Each
one of us, under the unceasing pressure of revolutionary ideas,
falls at times into a state of intellectual helplessness. Today it
is possible to see clearly. I think the older members of the
nobility will do so too. The desired transformation of the
nobility into a new and modern form has not taken place, and
will not. A number of individuals of old family have made
their way ahead with the help of the party. But they have
succeeded only because they have adopted the universal cynicism of the Nazi leaders, and have joined in the unscrupulous
competition for power and influence. They have been cor-
rupted, like all who touch Nazism. They have not succeeded
in reforming the institution of nobility; instead of that, they
have themselves sunk to the level of the gangsters. Those who
give that gang a little finger will find in the end that they
have given their whole arm. The novice in the gangster clubs
starts as merely a look-out man. His career ends with mur-
dering a policeman at the ringleader's order. There is no cutting adrift from that world. This all these young men with
historic names, who parade today in the higher ranks of the
S.S., have discovered. From the leading representatives of the
Christian nobility we used to hear now and then a protest
against particular Nazi acts. In the course of years even this

opposition was silenced. Is the demoralization complete? Is the tradition dead?

5

"UNA TERRIBILE"

OF AN ENTIRELY different nature are the ambitions of a social class which is credited with leadership, though it does not lead so much as affect to lead. The so-called "good" or "high" society of every country is extraordinarily blind in its judgments, and thus does a good deal of harm. It has no sense of proportion; its members lead a rather irresponsible butterfly existence, and engage in politics less from any will to power than from the love of a gamble and the desire to be considered persons of importance. For a time, according to their tastes, they find either Hitler or Bolshevism vastly interesting. Idly passing judgment on everyone and everything, they defeat the attempt at more serious judgments. Were it not that these self-important busybodies spread confusion everywhere, it would be unnecessary to take them seriously. In such critical times as ours, however, "good society" becomes a revolutionizing element.

But has Germany ever had a "good society" in the same sense as other nations? Perhaps not with the fixed criterion for admission and exclusion, or with the extent of undisputed membership, to be found in the Western European countries with their ancient social traditions. Thus the so-called "good society" in Germany did not exercise the same influence, because it was not a uniform factor for either good or evil. But however great or small its importance in Germany, one thing it did do—it made Hitler appear harmless in the eyes of the world. It represented the leader and the personnel of the National Socialist revolution as clumsy, youthful excrescences on a movement that deserved support for its healthy aims, young people who could be civilized by gradual education.

By this "good society" I do not mean only the group who financed Hitler and his movement in its early years—Frau Bruckmann, Frau Bechstein, Frau Wagner—but also the elements in society who, during the period immediately preceding and following the Nazi seizure of power, tried to make Hitler and the National Socialists socially presentable.

"Of course he doesn't know how to behave. He'll spend hours with a single guest out of the company. He has the bad habit of always lecturing, even at a social gathering. Poor Hitler! We must help him. Naturally women have never played a big part in his life. How could he find time for them amid his great work? Of course he is clumsy and awkward and shy! Well, I like shy men who still get embarrassed, men who have not forgotten how to blush. Have you noticed how he will suddenly turn pale? All the blood goes out of his skin. Then comes a sudden red flush. I think they call it vasomotive disturbances. We must help Hitler. It's time he acquired a good presence. Of course, what he wants is a woman's help."

The speaker was Frau von D., a well-known figure in Berlin society who had placed her house at the disposal of a club of a highly political nature. She was visiting me with her stepchildren, who were landowners in former West Prussia. She found everything amazingly interesting. It was a pleasure, she declared, to be alive, especially in these times.

"Our dear, splendid movement!" she exclaimed gushingly. "It will shed all its dross. I'm certain Hitler will ripen into quite unblemished, austere greatness. He will grow. He grows with every new task imposed on him, every new obstacle in his path. Just imagine what he was and what he's risen to! What opposition he has overcome! I always admire him and his men for that. They've all worked their way up. And what work they get through! I'm always saying to my son, where do they get the strength and energy for it? Are we all so degenerate that there's not one of us who can do the things they do?"

I answered the voluble lady with a few observations to the effect that I considered it very necessary to criticize both Hitler and his movement, and that there was grave cause for anxiety as to what would come of it all.

"Amazingly interesting," she replied. But clearly she thought my criticism was a trap, for she kept up her rhapsody. She complained that Hitler no longer had time to come to tea with her as he used to do. He was making it very difficult to help him. I said I thought it was most unlikely that Hitler had any desire to be lionized in society. Probably there had been times when he tried to make social connections, thinking that he could use them for his own purpose. But I knew from his own mouth what contempt he felt for everything connected with "good society."

"Oh, what a pity!" exclaimed Frau von D., with exaggerated simplicity. "But you mustn't destroy my belief that I, too, can help a little toward Germany's resurgence. What I try to do is to bring these new, young elements into touch with us old folk. We, too, surely have something to contribute. We can help with our experience and our social connections. Think how we can help to gain recognition abroad for our new Germany."

Frau von D. told me all she had done for National Socialism, and how she had worked for a better understanding of it in England and France. "I only wish Hitler knew how much he owes to our efforts abroad. It's we who smooth his path everywhere and open the houses of 'good society' to the new men. Do you know England? How important it is that there should be no misunderstanding, there especially! How important that they should regard Germany's rise with benevolent tolerance! I have enlightened all my many friends there. I am a busy correspondent, you know. 'Don't worry,' I write to them all. 'Don't get anxious about what's going on here.'

Then I quote Goethe to the effect that whatever wild shape the fermentation may take, it produces the wine in the end. I tell them that it's always easy for things to look queer in Germany, but no one need be disturbed about it. Let the young people sow their wild oats, I say. We've got the movement well in hand and we can guide it."

I asked whether she really considered Hitler and National Socialism as harmless as she made them out to be.

"Oh," said the voluble lady, "harmless! What makes you use that word? Of course I know what Hitler wants. But do you think they'll let him do whatever he fancies?"

I asked her who, in her opinion, was to prevent him.

"Amazingly interesting to hear you say that," she continued with a laugh. "Good heavens, there's no limit to the things Hitler tells us! He's going to unite Europe, to drive England from the Continent, to divide up Russia. Not long ago he told one of my English friends that the greatest mistake made at Versailles was only to disarm Germany, leaving her all her industries. I thought I should faint when he said that, but my English friend only said, 'How interesting!' I'm sure he made a note of it and reported it to the Foreign Office long ago. But you don't seriously believe that Hitler really thinks of doing all these things? It's another sign of his greatness! Of course he only says such things to puzzle people."

I need not give more of this conversation. Frau von D. was a curious mixture of intelligence, quick comprehension, and futile energy, with such a gift of loquacity that after lunch one of my friends whispered to me indignantly: "Really that woman is *una terribile!*"

She was not the only woman who tried to make Hitler socially presentable and to de-revolutionize Nazism through the influence of society. All that really mattered to these people was to retain their privileges of rank and to remain at the top. Barely ten years had elapsed since they had experienced a social revolution. The Weimar regime had brought other social classes to the top, and these were by no means all parvenu revolutionaries. Among them were well-educated and highly cultured families, who were formidable competitors not only because of their wealth; they had political influence. The old high society existed mainly on memories of past influence. And now yet another class had come to the top. There were Goering and his Emmy, Goebbels and his wife (the lady fresh from the divorce court), to say nothing of all the uncouth proletarian *Gauleiter,* whose spouses, former cooks or maidservants, were now all fine ladies.

How, then, was the upper class to keep at the top this time? Why, simply by promptly joining up. No more futile opposition or holding aloof as in the Weimar days. It must join up, lionize the new bosses, place its social skill at their service! That effusive reception might enable it to guide their footsteps. These parvenus were always grateful for initiation into the secrets of polite behavior. They had no desire to make an exhibition of themselves. They wanted to be reckoned among the members of good society. Even if the men were indifferent, their overblown, corpulent wives, more or less cheated out of the springtime of love and life, were anxious to bask in a few golden rays of autumn sunshine.

There were all sorts of ways in which the members of society could render political service. They could make contacts and connections, and act as safety valves for relieving the pressure. Through their personal friendships they could correct mistakes and remedy false steps. That involved creating opportunities of drawing nearer to these men of power on the human side. It could not be done at meetings or ceremonial receptions. But privately there would be opportunities to put them right, give them bits of advice, explain things to them, and intrigue. In short, establish the important petty frontier traffic between the political and social spheres. Otherwise there was danger of extinction, of sharing the fate meted out by the Bolsheviks to the entire Russian aristocracy and middle class.

So, at least, good society thought. But the Nazis upset all its calculations. The methods by which good society endeavored to instil moderation into them were as ineffective as the bribes by means of which others hoped to master them. They simply joined in the game and played any absurd part required of them; they managed to kiss hands neatly and to wear dinner jackets properly. But they remained what they were. And the upshot was very different from what had been intended. It was virtually the end of "good society." The members of society not only lost all distinction; by acting as matchmakers between the old and the new times they sacrificed the last shreds of their importance.

III

DIPLOMATS, DELUDED AND DELUDING

1

"LITTLE MAN, WHAT NOW?"

DID THE GERMAN Foreign Ministry have any political plan? Stresemann was supposed to have one; certainly Brüning had very definite ideas of his own. But neither Papen nor Schleicher had any definite aims in foreign policy. They just waited for things to turn up. To ease the situation, and to watch out for a chance of getting their elbows in anywhere—those were the principal ideas with which Hitler's two immediate predecessors at the Chancellery had approached the delicate field of German foreign policy. Not a soul at the Foreign Ministry knew, for example, what were the objectives in external affairs of the Hitler-Papen-Hugenberg alliance with the Reichswehr. The departmental heads were men of routine, not of any broad conceptions.

The German Foreign Ministry was, no doubt, the instrument of a policy, but it pursued no policy of its own. That was why it was defenseless against the demands of the Nazis. It fell in the end to the level of an office of experts.

Von Rheinbaben was a prominent German Democrat who had been one of the Under-secretaries (or State Secretaries as they are called) in the German Foreign Ministry, and an expert for the League of Nations, under the Republic. I have recently learned that von Rheinbaben's participation in Germany's Nazi course has been carried to the length of his appointment as head of the Gestapo at Lisbon. Herr von Rheinbaben was a younger colleague of Stresemann's. Nothing shows more clearly the crazy irrationality and the nihilistic character of Germany's course than the personal careers of such men, who collaborated with the best leaders of the German Republic. He was anxiously concerned under the

new regime to maintain his standing and to keep in good
odor, and he seized the opportunity of Germany's withdrawal
from the League to go on a lecture tour, making at the same
time a round of calls with a manifestly changed coat. In the
course of his tour he came to Danzig. He did his utmost to
make out a case for the fateful step that had been taken; he
spoke in favor of the League, he spoke against it; and he
ended with a tortuous declaration of love for the new policy
of accomplished facts.

I felt it desirable to say a few things at the end of his lecture, because the Nazi party was demanding that Danzig
should copy Germany's action and break with the League. I
spoke without preparation, and began by making use of the
title of that best-seller of the time, "Little man, what now?"
What were we little men to do, I asked, in our dangerous
proximity to the great? I offered a sort of apologia for the
League, reminding my hearers of the protection we had enjoyed from it. Many things about it had been disappointing,
and not only to seekers after protection like ourselves. But it
represented a beginning that should be persisted in and turned,
as soon as possible, into an instrument serving a truly just
peace and the needful co-operation between nations. It would,
I contended, be a great and perhaps an irreparable loss if this
first attempt at an institutional safeguard for an international
and supernational sphere of legality were lightly permitted to
collapse. I concluded: "We may be small men, whose voice
is barely audible if at all in the concert of the great; but we
mean nevertheless to go our own way. We took steps to defend ourselves against invasions of our rights, and we found
friends at a time when we were in a difficult situation. We
must not let our heads be turned now that Germany's star is
once more in the ascendant. We must not turn our backs on
friends who took pains to help toward a just reconciliation of
interests at a time when that help was needed."

It was a curious situation. After the speeches we had a social gathering. Here the roles were exchanged.

"It's easy enough for you," confessed the Weimar Democrat, "but I am not free to say just what I think. Of course I agree with everything you said. It would be an irreparable disaster if the League were smashed. The world would never summon up the courage to set up another institution of the sort. But I hope Germany's withdrawal is not definite. We must cautiously bring her round again. That's been my view all along."

It might perhaps have been possible to do this if men like von Rheinbaben had had a little more backbone, instead of each finding reasons of his own for hurriedly seeking the favor of the new lords.

This episode illustrates the difficult position in which we were all placed in the new Germany. At a time when the more responsible elements among the new men in power were beginning to get abreast of their duties and to adjust their political ideas to realities, it was precisely the men of the old governing party, the Democrats and other firm supporters of the Weimar system, who, in their panic fear of being shut out under the new regime, threw themselves into the arms of the Nazi extremists, showing readiness to go even further than the "wild men" in order to give clear evidence of their national spirit. It was these elements that interfered with the hoped-for maturing of Nazism and actually promoted its radicalization.

I knew a good many of the officials of the Foreign Ministry and the diplomats. At first they were all indignant at the "incursion of the barbarians." There were complaints everywhere of "broken china." It was noted with vexation how carefully tended political connections were being jeopardized or destroyed.

But gradually this first reaction gave place to other ideas. It was discovered with astonishment that foreign administrations were putting up with the roughness and the unmannerly pushfulness of the new men, and were obviously impressed. There was no deterioration of relations after all! On the contrary, in many cases there came an actual improvement. It was discovered with amazement that many things were put through that had been simply unattainable under the cautious methods of the old diplomacy. So that was how things stood! Well, then! Give the new methods a trial! So hostility and apprehension gave place to admiration. Men of the old school began to enjoy the new technique and to apply it with a will. They abandoned their carefully chosen phrases, and began to use the Nazi style. A strident and aggressive tone began to appear in conversation and in official intercourse.

Then there were men like Radowitz, who just shut their eyes to all sorts of things and fixed their attention on one or two alleged good aspects of Nazism as the last hope of their declining years. So, narrowing their vision, they forced themselves to be loyal and trusting collaborators, telling one another cheerfully that all would be well in the end. There were officials who resigned themselves to collaboration because they came round to the view that they were not entitled to influence the decision of political issues. Among these were diplomats of the old school, like Köster, who made no secret of their personal opinion, but nevertheless loyally represented the new official policy. How they managed this autotomy, this self-dissection into a critical private individual and a dutiful and obedient official, is one of the mysteries of this sort of diplomatic soul. I asked a friend of mine, Minister of one of the Legations, what was his attitude, and he replied:

"It is not our business to determine the course of policy. It is our duty to be loyal officials. We were just as loyal to the Republic. We are habituated to representing policies against our own better judgment. We are not even privileged to prevent a collision between our convictions and the policy we are to represent by voluntarily resigning. There are situations in

which our resignation might inflict the most serious injury
on the Reich. It is our duty to practice self-suppression to the
very utmost."

I think we do an injustice to many distinguished men and
men of high character when we suspect their motives in continuing to represent the Reich under the Nazis. But the motives were not so honorable in every case. The line of reasoning
of many who offered their professional services to the new
rulers was very simple. "The thing will go on anyhow," said a
young Foreign Ministry official to me cynically—a particularly
able man who saw the opportunity of a great personal leap
ahead. "If we don't take part in it, other people will. What
would you have us do? Resist it? What would be the good of
that? There are men waiting to jump into our shoes—queues
of them, reaching to Unter den Linden. They will not only
do the things men like us do with repugnance, they will do
any dirty thing they are told to. They will set no limits to
their servility. No, old man, what other people can do, we can
do just as well. I have no hankering for needless personal
sacrifice and martyrdom. We can at least offer greater efficiency."

Other men spoke less candidly. A man I had known for a
long time came home from service abroad just at the moment
of my resignation. "What!" he said, indignantly. "You are
going now, of all times, just when things are moving at last?
You must be mad! It was possible to be mistaken about the
Nazis at first. I confess that I regarded them as a body of wild
men. Abroad we could only see the damage they were doing.
But you have been in their midst all the time, and you know
what they are aiming at. And now, when we can see how
well they know what they are up to, you are making off!"

I replied that we had evidently been moving in opposite
directions. "You used to jib at my nationalism in a friendly
way, and I at your pacifism. I seem to be fated to fall out with
whatever is the current view. You are luckier—your personal

views seem to move in harmony with those of the majority. I congratulate you on your new nationalism."

When I think of all the men I knew who turned their coats, beginning with furious denunciation of the Nazis, then showing hesitant approval and finally energetic enthusiasm for them, it seems impossible to set them all down as concerned simply to save their skins or to push their way ahead. There were, of course, some complete cynics among them, like the high official who joined the Nazis and gave his friends the simple explanation that he had been "all my life a cynic." Such candor had at least the merit of honesty. To men who were content with that standard, there could be no difficulty in first jumping over every obstacle in the steeplechase of the Weimar Republic and then, when the time was ripe for a move, elegantly jumping the broad ditch that divided the Weimar system from the new regime. Under-secretary Meissner, for instance, was an imposing pillar of the old system, the very symbol of deeply-rooted, genuinely democratic allegiance to the pre-Nazi Germany. Yet he was able to serve Hitler with the same devotion with which he had served Hindenburg and Ebert before him.

But there were not only the high officials who were working to prevent the worst; there were also the many patriotic laymen who were gradually compelled to recognize that, vile and disgusting as it was, Nazism had at least finally broken with the petty shifts and humiliations of the "policy of fulfilment." The fetters had at last been cast off; suddenly it had been proved that they were not steel at all but just wisps of paper. Thus the knowledge of the true character of the Nazis was outweighed by love of Germany and desire to see her strong, and by the feeling that Germany's hour was now striking.

In the first two years of the regime I found no one at the Foreign Ministry who was a real National Socialist: the general feeling was an ardent desire to see the fall of the party.

The only Nazis were the clerks and porters, the messengers and charwomen. The first "cells" were formed by these and by ambitious subordinate officials. These people carried on a grotesque and intolerable activity as spies and informers. They gave me, as a fellow Nazi, a particularly friendly greeting when I called at the Ministry. It was not least in order to make an end of this dangerous and mischievous development that the entry of the higher officials into the party was welcomed. The final impulse to abandon opposition in the Foreign Ministry came from the menacing growth of new departments that were interfering in foreign policy—the Rosenberg organization and the office set up by Ribbentrop.

Could the Foreign Ministry have done what the Reichswehr successfully did? The Reichswehr defeated the attempt of the party troops to capture the leadership of the new armed forces. But could the Foreign Ministry prevent Ribbentrop's organization from one day being declared the actual Foreign Ministry, the existing Ministry being reduced to a politically impotent office of experts? The only way to prevent this was to abandon all opposition! Only in this way could the Ministry retain a certain influence. These were the ideas at the back of the complete capitulation of the Ministry, headed by Neurath, to Nazism. After Hindenburg's death it had been too late to embark on a struggle. There was no possible leader left.

All these high officials, with their fine culture and their careful bringing up, were at bottom nothing but little men, with the same anxious question on their lips that oppressed every underling at every hour of those days of suspense— "Little man, what now?"

2

A FOREIGN MINISTER

THERE WAS A suggestion of friendly warning in Baron von Neurath's parting words as he accompanied me to the door. "After all," he said, "you are a German like the rest of us. The Opposition will be tumbling over one another in their eagerness to get hold of you. I advise you to hold back, and to offer them no encouragement. You are surely with me in wanting Danzig to remain German."

I replied that I had never given any occasion for doubt of my loyalty to my country. But I should have to decide for myself what I should do, or not do, in the days ahead of us.

"I am extraordinarily sorry," said Neurath more than once, "that it should have come to this. In my opinion it could all have been avoided."

I quote these farewell words of *Freiherr* von Neurath, who at the time was the German Minister for Foreign Affairs, because they seem to me to offer the key for the comprehension of the really tragic self-abasement of this finely cultured, independent-minded South German aristocrat. As taskmaster of the Czech nation, he was an impotent figurehead, contenting himself with the shadow of a power of which he had not a trace, and making himself the agent of terrorist decisions against which he had no means of protesting. Now he has been relieved of his part, to make way for yet more ruthless terrorism. He has fallen from crag to crag, this genial, courteous diplomat who at one time was universally trusted and liked.

It is only too easy to explain such cases as the outcome of personal ambition and hunger for power. This genuinely patriotic German had fallen into the error of countless others who felt it their duty to hold out, and to put up even with personal humiliation in order to prevent the worst and to be at hand when the Nazis would come at last to the end of their tether and the day would come for their public disgrace.

It was possible to hold to such a hope only if one had quite definite ideas as to the part the Nazis were playing in the great process of the German Revolution.

In the course of a series of lengthy conversations with the German Foreign Minister it gradually became clear to me that he had no conception of developments in Germany and of a constructive foreign policy. He was pursuing a happy-go-lucky, hand-to-mouth policy in blithe trustfulness and excessive optimism. Neurath was beyond question a man who meant well. His cultivated tone and South German grandee's style lent a certain dignity to his heartiness of manner. His sanguine temperament was his outstanding characteristic. He was perhaps superficial. His intellect did not seem to be on a par with his other qualities.

He was much too confident in himself to have any doubt that he could tame the savage Nazis by gentle compulsion. I watched him at Geneva, on the first and only occasion of the public appearance of members of the Nazi Government at the Assembly of the League of Nations. He guided their steps on that slippery parquet with much the same sort of tender concern as an aunt taking her nieces to their first ball. Let the Nazis make a public exhibition of themselves? Nothing could have been further from his mind than such intriguing malice. I had been invited with Goebbels to the house of the German Minister to Geneva; Sir John Simon and M. Paul Boncour were there. Neurath took endless pains to train the Nazis in diplomatic manners. He arranged for Goebbels to have a heart-to-heart talk with Boncour. Goebbels insisted at length on the genuineness of the Nazis' Socialism and their harmlessness in world politics.

At Geneva, as everywhere in the years that followed, Neurath lent his prestige and the confidence he personally inspired

as cover for the Nazi enterprises. He did not do this in order
to make himself indispensable. I am perfectly sure that he
acted from the highest of motives: he was trying to train the
Nazis and turn them into really serviceable partners in a
moderate nationalist regime. He considered the coalition of
the German nationalists with the Nazis to be essential. He
felt that it was his duty to make the best of the Nazis, and
this could not mean getting rid of them as quickly as possible.
He regarded himself as the protector of a young and undisciplined element out of which he flattered himself that he
could form a politically serviceable one.

The pride natural to him and to many of his fellow aristocrats, their awareness of the strength of their social position,
led them to underestimate the dangerousness of the Nazis. It
seemed to him to be essential, and a patriotic duty, to try to
educate these fellows, and in Germany's interest he made the
attempt, patiently and with great self-control. His good will
was undeniable. Plainly he was out to make Germany great
and respected once more, and to prevent rash experiments
and wild adventures in foreign affairs. Yet, in spite of their
good will and good intentions, men like Neurath bear a
heavier responsibility for the European tragedy than the brutal,
uneducated Nazi leaders, men from the lowest depths of
society. What could they know of foreign policy?

I always looked forward to talks with Neurath. His candor
and cheerful confidence inspired trust and reliance in him.
Personally I always found him most friendly and helpful. He
certainly exerted a moderating influence upon Hitler at the
outset of the Nazi regime, and succeeded in preventing the
wildest escapades of Nazidom in foreign affairs, or at least
getting rid of their worst features. Hitler proved amenable in
foreign affairs at first, and Neurath drew the conclusion that
as time went on he would succeed better and better with his
"process of education." He thought he had the power to "draw

the poison fangs" of the party, as he put it, and to train its young men to be colleagues worth their salt.

"Just keep up your courage and don't lose patience," he said to me once, clapping me on the shoulder in his cordial, avuncular way. I had been lunching with him in the historic rooms in which Prince Bismarck had lived so long. There were only a few of us, the baron and baroness and two or three diplomats. I expressed apprehensions about the future of the youth of Germany, and the dangers their present development involved, but Neurath insisted that he was optimistic. "Let things take their course, my dear Rauschning, let them take their course. Five years hence nobody will be troubling about these difficulties."

Not five but eight years have passed since then, and the problem of the German youth has not solved itself. On the contrary, it is of great concern to everyone who has not become blind to the spiritual and moral ravages wrought by ten years of training in revolutionary violence. Neurath is not the only man who has failed to tame Nazism. He must soon have realized that his influence was diminishing instead of increasing. Hitler applied his own technique to foreign policy, a technique no diplomat of the old school could follow. Sinking lower and lower, this well-meaning protector of the Nazis, with all his appreciation of independence of mind, ended as protector of the subjugation and persecution of a nation.

Before the Nazi regime was two years old, Neurath had become little more than a fifth wheel in its cart. I met him soon after the massacre of June 30, 1934, at a prolonged official discussion with Hitler. In Hitler's presence the big, corpulent man had become painfully like a smart young subordinate on pins to make himself useful. Even then he had still to start on the path of real humiliation.

"After all, you are a German like the rest of us!" Before these farewell words Neurath had explained why he regarded my conflict with Nazism, which had led to my resignation, as egotistical, undisciplined, and entirely needless.

"One has no right to throw up the sponge in such a situation. Why did you let this conflict come? I am sorry I was not in Berlin to advise you against it," he said. He had just told me that Hitler refused to receive me to make my report to him.

I replied that I considered I had plenty of solid reasons for permitting the conflict to come. It was not a question of personal differences of view, but of the line to be taken in our foreign policy; if the present policy was continued it would inevitably lead, at Danzig at all events, to irresponsible adventures.

"The decision as to our course in foreign policy lies exclusively with the Fuehrer," replied Neurath. "Besides," he added less tartly, "don't you see what difficulties you are making for the Government of the Reich through the distrust your resignation will arouse everywhere?"

I retorted that I should feel happy if these difficulties at least had the result of slowing down Germany's pace in foreign affairs.

"It is the patriotic duty of each one of us," said Neurath dogmatically, "to submit to discipline. In the past it was considered honorable to act in accordance with one's lights and one's conscience. There is no need for me to tell you that there are situations in which the patriot no longer has any right to insist on his own better knowledge and judgment."

The attitude that prompted those dicta clearly reveals the motive that led Neurath to pursue the path of patriotic duty, as he misconceived it, to the bitter end.

3

KEEPING ALL AVENUES OPEN

IT WOULD BE absurd to describe Neurath as a wild nation-alist steering straight for a war of *revanche*. He certainly had no intention of deceiving other countries as to the insidious schemes of the Nazis by the play of his simple goodhearted-ness. He was, nevertheless, used to that end by the Nazis.

At a later time such men as Neurath lost every stable criterion of personal responsibility. They allowed themselves to be unscrupulously made use of, dignifying their resigned silence by some lofty euphemism. They also lost the sense of the politically reasonable and possible. I can offer a few re-marks on the initial stage of this process.

It could hardly be said that Neurath had any program in foreign policy. In our conversations, however, he did give me a few disconnected indications of the broad lines of his policy, so that I was able gradually to obtain a coherent idea of it.

He regarded the League of Nations as a harmful political element. In his view it served only to confuse the situation. It was not so much that it was the instrument of an anti-German policy; his objection to it was based on his general view of the State, national or other, which he regarded as the ultimate subject of the political will. The constitution of an organized society of nations over and above the State was, he considered, a utopian proceeding that falsified realities and needlessly complicated problems.

One day I asked him when Germany would return to the League. He looked at me in some surprise. A lot of water, he said, would flow under the Rhine bridges before that hap-pened. The League would have to undergo radical change; the existing League could never become an instrument of German policy.

At another time he spoke of the first aim to be worked for—to attain without complications the point at which Germany would once more be a great center of power and able to exercise her magnetic influence. "We must expect in the years to come a shifting of the center of influence of the European States. The tendency to wider fields of force is imposing itself. The smaller States will not be entirely absorbed, but they will lose their importance as sovereign entities, and will group themselves round the center of a wider system, in order to continue the development of their political and economic life under favorable conditions. There is no stopping this process. It is in harmony with the modern movement in every field, with the consolidation, for instance, of greater industrial units."

I asked what sort of demarcation of these new political units seemed likely.

"It is quite idle, and serves no practical purpose, to consider that. This sort of change cannot be theoretically determined in advance. It is a complicated process of actual growth. It adjusts itself in the face of opposition. It profits by chance opportunities."

I asked in what direction these political fields of force might be expected to develop, but Neurath objected to this, too, as a useless speculation.

"I will have nothing to do," he said, "with any questions of so-called 'orientation.' The chatter about eastern or western orientation, about a policy of alliance with Russia or against her, is harmful. It is much too soon to think of tying ourselves down. The things that are possible today are tactical alliances, not coalitions and still less federations. We must be prepared for surprising changes of front. We have many opportunities, and nothing could be more senseless than to allow ourselves to be deterred on general grounds from taking advantage of them."

On this occasion I forgot to put a question of which the

crucial importance only occurred to me later. At the back of these indications of policy I thought at the time that I could detect a conception that tallied on important points with my own ideas of the future course. The question I omitted to put had reference to the extent of these "fields of force"—these novel systems of protecting Great Powers with a clientele of small States seeking *Anschluss* with them. Neurath seemed to leave it entirely to the magnetic power of the particular center of political force to determine the greater or lesser extent of its new federation of States. This seemed to me to be likely to create the temptation to pass from a policy with limited aims to a political dynamism acknowledging no limitations and accordingly aiming at a maximum of power and territory. A popular expression for this unrestricted policy was *hochschaukeln,* "swinging up"—meaning that by sudden turns and drastic adjustment to each favorable position Germany must work herself out of her difficult situation as Prussia did before her.

Neurath was well aware of the revolutionary character of the world crisis. Sanguine as he was in other respects, he did not treat the crisis as merely a transitory economic depression. He was far from regarding it as an outcome of the Versailles peace treaty and the world war. In the conversation in which he expressed himself so optimistically as to the early removal of all the troubles and difficulties of the moment, he showed how thoroughly he realized the actual forces at work in our day. We were sitting after lunch in the embrasure of a window overlooking the historic old Chancellery park, with our coffee and a wonderful Swabian raspberry liqueur.

"We are in the midst," he said, "of a great revolutionary transformation of all our relationships, political, economic, and social. Technical progress has not only narrowed our territorial spaces; it has changed our political and even our spiritual circumstances. In the face of the new military resources of power, small States and insufficiently industrialized nations are absolutely helpless. Only great States with vast technical resources are capable of defending themselves and so of maintaining full sovereignty. It would be folly to refuse, on sentimental grounds of historic association or for the sake of a supposed democratic justice, to admit this change in realities. From now on there will always be degrees of sovereignty. We must aim at creating new groups of forces and a balance between them. There can be no revival of the old European Balance of Power."

He explained his tactics to me again and again: "Avoid giving needless offense." He welcomed the new Polish policy, and praised my successful effort in the matter of Danzig. "But," he said to me, "don't commit yourself too deeply. You are inclined to turn your pro-Polish policy into a system. Don't do it. Keep your elasticity. Systems narrow the vision. Don't lose sight of the whole. We are still far from being able today to decide for or against Poland."

He never tired of the theme that our first duty was to keep things moving, and not to allow ourselves to get stuck in a bog. This was a revolutionary policy in Conservative guise— a sort of "muddling through," but with a sharp revolutionary point. Neurath was a realist or a skeptic, more or less in the ordinary sense: he regarded the egoism and the pursuit of power of each individual Great State as the only true basis of policy. The sphere of international relations was not to be formed, in his opinion, by utopian ideas of right, but by the interests of the Great Powers. "Keep all avenues open"—that was a maxim he repeatedly impressed on me.

But he stood for a policy that avoided every warlike complication as far as possible. He showed this in expressing his satisfaction over the improvement of German-Polish relations. "Do what you can. It saves us needless wars. There is nothing that cannot be attained by peaceful means amid the changes in the world around us. The need of the small States for protection, and their interest in economic and social progress, are motives enough in themselves to produce a vast improvement in our political situation."

Common interests were in his eyes the best regulative of inter-State relations. I talked once to him about the fate of the German minorities in Poland, and mentioned with regret Colonel Beck's public denunciation of the Minorities Treaty at Geneva. Neurath replied that high-flown treaties and international legal decisions had not settled a single dispute satisfactorily: there was only one possible way of coming to an agreement over these problems—by negotiation between State and State on the strength of the existence of other and more important common interests.

From my talks with Neurath I gathered that he was firmly convinced of the internal weakness of France, and of the great changes in international affairs that would result from it. He believed that it would be possible to arrive at a friendly delimitation of spheres of interest with Great Britain. Perhaps his optimism in this case was only assumed. I heard of other statements of his in which he expressed himself as very skeptical in regard to Britain. But optimism and a measure of recklessness seemed to him to be indispensable ingredients of any active policy. "We're playing with big stakes"—this was the current phrase in the corridors of the Foreign Ministry. Playing with big stakes implies recklessness.

"The world has been set in motion once more," he said once. "Whither we are going we do not know. But the world is moving. Do not let us imagine that we can do much to control it."

In the end Neurath showed me the cold shoulder. He was not inclined to put himself to any inconvenience on my account. I learned from a mutual friend that Neurath had indignantly refused to expose himself on my behalf. "If he cannot manage his own men," he said, "we are not interested in him. We have other people to look after. It is all we can do to maintain our own position."

It was quite true that the members of the bourgeois nationalist groups had plenty of reasons for not prematurely exposing themselves. One reason was the hope of becoming the chosen heirs of the Nazis when the regime had finally and completely exhausted its usefulness, as it was expected that it might do at any time. Moreover, Ribbentrop's star was in the ascendant. Neurath's position was insecure. Difficulties and conflicts could be seen ahead which would make it necessary to be prepared for political changes. If the resistance from foreign Powers became too strong there would be nothing for it but to put a stop to the present course, bring down the Nazis, and work for a tolerable general settlement. So long as there was a chance of effecting this, no one could afford to jeopardize his personal influence. In the view of Neurath and his friends the revolutionary élan of the Nazis must be made use of in foreign policy as long as it continued undiminished, that is to say, until it had been worn down by the natural obstacles it faced. The time would then come for liquidating the party and returning to a foreign policy of moderation and to normal constitutional conditions at home.

Unhappily that moment never arrived. It was not Germany's fault. She found no opposition. All the avenues were open—wide open, and unguarded.

4

THE ADMINISTRATOR OF THE LEGACY

SOME OF THE initiated in Berlin thought that under the new regime von Bülow, the Under-secretary of State, might become the real controller of the Foreign Ministry, thus giving the Ministry the same virtual independence of the Nazi party which the army still enjoyed, and confining the wild waters of the new nationalist policy within secure embankments.

Bülow was himself one of those who thought this. He was a man of rather striking appearance, with plentiful white hair and a still youthful face; an intelligent man with a tendency to craftiness; cold and composed.

Neurath was surrounded with a certain atmosphere of benevolence. With Bülow one had to be constantly on one's guard. Neurath virtually guided the first awkward steps of the new rulers, and hushed up their stumbles. Bülow mercilessly allowed anyone to stumble. He was out to get rid of anyone who in his opinion was likely to bring new disasters upon Germany, and who stood in the way of a sound plan for Germany's greatness.

I did not often meet Bülow. My Nazi *Gauleiter,* Forster, was indignant at what he considered the arrogance of that reserved and formal representative of a "criminal regime of reactionaries," and I was thus led, perhaps, to overestimate Bülow's importance. He was, in any case, not to be drawn from his pose of superiority and reserve, and least of all with anyone who shared his reserve and met his courtesy with its due equivalent. Perhaps the only way to upset the composure of such men was deliberately to break through their atmosphere of carefully maintained dignity and to behave with thorough unmannerliness. To bluster, to let oneself go, to play the savage, the semi-maniacal, unbridled man of violence, was the well-considered method of the Nazis—Forster had advised me to adopt it—in order to get the better of "lofty aristocrats" like Bülow. I can well imagine that that sort of treatment would baffle men of Bülow's cast.

I had an encounter with him over a lecture I had given in which I made constructive suggestions with regard to the Polish agrarian reform. In view of the social conditions in Poland it seemed to me that the settlement of Polish peasants on the part of the great estates was, within due limits, a reasonable and needed policy. Perhaps I had failed to make my meaning clear; in any case, the big German landowners in

Poland complained of my statement. They regarded it as a blow in the back at a time when the Germans were carrying on a hard struggle against the expropriation of German estates. I had made no mention, however, of the oppressive use of the agrarian reform for the purposes of Polish colonization on German estates.

Von Bülow had sent me a rather severe note in which he expressed the utmost regret for my statement as in direct opposition to the standpoint of the Reich, which, he said, rested on a sound legal basis. I called on him in Berlin and gave him the actual gist of my statement, adding that I was rather surprised that the Reich Government should attach so much importance to the formal maintenance of its past standpoint and so little to the need for showing a better realization of the vital needs of a State with which it desired to cultivate friendly relations. On the point at issue I could only say that I should be the last to advocate anything in the nature of so-called "agrarian Bolshevism."

"There is no need," replied von Bülow, "to go into the point at issue. I entirely understand and approve your motives. I don't doubt for a moment that you had no intention of speaking in favor of the principle of the partition of the great estates. But what you said gave room for misinterpretation and is capable of being made troublesome use of by Poland as a weapon against the Reich and an argument against the standpoint hitherto taken. It is one of the elementary principles of political life to give away nothing without some return."

I rejoined that it seemed to me an elementary requisite for any rapprochement toward a former opponent to understand the political ideas of that State better than in the past, or at least to give evidence of readiness for that better comprehension. That, I said, was the purpose of my statement.

Bülow made a complimentary gesture. He repeated that nothing was further from his mind than any idea of discussing the motives of the statement complained of. "But it seems doubtful to me whether, even from the point of view of an understanding with Poland, such a statement was of service. To attain an apparent understanding by giving up material or even merely moral rights that have long been insisted on is a success of doubtful value. The improvement of feeling that it may bring may very easily be wiped out again."

It was rather startling to find Bülow hinting, however cautiously, that the improvement of relations between Danzig and Poland was in his opinion neither a useful nor a lasting achievement. I said a little tartly that I knew that improvement to be in the interest of the Reich and to have perceptibly eased the position of the Reich Government. Bülow replied, dropping his voice almost to a whisper as he proceeded:

"An accommodation is certainly desirable, but the efforts to achieve it should not be pushed too far. I am entirely in favor of a firm policy toward Poland, and of not giving up any of our rights. I am bound to say that your agreement filled me with apprehension—I did not like it at all. I'm not going to repeat all the objections that have been made against it; but I have the impression that Danzig rights that have long been successfully upheld have unnecessarily been abandoned. On looking closely into it, it is clear that the Danzig-Polish détente has been purchased at a very heavy cost to the common interests of Danzig and Germany."

After these preliminaries Bülow gave me some carefully wrapped up advice which I regarded at the time as the rather overweening and biased view of pure officialdom. Clearly, I thought, Bülow either could not or would not go beyond the conventional attitude of the department. Later I corrected that judgment. Bülow was carrying on beneath the surface a tenacious struggle against the new and inexpert policy which, in his view, was frivolously and recklessly destroying all the laboriously acquired opportunities for solidly constructive political work.

"I am skeptical," he said, "of the advantage of any political demonstration of so-called good will toward the Poles. I am not prepared to give anything material in return for the phantom of an understanding. Poland never gives anything away unless the difficulties of her position compel her to do so. There is no reason at all why we should pursue a policy of advances to Poland. Any improvement in her situation only brings new demands from her. I value your publications on Polish issues," he added; "they prove your expert knowledge of the subject. I assume, therefore, that you share my opinion that Poland will recognize the rights of other parties when she sees that she has no alternative.

"I must warn you," he continued, "against any impulsive action. Big moves often bring big setbacks. Foreign policy consists before all else of self-restraint. It is never possible to make as much use of a favorable situation as might at first be supposed."

I objected that in the new policy of the Reich for Eastern Europe there was no question of making use of a favorable situation, but of creating in the Polish agreement an instrument that might produce one.

"I do not share the view," Bülow replied, "that the new policy offers the key to any important developments. Until recently Poland was completely isolated. The natural thing should have been to take advantage of this isolation, and not to place Poland gratuitously in a tactically favorable situation which is now permitting her to break through the ring that hemmed her in. A change has been made in a policy that had proved up to now to be the right one and had produced useful results."

He felt that it was well to point out that too much must not be expected from surprise changes in policy. Impulsive actions and eras of conciliation had never yet produced the permanent success hoped for. They had remained mere episodes. "The German-Polish conflict is based on a natural conflict of interests, as past history has shown. Both nations lay claim largely to the same territories. Poland aspires to be the controlling Great Power in Eastern Europe. Such dreams of national greatness are not given up because of a few friendly concessions from the chief rival."

Bülow went on to say that he had nothing against a détente with Poland as a tactical expedient. But it was impossible to say in advance how far we could get ahead by means of it, and consequently we should not give up any important positions of our own.

I pointed out that Poland could not find a really interested partner either in France or in Great Britain; thus I could well imagine that a German-Polish alliance might offer great advantages from Poland's point of view, even if it entailed the sacrifice of some of her national aspirations.

"Don't misunderstand me," said Bülow, "if I decline to enter into speculations of this sort. There are various political tendencies that reappear time after time in the history of a nation. I recommend that you study them. Otherwise we run into the danger of falling victims to one-sided conceptions that produce no less unhappy results than the utopias of doctrinaire politicians."

On later occasions Bülow gave me no more insight into his real views than at this time. His rather mannered closeness led me to suspect that the secret of his whole policy lay in the cultivation of elusiveness. Shortly before my resignation I had a conversation with him in which he treated me with the most courteous and most complete disdain. His arrogance made him blind to the real dangers. He was one of the persons in influential positions in the Third Reich who greatly underestimated the importance of Nazism. In every weakness it revealed and in every small blunder it made they thought they saw signs of the disintegration of this hated regime. They remained passive, letting it be understood that they did not want to disturb that process. But decisive victories are not to be won on the political battefield, any more than on the military one, by a strategy of passivity.

My friend Werner Otto von Hentig was a passionate opponent of Bülow personally. Hentig exerted himself to convert the younger diplomats to his idea of the members of the Foreign Ministry becoming a personal élite closely united together, implying the autonomy of the Foreign Ministry as a political corporation. Personal rivalries and enmities were much more characteristic of the life of the Foreign Ministry than any idea of team spirit or unity. Such a unity could have been attained only if the Ministry had possessed not merely a strong caste spirit, or at least a special professional ethic, but the sense also of a great political mission.

This it never had. It was an arsenal of political experience. But together with that asset it carried along all the lumber of a political heritage of two generations, a heritage rich in errors and misguided aspirations.

5

TRAGIC CONFLICT

BÜLOW WAS A tragic figure. With his deep sensitiveness, he was placed in the typical dilemma of our time, for which the individual can no longer be held responsible. He was one of those who were robbed not only of the fruit of their labors but of the meaning of life. Fear of that fate has made many men do things they would never have defended in other circumstances. Bülow was a nephew of the well-known Chancellor, but he was no admirer of Prince Bülow's policy. In consequence of the verdict pronounced in the Treaty of Versailles he had resigned from the diplomatic service and taken up the fight against the "War Guilt Lie" that laid on Germany the exclusive responsibility for the first world war.

Bülow was a German patriot; perhaps he was what is called a nationalist. Germany's equality of rights with other nations, and the full restoration of her sovereignty, were for him the obvious fundamentals of German foreign policy. This did not imply fresh adventures or preparation for war, but on the contrary a stern and tenacious policy of evolutionary advance within the terms of existing treaties, using such resources as Germany's legal position permitted. Bülow's opponents complained of lack of initiative and imagination in his policy, and of his personal lack of vitality. But he deliberately refused to adopt methods that promised rapid and spectacular but only temporary successes.

He had been able to fight with a good conscience against the myth of Germany's sole responsibility for the last war. His situation became tragic when he found himself involved in a policy that could not fail to produce a new war—this time with Germany, or at least her existing regime, undeniably the sole culprit. He fought against it, but there was little that he could do. He was finally placed in the same dilemma as every other despairing patriot in Germany: if he could have brought himself to take such a step, he could gladly have called in his country's ex-enemies as allies against his country's Government. But Bülow could not justify to himself a conspiracy with foreign Powers against his own country, even in her own interest. And even if he had, he would not have found among the Western Powers a partner qualified to engage in so mighty an enterprise. Their politicians in power were at best correct mediocrities, with not a man among them of the genius and daring required for a policy that transcended the ordinary.

Bülow was symbolic of a large class of good patriots who tried to reconcile their German nationalism with a sense of European solidarity, and to avoid the political mistakes of the past. Such patriots stood between two camps. On one side of them were the utopian pacifists or national masochists, ready to go to any length in self-abasement and self-pillorying in order to gain favor abroad; on the other side were the unscrupulous adventurers who would stop at nothing in their pursuit of power.

Not every patriot had Bülow's good fortune in escaping through death from the ultimate humiliating capitulation. Moltke, the German Ambassador to Poland, was a reserved, refined, able, and in the best sense aristocratic man. I had two or three talks with him on our Polish policy. At that time he was very skeptical of the Nazi policy toward Poland. He did not regard the Poles as treaty partners with whom a broad peace policy could be attempted. His opinion of Pilsudski, too, differed entirely from mine. He told me of a talk he had with the Marshal in which Pilsudski gave him the impression of a dying man no longer in full possession of his faculties. But Moltke, in spite of his dislike of Nazism, played his part later in the policy that brought the war.

There are officials who regard it as their duty to suppress their own personality altogether. They will go so far as to "submit with the utmost respect" that they differ from the policy they are ordered to follow. Having thus "placed on record" their dissenting view, they are content. They have done all that their conscience requires of them, and can play their part without further protest even in a policy of which they deeply disapprove. But in this German tragedy there are men of another type. These are the men who are haunted by the fear of being robbed of the whole meaning of their existence, of their life's work, or what they so regard. The ambition underlying this attitude is of a higher character than that of the base and primitive careerists who are out simply for personal advancement. Beneath it is the modern identification of a man with what he regards as his "work," the breathless anxiety lest others rob him of what he has set before himself as his real task in life, and even perform it better.

I do not know whether this fear is to be found in other nations, but it is widely prevalent among the educated elements in Germany. It was given unvarnished expression by a man with whom I used to have a good many ideas in common, Karl C. von Loesch, a man of influence among the *Grenzund Auslandsdeutschtum,* the Germans beyond the frontier or abroad. By means of such publications as the periodical *Volk und Reich* he had done much to prepare men's minds for the idea of a "Greater Germany" and a Central Europe under German leadership. These ideas had nothing to do with any new imperialism. They had nothing in common with the Nazi policy, now in operation, of dominating and subjugating the non-German nations in Central Europe.

Thus Loesch was by no means *persona grata* among the Nazis. His political ideas were placed on the Index like those of all whom the Nazis regarded as their forerunners or as rivals. He tried to secure a new field of operations, and went about lecturing. I attended his lecture in Danzig, in order to show that though he was under a cloud our old friendship was not affected. But instead of an ally in my fight against the Nazi extremists I found him an entirely changed man. His ideas went far beyond anything that the Nazis had so far advocated in public.

The huge, massive form of this politician, with his round face and large, sensual mouth and Slav cheekbones, gave the impression of a Tartar. A forcible personality; yet he had voluntarily condemned himself to advocate a policy that went against his instincts.

He must have sensed my wonder at this when we met after his poorly attended lecture. "What!" he said indignantly. "Shall I let these swine do me out of things I have fought for for years?"

He developed his view of the weakness of the League of Nations, and of all the political forces of that time, so that I asked him in astonishment:

"Do you mean to say that you think the time has come for a German war of *revanche?*"

"Rubbish!" he said. "But our day has come. We can do the things we have only talked of so far. Are we to let other people do them instead?"

He gave me details of the intrigues of place-hunting Nazi underlings who wanted to push him aside. Since then von Loesch has landed in the Foreign Ministry. I have no idea what he does there.

The belief in a personal "mission," the self-identification with a "task," is one of the many secret faiths or substitutes for religion to which at times of acute crisis men of all sorts turn as a last refuge.

Even more striking than this impulse to cling to something concrete for support at a time of universal collapse and nihilism are the amazing vistas of boundless opportunity that seem suddenly to open. Ignorance, charlatanry, unashamed and brutal encroachment, won everywhere in Germany an easy victory over knowledge and responsibility, conscientiousness and loyalty. "Here in the Ministry," said my friend to me in self-mockery, using a bit of genuine Berlinese, "we have 'tumbled out of our slippers'—we have been entirely put out of countenance. Why? I will tell you! Nobody imagined anything approaching all this to be possible. But the magic has worked! And worked magnificently! Shall we not join in? It is as easy as pat, and 'justifies the highest expectations.'"

The explanation is not, to use the phrase of a recently published English verse, that the "beast in the German" has suddenly emerged, and will emerge again and again through all time. What has happened, and always will, is the revolt of the suppressed beast in man, trying to throw off the fetters of civilization. Once more, as at every great historic crisis, the fragility of a higher humanity has been revealed as our accustomed environment has collapsed in ruins about each one of us. Our whole world of conventions and agreed rules, once those rules have lost their accepted validity, becomes nothing more than a dream, and we are left defenseless in the world in face of the brute struggle for existence. Was it the Nazis who destroyed that world of conventions? Did they really do more than profit by a destruction that had already been long at work?

6

THE LURE OF ADVENTURE

THE MASS OF inherited political ideas and aspirations which the German Foreign Ministry administered as trustee included the stage properties of the political drama which had ended so tragically in the last war and the Treaty of Versailles. I mean such conceptions as the traditional policies for Southeastern Europe and Asia Minor, for the Ukraine and the Caucasus, and for India and the Far East. They included, for instance, Papen's tortuous activities in America, and also the political devices of conspiracy and corruption, subversive activities in countries regarded as potential opponents, and the stirring up of full-scale revolutions.

In all this the machine itself influenced the political line of thought. Existing practice, and political expedients already in use, guided departmental views and ideas. Beneath the surface of a policy of fulfilment and of loyalty to the League of Nations there still remained the undertow of all the ideas and schemes of the last war. With the change in the regime all these old ideas and schemes reemerged from obscurity, to be hawked about by astute and interested persons who saw their opportunity coming—the retired experts on colonial questions or questions of the Near and Far East, the specialists for the Arab world, the professional conspirators, the restless practitioners of dangerous living. These people all crowded into the Nazi party in order to persuade its leaders of the importance of their special field to the future of Germany; and they also made use of their connections with the Foreign Ministry in order to stimulate its professional jealousy and to interest it in their activities if only to prevent them from falling entirely into the hands of the wild men of the party. Not so much time had passed since the war as to prevent most of the personal ambitions it had stimulated from still being felt by men who recalled the war period as their time of glory. The ending of the war had thrown these men out of the saddle, to wait year after year for some new chance of returning once more to their old, their real job.

Among these surviving relics of the last war was no less magnificent a personage than Skoropadsky, Hetman of the Ukraine, whom the German Supreme Army Command had declared head of the independent Ukrainian State, and who had lived in exile in a suburb of Berlin since the war. I mention him because I found to my astonishment not only that Rosenberg, the head of the Nazi "Foreign Office," still followed the Ukrainian policy initiated by the Supreme Command, but that that conception was still kept in mind even by the cautious Foreign Ministry "in case anything turns up."

One day the Hetman's son came to me at Danzig with a confidential introduction from a personage at the Ministry, and asked for assistance for the staff which the Hetman had been maintaining in England. Exchange difficulties were making it impossible at the time for the Foreign Ministry to supply the needed funds in foreign currency. Would Danzig, then still in a position to make international payments without restriction, come to the rescue? The young man, an engineer by profession, offered me the use of his connections in London for the purposes of Nazi propaganda. They had, he said, a wide network of personal connections. Some of his people depended on regular subsidies.

The young man had interesting things to tell me about the possibilities of underground propaganda. I made inquiries in Berlin, and learned that it would be in accordance with the wishes of the Under-secretary of State if the Ukrainians were given temporary assistance. Thus even the very correct von Bülow considered it worth while to maintain the old stage properties in working order and to keep them together in readiness for fresh performances.

This did not suggest any new general policy, but rather that the department was still inspired by the ideas of the past. To try in this way to "preserve continuity of developments" was a sign not of creative leadership but of sterility. They never got out of the rut of the accustomed policy, but fell automatically into the same lines of thought that had already been fatal to Germany.

A man of more original mind, able to get away from all the lumber of antiquated ideas and methods and to point the way to a new and strong foreign policy, was Werner Otto von Hentig whom I have already mentioned. I should like to say a little more about that extremely capable German diplomat, perhaps the best horse in the Ministry's stable. He illustrates as effectively as anyone could the confusion of thought and feeling that took hold of the best men in Germany, finally landing all of them in Hitler's camp, and this at a time when there could no longer be any doubt where that mad dervish was leading. At first Hitler had filled them with utter repulsion, but then he gave them the opportunity of realizing their wildest professional dreams. That sort of temptation is more difficult to resist even than the charms of an attractive woman.

I remember an hour's stroll with Hentig on a spring day amid the fresh green of the Berlin Zoo, shortly before he went abroad to take up a new post. He was going with reluctance. He revealed the despair of the man of creative spirit who sees his opportunity irrevocably passing. He spoke with passion of his ideas of a broad German policy of peaceful evolution. He denounced the revival of the Hohenzollern policy of adventure, of hysterical enthusiasms and lightning decisions. We spoke of the chances of upsetting the regime, and discussed plans and personalities for a new coup d'état.

Hentig was living with a friend who was carried off by the Gestapo on June 30, 1934. I do not know whether this man was executed. If Hentig had still been in Germany he would, with his impulsiveness, have shot the Gestapo official and have had to flee the country. Fortunately he had left Germany a few days earlier. But perhaps it was not so fortunate for him. In exile, with his energy and initiative, he would have succeeded in time in organizing formidable opposition to Nazism.

This same impulsiveness had brought him into difficulties in private life that had interfered with his professional career. He was a man of great activity both in sport and in the things of the mind, highly trained and highly educated, and his gift of inspiration showed itself in his relations with younger or inexperienced officials. For some time he was responsible for the training of the young diplomats. He worked with them in labor camps, came into close contact with American work-students, and had original ideas on the subject of the professional training of diplomats. He was eminently what men call a good comrade.

On that afternoon he expounded his ideas to me. He considered that the new State must on no account become a centralist power. He spoke with passion of his opposition to dictatorship, tyranny, and omnipotent machinery of government. As regards the "national rising" under the Nazis, he admitted that it had got rid of the evil system of pseudo-democracy with its tyranny of a majority coalition. What was needed in his view was the creation of autonomous centers of

seemed to me and to others to be capable of securing for the Ministry some such independent function as the army then possessed. Instead he had to content himself with fourth and fifth rank posts.

On his return he succumbed to the universal temptation. The German world had totally changed; and he capitulated. He returned to the ideas and the tasks in which he had distinguished himself as a young diplomat when he had been entrusted with a mission to Afghanistan—the tasks of rousing the Arab and Mohammedan world against Great Britain. He turned back from his own ideas of a fruitful German policy, and re-entered the world of adventure.

What was it that induced such men to cast aside their own wiser views like an old-fashioned coat, and to put on the newly tailored uniform of the legionaries of world conquest? Were they one and all so unsure of their own ideas? Was it immaturity? Was it ambition? Or is it not more likely that it was just the attraction of a great adventure?

7

LEVIATHAN AND BEHEMOTH

TWO NIGHTMARES BROKE into the sound sleep of the German Foreign Ministry. When he came into power Hitler had to give President Hindenburg an undertaking not to make any changes in the staff of the Foreign Ministry. He kept the promise, but did something else. Out of the many branches of the Nazi party organization, some which dealt with foreign affairs grew into independent departments. There came into existence not one but a whole collection of enterprises that entered into rivalry with the Foreign Ministry.

Who in the Third Reich was not concerned with foreign policy? Every party formation, from the Hitler Youth to the

S.S., had its department for foreign affairs, its information department, and so on. The officials of the Foreign Ministry did not take these activities seriously. They felt satisfied that they would put the fellows in their place. They had done so with the wild men of the Weimar regime, of whom there had been plenty at first. If this had been possible with intelligent men, some of them with experience of the world, it should be easy with the uncouth and uneducated Nazis. They were a perfectly illiterate lot. Their *faux pas* were a source of continual amusement.

But the new men's *faux pas* did not interfere with their activity. Their illiteracy abated nothing from their dynamism. The officials of the Foreign Ministry had failed to realize that while it had been possible to manage the new men of the Republic, men of intelligence and good will, it was not an easier but a more difficult task to get the upper hand with a set of politicians of the type that, in their opinion, could be looked down upon as "illiterate." Hitler and his associates were well aware that the bureaucracy had diverted the revolution of 1918 into moderate channels. They knew that Mussolini's revolution came within a hair's breadth of failure through the passive resistance of the Italian officials. The leading cliques of the Nazi party had therefore developed a system of tactics with which to overcome official obstruction.

Of the two nightmares that preyed on the Foreign Ministry, the master of the Ribbentrop Office finally won. Rosenberg did not achieve his ambition to control foreign policy. A good part of his stock of political ideas, however, retained their influence. Outside the party Rosenberg was never taken very seriously as an individual, and he had no particular prestige within the party. He was just a writer, not a practical politician, not a man with the gift of leadership, not a subtle tactician. He was slow-going and commonplace. His visit to England was an utter failure, and Hitler never forgave the fiasco of that visit. Hitler's anger at Rosenberg's pitiable show in London was the beginning of Ribbentrop's career.

I had several talks with Rosenberg. Undoubtedly he is, in his way, a versatile man, full of ideas and very well read—the typical amateur of every field, and yet with an undeniable flair for ideas that sound new. His *Myth of the Nineteenth Century,* a book more quoted than read, continues the line of thought of Houston Stewart Chamberlain's *Foundations of the Nineteenth Century,* that much-read book of thirty years ago, in the same way as Hitler's policy continues that of William II. Chamberlain's book provided mental nurture for the German youth for a quarter of a century, Rosenberg's for barely five years. Today the young have gone on to other, sterner textbooks. But Rosenberg remains in the public eye through his policy of an anti-Bolshevik crusade. Here is the genuine Rosenberg, the Balt. He sees in Russia the great apocalyptic beast Behemoth, the land monster which must be destroyed if Germany and the world are to live.

That was the sort of thing he was saying when I met him at the outset of the Nazi regime. Rosenberg had just moved into new offices. The *Völkischer Beobachter,* of which he was editor, had become the Government organ. He was surrounded by indescribable disorder. In the business part of our talk I found him helpless and entirely at sea. His defect in speech irritated me. As a Russian he was unable to pronounce "R," and turned it into L. His typically Baltic face, and the familiar Baltic accent with which he spoke, both attracted and repelled me. He began to brighten up only when we left administrative details and started talking on general ideas. He thawed then, and became in his way attractive. He was loud in complaint about the tendencies he could see everywhere to welcome a pact with Soviet Russia. He was the only one, he said, who had personal experience of Russia. There was nothing he could do but go on warning people, but they did not seem to hear him. They were trying to force Hitler away from the straight line of his policy. Germany could not prevail against the West; her future lay entirely in the East.

I objected that according to Hitler's *Mein Kampf* France's military power had first to be destroyed before the German march to the East could begin—both of them, incidentally, ideas that filled me with apprehension.

Rosenberg replied with vehemence that all these ideas were out of date. He had no idea of seeking a conflict with France in order to destroy her military power. France would sink step by step into the obscurity of a second-rate Power of her own accord, without our moving a finger. It would be idiocy to interfere with that process. It was very different with Russia. There, as anyone could see for himself, a new military power was rising with almost unlimited resources. If the new Russia was allowed to consolidate her strength and fully develop her military machine, there was no possible coalition of Powers in Europe that could withstand her.

Rosenberg passionately denounced the suicidal folly of proposing to come to an agreement with such a Power as Russia. Russia was now going through the process through which Germany passed in the nineteenth century. A passive, contemplative nation of religious dreamers, a peasant country, was turning into an industrial nation of active, matter-of-fact, realist men and women. Bolshevism was neither here nor there; the dangerous thing was this transformation of the Russian national character. A similar change in the German nation had produced the wars of unification of the last century and finally the world war.

"In Russia," he continued, "things are moving much more quickly. Already Russia, and no longer France, is the greatest military power in Europe. In another ten or twenty years of this process there will no longer be any possibility left of resisting a vast Asiatic wave of conquest. The devilish thing about the whole situation is that Russia has forged herself a type of weapon with which she can wreak destruction at any time in the very heart of her enemy's territory. Such is the purpose of the Communist organization in every country of the world. In this way Russia maintains troops in each country, who will divide counsels and cripple the will to resistance, and will be able to carry out sabotage on a gigantic scale."

There is no question that what Rosenberg described as a new Russian weapon served as the model which Hitler so cleverly adapted to his own purposes. The Nazi organs of propaganda, the Fifth Columns, and political warfare as a whole grew out of the lessons men like Rosenberg drew from the Russian tactics. At that early time he declared to me that Bolshevism would become the cover for a new aggressive Russian nationalism, and that the new revolutionary wars which Russia would later carry on for the conquest of the world would be conducted partly with entirely new weapons.

"In Russia," he said, "a military power is developing of which no one appreciates the danger. It drives me to despair to see people everywhere ready to conclude an agreement with Russia which will further strengthen her."

"Does that mean," I asked, "that you consider the main political end to be the destruction of Russia as a centralist Power, the breaking up of the Bolshevist State, unitary as it is in spite of its name, into a series of national States?"

"I am in favor of a straightforward policy," replied Rosenberg. "But if we pursue it, shall we be able to find friends and form the great circle of States that will represent a new Europe instead of the Russian and French hegemony? Germany's only really dangerous enemy is Russia. The dangers threatening from Russia in every field are mortal. Social, intellectual, political, and also military dangers. Such political dangers as are supposed to exist elsewhere are largely imaginary. In order to conquer Russia, any alliance is justifiable. Our natural ally against her is Great Britain."

Joachim von Ribbentrop's view was the very opposite of this. I can give no personal impression of him. So long as I was active in politics he was an obscure man in the background. Today he is, with Himmler, the most important man in Germany. He is the exponent of the extremists. Today he dominates Hitler. All I know of him has been told me by men who see in him a dangerous opponent. That may not be a good point of departure for the formation of an objective judgment. But we are concerned here only with one fact.

In Ribbentrop's opinion the enemy Power that must be destroyed, because it is the only bar to Germany's domination of the world, is Great Britain—the other apocalyptic beast, Leviathan, the sea monster.

On the surface there is no greater friend of Britain than Ribbentrop. He still has friends in England who see in him the man who has tragically been prevented from fulfilling his true mission, the uniting of the two nations that are destined to close co-operation with each other—Britain and Germany.

In reality this was no more than a subtle pretense. Ribbentrop's office, financed by "private contributions," had the express object of making use of every means in the world to destroy Britain. It has done a great deal of work to this end.

Ribbentrop has made obvious mistakes in his judgment of England; on one point he has been right. The universal power of the British Commonwealth, straddling the world, prevents any attempt at world domination. So long as that ubiquitous naval power is unbroken, Germany cannot emerge from her confined continental situation and rise to leadership as a Power. The dissolution of that sea power is an impossible enterprise for a continental land power. It calls, in any case, for special tricks. If the wakeful eyes of the sea monster cannot be closed in sleep, all other efforts are vain. An assault on the monster after putting it to sleep—as in the ancient Greek myth—seems to me to have been the purpose of Ribbentrop's subtle policy. But he did not manage to croon all its eyes into a drunken slumber. A few of them remained open.

In the course of these two struggles against Behemoth and

Leviathan, the cautious men of the Foreign Ministry were gradually poisoned. They stood out against the acceptance, lock, stock, and barrel, of such political aspirations as the destruction of the British Empire. But, they said to themselves, there is something in the idea. Britain's world domination, they said, is not only tiresome, it is quite out of date.

The continual repetition of ideas of this sort slowly has its effect. It corrupts men's thinking and weakens their judgment. A few years later, when the Nazi regime had acquired legality by the force of custom, the views of the wild men gained the day over the rational outlook of the officials.

8

GROTESQUE MISCONCEPTION

RIBBENTROP AN ENEMY of England? The man who gained so many friends in the country, or thought he had? Always busy denouncing Communism as the world's enemy and trying to bring Britain over to the side of the "young Powers"?

It helps little to attribute his policy simply to vaulting ambition and wounded vanity, or to harp on the fact that he traveled for a champagne firm. There are much deeper reasons for the fatal character of his policy. It was rooted in the ideas prevalent in nationalist quarters in Germany.

Ribbentrop belonged through his bringing up and by his own inclination to the nationalists. We have no right to doubt the genuineness of his patriotism, although he must doubtless be reckoned among the most evil types of the Nazi leaders, and in his pernicious influence on the same level with Goebbels and Himmler. He was untouched by the motive that accounted for the radicalism of many prominent Nazis— the urge to escape from their precarious existence and rise into the ranks of the *beati possidentes*. This man had already achieved material success. He had had good fortune; and such good fortune does not come without talent and industry. In his youth he had revealed both talent and initiative. He knew how to make himself liked. He had had the advantage of a good education, and had experienced the success of the self-made man who, working without connections and in a foreign country, makes his way to the top.

His start in life in Canada as a young man, before the last war, ran counter to the conventional ideas of those times. In the class in which he grew up it was considered hardly respectable to have to go "across the big pond" and start from the bottom, instead of entering on a normal career as an officer or in the higher civil service. Perhaps this individual start in life, this early contempt for convention and social prejudice, may help to explain certain characteristics of his policy. But the desire for outward success and distinction, the over-assertiveness born of a secret sense of inferiority, the insincerely exaggerated optimism of the commercial traveler crying up his goods, his habit of killing time on his journeys from town to town by spending his leisure in bars, incidentally acquiring social tricks and talents together with some inclination to sharp practice—all these elements of a plausible summing up of his psychology do not fully explain Ribbentrop's policy. Nor has he the fascination of the unusual. There is nothing about him that could be described as demonic, however much he may try at times to create that impression. He is a scintillating mediocrity, able to bring many qualities into play, capable of personal charm and of a brusque affront, versatile, alert, even audacious, but without the intuition of the really gifted.

He has never been a National Socialist in the ordinary sense of the term. He agreed to become a member of the party at the instance of the notorious Count Helldorf, though only in secret, because, as he put it, he had many Jewish customers and could not afford to belong openly to the party. His nationalism is not of the Nazi type. It would not be accurate to describe it as middle-class nationalism. It is of a very extreme type, but its origin was entirely different from that of the nationalist hopes which Hitler had conjured up out of the fermenting refuse of Germany's despairing lower middle class.

In the early summer of 1938, after the occupation of Austria, I met in Switzerland a former acquaintance who belonged to the extreme nationalists and had very much the same outlook as Ribbentrop. He was neither an active party man nor an official. We met by chance by the lakeside at Zurich, and it was not a place where he could talk to me with comfort: he had no desire to compromise himself and get into the Gestapo's registers. We agreed to meet on a steamboat making a moonlight tour of the lake.

We took no notice of each other until some time after the start. The passengers were almost all of the clerk or shopmen type. They were all Swiss. We were able to talk without disturbance—until a well-meaning young man, with plenty of self-confidence, spoke to us because he noticed our northerners' German. He took it for granted that we were Nazis, and told us proudly of his journey to Berlin on the invitation of the German Consul. Germany and Switzerland, he declared, would soon be one now; Switzerland needed something like Nazism.

My companion led him on. In his candid and hearty Swiss style the young man brought out all the stock phrases of the Nazism of the period on the struggle for power. "We are getting on," said my acquaintance to me with a wink. "See how we are gaining friends."

Later we sat out of doors over our wine in the twilight at a holiday resort, while the young people danced. My acquaintance said to me:

"Do you see what is up? You placed your hopes in the West. So did many of us until lately. But the Austrian business has made an end of that. Do you still place your trust in the West? You will have many more disappointments! We know exactly what we are doing. He who gives up finds no ally. The people who think like you, the people who have been afraid of a fresh disaster, are gradually dying out among us. For anyone with that outlook it ought surely to be puzzling to see how Britain and France, and the little ones like Switzerland and Holland and Belgium, take everything lying down. It is not seven years since they were all shouting, big and little alike, 'Not one step outside Versailles into the land of freedom!' That was the song in those days, when Brüning and a few others were trying to achieve by peaceful, 'Western European' means, what Hitler has now, in his low-down way, carried to success. And your Western Powers have swallowed it all! The cautious Brüning was set down as a cut-throat, with designs against the peace of the world. And what do you find now? Why is everything suddenly running like clockwork? 'There you are!' say our people at home. 'Well, why not carry straight on in the same style?' You see, that man Hitler has been justified by results! I tell you, he will go on getting his way. Our opposition element is dwindling like snow in the spring sunshine. And what do you suppose people of sense think here, about what to expect in the future?"

I replied that, so far as my friends and I were concerned, we had not opposed Nazism out of fear that it might fail. If that had been our reason, Hitler would have been justified in denouncing us, as he had done, as faint-hearts. "But a policy of this sort," I said, "is bound to come to grief, and not only because of the opposition it will arouse; even if it shows every sign of succeeding it means disaster for us all, victors and vanquished alike."

"Draw it mild," protested my friend. "Why should you damn it outright like that? What else has national policy ever been? Make the most of your opportunity, go for the big prizes! So much at all events this new man Ribbentrop has

understood. We have such a chance as will never come again.
The others are asleep. It's no business of ours to wake them
up; let them sleep on! Meanwhile, old man, we go ahead. At
last, for once in our history it is not we who are asleep! Push
ahead and push hard! That's the motto for us. Nothing else
matters.

"Who is going to stop us? Your democracies? Have *they*
ever done differently? They have had *their* opportunity! And
they did not let it pass. Today it's our turn. Our turn, and
shall we not take it? Is politics suddenly to become this time,
for a change, a moral occupation? Let's have fair play all the
time! And that means that they must be able to lose in a
decent spirit!"

We went on arguing about the widespread view in Germany that the Reich was being saddled by its ex-enemies with
what they regarded as a peculiarly German crime, although
they had themselves done exactly the same in the past. "Men
don't change," said my companion. "And politics doesn't
change. Success is always the criterion. Your democracies believe in moral progress. They still imagine that they can unite
the faith in progress with Christianity, and they think themselves particularly good Christians. We don't share their belief."

It was love's labor's lost to attempt to persuade my companion that only a policy of peaceful compromise can have
lasting results. "No results at all," he insisted, pointing once
more to Brüning's policy. "You won't get any at all. You
imagine you are marching on and you are just marking time.
Good God, is it really so difficult to see that we are simply
bound to do what we are doing? Will the English prefer to
see the Russians master of Europe rather than a powerful
German Reich? I wish them joy of it!"

My companion sang the praises of Ribbentrop. "He at all
events knows how to talk to England and France in order
to be understood. All those pseudo-strong men, Neurath,

Weizsäcker, good honest nationalists of yesterday, who wanted
to see Germany great and powerful, are too hesitant, too slow,
too full of inhibitions, and ever since Versailles they have
suffered from national inferiority complexes. Think, man!
Are we to come too late? Our 'world-hour,' as it has so finely
been called, is today. Tomorrow it is the Russians' turn. Everything in its turn, old chap. Nobody can deny that in all the
world there are only the two of us, we and the British, who
really count. The third party, who will be the heir of us all,
stands in the background—the Russian. But there's time for
that yet. He can wait. First comes the German episode."

"There," I said, "I think you have hit it. 'Episode' is just
the word. It's all it will be—and an episode which everyone
will recall with horror."

"Do you suppose the Napoleonic period was a particularly
rosy time for people like us? Or Cromwell's time? We shall
run the race! Don't miss the fun!"

I replied that I could well imagine that that was Ribbentrop's policy, and I said a few things in criticism of it.

"His policy? Call it primitive if you like! What of it? But
why do you abuse the poor man for it? He has managed to
swing himself up to the top. Perhaps he will do the same for
Germany. Give him a chance! He is a smart youngster. We
need that type if we are to get on. Do you suppose they could
make use of men like you and me for the job? Ribbentrop is
a magnificent instrument. He simply confirms the things that
Hitler knows by intuition. He has got to the root of the
mystery."

"What mystery?"

My companion replied with a new attack on what he called
my faith in the West. "Morality," he said, "is impotence."

I made no reply to that dubious apothegm.

Returning to our subject, I said it seemed to me that there
was a terrible misunderstanding at work. Even assuming that
Russia might one day become a menacing military power

(though it did not seem likely to me that the primitive Slav and Tartar peoples could be formed into a conquering nation) —even if we had cause to fear anything of that sort, then for that very reason our one and only chance was to stick to France and England, and cast in our lot with the West of Europe, instead of continually playing an ambiguous game between East and West.

"And become just so much as Britain and France will permit—the miserably paid, miserably treated policeman for the wealthy possessing Powers. No, my dear sir, we are a world on our own. We have nothing much in common with either the West or the East. But I don't think there's anything to be gained from these philosophical wrangles. Our struggle for existence does not permit us any sentimentalities. When we have come out on top, we can begin to think about striking a moral attitude."

I asked about the great reshuffle that spring, when Neurath resigned and General von Fritsch was retired. That, I said, seemed to me to be the final preparation for the step to extremes, to war.

"The inevitable step," replied my companion. "It will liquidate the last bunch of dodderers. Immense, the way the man has grasped the nettle once more! While actually on his guard against an attack from his enemies abroad, he has delivered a mortal thrust against the old regime at home. The military, as always with us, have shown themselves as dull as dull can be in politics, dull and slow-going. Now we must just go our way to the end!"

"What sort of a way do you think you see?" I asked, adding that it seemed to me that only one conclusion could be drawn from the events of recent months, that the extremists, the radicals, had won the victory over the scanty vestiges of prudence.

In Germany today, my acquaintance replied, it was impossible to stop to consider what was extreme or what was moderate. France and Britain had waited too long, had held back with their concessions until too late. It was they who had driven Germany to extremes. "We were ready for what you call moderation. Brüning made our offer. It was not accepted. Do those people wonder if they get from the forest an echo of their own shouting?

"I know what you mean," he continued after a pause. "In Europe, you tell us, extreme solutions do not last. The West is the land of moderation. We have heard all that. But I tell you, that time is past. There is no longer a West. We have all helped to bury it."

"Do you realize that it will mean war with Britain and America?" I asked.

"Britain," he replied, "ought at least to allow us, before it is too late, to take the place that only we can take. But do you expect her to do so of her own will? We must simply place her in a position in which she has no choice but to give us a free hand. England will never again go to war," whispered my companion. "Think of me when the summer is coming to its end."

"What do you mean?" I asked.

He shrugged his shoulders. "Ribbentrop knows whom he is dealing with. It may be that his trade of champagne tout was very useful to him. He has his connections. He made good use of his time as Reich Commissar for Disarmament Questions. He gave us first-class tips on how far we could go in arming."

I tried to make it clear that the day would come when England would rise against Germany as she rose against Napoleon.

"Do you know England?" he asked me. "Ribbentrop does. One has to know how to put things to those English. Then they will agree to anything. This England will die away in peace, a nation that has lived its great life to the full. It will make way for us. Peacefully, or pretty well so."

"You are more likely to drive the English into the arms of the Russians."

"Rubbish! They have got to keep the peace. They don't want to part with their possessions. Their workers will not give up anything of their high standard of living. That makes them weak. You shake your head. Just go across the Channel. You will not find yourself back again in the fortunate land of your youth. Here and there you will find yourself right back in the less fortunate thirteenth century. A country in which the very door-handles have to be turned the wrong way. Where there is an aristocratic republic without any genuine, belted aristocracy. Where earthly success is regarded as the sign of God's blessing. All that blend of primitiveness and decadence! It won't last much longer. You doubt that? You think the elements that have formed and maintained that great Empire cannot be a mere matter of routine. Go on doubting! All the same, it is just routine that holds the whole structure together. Give it a poke and it will collapse."

"Good God! Is that what you really think? Is that the wisdom of your lord and master Ribbentrop? What a grotesque misconception!"

"Don't get excited. Things are going already according to plan. The British *have* capitulated. They did not march on account of Austria, and they will not for Czechoslovakia. And once they have abandoned their friends in Central Europe, no one will trust them any longer. One day they will be alone. That is the situation into which Ribbentrop is maneuvering them."

"And what then?"

"Then? There's no then! They are capitulating once for all, and leaving the way free for us."

IV

CAPTAINS OF INDUSTRY AND ECONOMIC VISIONARIES

1

CAPTAINS OF INDUSTRY

IN THE WINTER of 1938 I talked with a well-known German industrialist who had left Germany. He was a "non-Aryan." Our discussion took place just after the terrible pogrom in Germany, in which his sister had been barbarously treated, and what this patriot (he was one, in the truest sense of the word) had to say on Germany's destiny made clear to me a thing that until then I had found inexplicable, though I had frequently met other captains of industry—the ideas of these industrialists.

"Really," observed this man with a tinge of bitterness, "but for its persecution of Jews and its war on Christianity, this Nazi movement might have gained the world!"

He was certainly not a camouflaged Nazi, nor a pan-German or imperialist. He was one of the many German businessmen who combined coolly calculating attention to business with a passionate belief in the mission of the German nation to become a world Power. The politics of such men are not based on their will to achieve economic power and wealth but on anxiety concerning their business affairs and future prospects. He is an unhappy, sorely stricken man, with much more of the real German in his nature than so many of his "Aryan" colleagues who remained in the Reich. The fact that this particular man was of Jewish origin, and had suffered a cruel break in his own career, is beside the present point. I am not quoting this conversation in order to prove that Germans of Jewish origin are no exception in the matter of what is called patriotism. What horrified me was the complete lack of political development and the primitive political notions of this successful, capable, shrewd businessman.

We began a serious talk as I was inspecting his collection of wonderful cast-iron ornaments and plaques dating from the beginning of the nineteenth century. I shared his interest in these things. There was a symbolic element in this renunciation of precious metals and expensive material in favor of artistic craftsmanship and inspired design.

I forget how, but we suddenly plunged into a discussion about current politics. S. began to talk about Hugenberg, the leader of the German Nationalists, whom he had known intimately, and his attempt to break the power of the Marxist trade union leaders.

"All this would have been quite unnecessary," he said, "if Marxism had not blinded the masses. The workman wants to be sure of a job, and the German workman is by nature the most intelligent, good-natured of fellows. Someone should have explained to him the situation we were all in. It wasn't just that we had lost the war. The roots of the trouble lay much deeper. I mean the origin of the crisis. The crisis was bound to come, war or no war. First there was this talk of the class struggle, which set the workers against us—as though we were not all in the same boat. We ought to have gone out for some sort of reasonable Socialism, instead of Marxism—the English variety, if you like. The workman must have his representatives; no one will object to that. On the contrary, we want someone to negotiate with; we are not reactionaries. But those doctrinaire leaders of theirs kept on trotting out some new-fangled notion every month. They gave the workmen no rest. There had to be continual trouble; otherwise they would have lost their influence. They never wanted a real understanding between capital and labor. They simply couldn't see that we are all holding on to the same lifeline. They didn't care twopence about the workmen really, they were only looking after Number One."

Another visitor observed that those men were at least infinitely better than the Nazis.

S. shrugged his shoulders. "It was quite right to make all these trade union officials, the big and little busybodies alike, look thoroughly ridiculous. When we had flattered these gentlemen into donning dinner jackets and tail coats we had begun to make progress. Fritz Ebert looked simply silly in a cutaway. The workers began to get sick of their own men."

"Is that why the Nazi carpet-baggers run about in brown shirts?" inquired my friend B. bitingly.

But S. was not to be put off. "It was my friend Hugenberg who hit on that idea. He was right. We just had to get rid of those fellows."

"And the workers got the Nazi bosses instead," interjected B. "Are they any better off?"

"In one respect, yes. At least the men can talk to them. They are not doctrinaires. They know you can't feed the fires without coal. We can't give work and pay wages unless we sell something."

"*Volksgemeinschaft!* National partnership," said B., scornfully bringing out that cant phrase of the Nazis.

I was dismayed to find a man who had seen behind the scenes, and who had been treated so scurvily, speaking in this way after six years of Nazi rule, and defending the disastrous blunders of his business colleagues.

"There is something else they have grasped," argued S. "They realize that we need a market for our goods and can't get it by bargaining. The only way is to conquer it, either by war or by superior business methods. It depends on circumstances which course you take—generally a bit of both. We need Europe, and we need the East. German industry can supply all Europe and half Asia. It not only can but must do so, or it will run at a loss, which means unemployment for some workers and bad pay for the rest. The home market is only a stopgap, a makeshift. Everyone inside and outside Germany knows that quite well. We've got to get rid of the petty, dry-nursed, unfair competition of all those new States, or control their outputs, if you prefer to put it that way. There's room for only one big industry, and that's the German industry. That is the actual truth of the matter. It's war to the knife, and we or they must go under. We can't afford to be merciful. The solidarity of the workers breaks down at that point, and pacifism as well. There's bread and work either for the German workers or for the Czechs and Poles, but there's not enough for all of them. The others will have to go back to the land or find something else to do. Industry remains our monopoly, and our workers are just as interested as we are in seeing that it does. National Socialism has done its job if it does nothing more than drum that into their heads."

"So you mean the worker has got to be a nationalist," interrupted B. "Which means that National Socialism is right and international Socialism wrong. It seems to me that it may be more difficult to reconcile the interests of nations, States, and classes, but it offers a more permanent solution. At least it doesn't lead to war, which your way makes inevitable."

"Other countries did the same before us. They did it in their own fashion, and perhaps that's why you overlook that fact. All they had to do was to cut themselves off from the world economic system. They no longer needed to conquer markets. They had done that in the past, and are thus in a fortunate position. They have their own natural *Lebensraum,* their 'living space,' and it suffices for them. That's why they call themselves democracies today, and love peace and liberty."

"The faults of the others are no excuse for our own," replied B. "No one denies that the British and the American tariff policies are largely responsible for all the trouble."

"We have no choice. The democracies find fault with our autarchy, but they themselves forced it on us by their own policy. Autarchy is an emergency measure."

"It's a pretext," replied B.

"Perhaps it's a preliminary condition to the creation of a really large economic region," argued S.

"A *Lebensraum*," I remarked.

"Call it so, if you like. Not a bad expression. It depicts the right of the stronger and more capable and more industrious to monopolize the space that is his natural sphere, at the expense of those who shut themselves behind their walls of protectionism and artificial promotion of industries by subsidies for which the taxpayer foots the bill. Really," concluded S., "this Nazi movement could have gained the whole world if it had not persecuted the Jews."

2

ESSEN CONVERSATIONS

"GERMAN INDUSTRY WAS really in a hopeless state," said the Secretary of the Mines Association at Essen. "It's not Reparations or the Versailles Treaty that is to blame, or the malice of enemies of the German people or 'international financial capital' or a 'world-wide Jewish conspiracy.' The real trouble is due to three causes. One is the continually dwindling market instead of an increased turnover. Then we have an extensively rationalized industrial mechanism, with a capacity considerably in excess of the requirements of a whole continent, and there are political and economic obstacles which prevent its proper exploitation. And then there are the increases in wages and social expenditure, pressing more and more heavily on us as the turnover falls. The consequences are insolvencies, no basis for price calculations, and a load of indebtedness, with the State as our last hope of salvation. It's absurd to say the heavy industries are inciting to war because they see no other way out; but we can see clearly the fate of all highly industrialized countries, even though we may not have been the first to see it. Year by year the process of production becomes more and more automatic, thus continually throwing more men out of work with no possibility of ever re-employing them."

"What can you do?" I asked.

"Turn our debts over to the Government, which will help us for a year or two," replied the secretary. "Reduce wages and cut out the so-called political wages, and decrease the social expenditure, so that perhaps we'll be better able to compete in the foreign market, although there's very little room left for free competition. But all this brings further disturbance of the home market. To adapt ourselves to providing merely for the home market, to isolate ourselves from the world and at least skim the cream of home orders, would be a miserable makeshift."

"A self-contained commercial State," I observed. "It was the gospel of our German philosopher Fichte, a hundred years ago."

"My dear sir, how can the home market absorb so huge an output?" continued my companion. "And an impoverished home market at that, with customers that can't buy. They're growing poorer every month. We should have to find artificial means of increasing their purchasing power."

"Plenty of quacks and charlatans have come along with their sovereign remedies," I said.

"We can't get far with tricks," he replied. "There's only one way to help us out. Give us a big market, a region for German industry to dominate, a *Lebensraum*."

"But how? By war?"

"Wars don't pay. The last one showed that. It was the great illusion. War is no good, but is there any other way of securing that region? A strong Germany," he concluded, "is bound to go ahead politically. We must arm. The country must be strong and united. Arming implies three things—cranking up industry, disciplining the workers, and stopping political agitation."

This was the tenor of a talk I had in Essen in the spring

of 1934 with a number of businessmen. I had been invited to address the Essen Mines Association. It was no easy task, because my audience wanted to hear nationalist sentiments—the return of German Danzig to the fatherland, and so on. But I could not afford any political indiscretions: we were engaged in delicate negotiations with the Poles. So I disappointed my audience. I spoke of the necessity of co-operation, of the peaceful penetration of political and economic frontiers, and of the great potentialities of a German-Polish rapprochement.

The dinner and the talk after it were more promising and important. The unfortunate Fritz Thyssen was in the center of it all. There was no enthusiasm for what had been achieved so far.

"What surprised me in your speech—really shocked me, I tell you candidly—was to find you calmly talking of co-operation with countries like Poland," said one of the industrialists. "Did you really mean it, or were you just saying it for political reasons?"

I replied that in my opinion there was no other way of overcoming our difficulties.

"There you are," said his neighbor to Thyssen. "It is what I have always said. We must drop our national prejudices."

"We've been discussing whether we should help on the job of modernizing the industrial plant of Polish Upper Silesia," another man explained to me.

I told him that I entirely agreed with the idea.

"It's not our business," said Kl., the man opposite me, "to complete the industrial equipment of our political adversaries."

"We've just done a big job of bridgework for Yugoslavia," said Thyssen. "It's the same old controversy—should politics fall into line with trade expansion, or should business kowtow to politics?"

"At a time when considerations of military security compel every country to attach the utmost importance to a highly developed industrial system, it's silly to help potential enemies to improve their industrial potential," exclaimed Kl. "Besides, the Poles are our competitors, and in five years' time their products will be undercutting ours in what remains of the world market."

"In any case you won't be able to stop it," I rejoined. "You'll only leave the business to other nations."

"Heaven forbid," he replied. "But no one will invest anything in Poland if we don't do it."

I replied that there seemed to me to be only two possible political lines. One was to prepare for a war. If we contemplated that, we should have to face the prospect of it being a world war, of much longer duration and on a far larger scale than the last one. That would be the inevitable consequence if we tried to destroy Poland by force of arms. The alternative was a peaceful division of work and markets, in other words a symbiosis and the strengthening of mutual interests. It seemed to me that the German Government had chosen this course, and I had come to address them as an interpreter of this new policy, which was bound to appear extraordinary to all nationalists, and to be distasteful to them.

"That's just the Stresemann game," observed someone on the other side of the table.

Thyssen defended me—though, he said, whether the new policy would be successful remained to be seen. "But it's perfectly true that we've got to find new ways to get Germany the space she needs for an activity proportionate to her size and productive capacity." Then he began to denounce the warmongering illusionists and the advocates of a policy of revenge. "If they shove another war on to me, I'll stop backing them."

"Do you think that'll help?" rejoined his neighbor.

We changed the subject. My hosts complained of the interference of Nazi officials in factory procedure. The guests cited instances, showing a somewhat petty point of view, from which they condemned the misleading of the workers and a certain amount of incitement.

"You're a Counsellor of State," they reminded Thyssen. "You can talk to Hitler about it. Things can't go on like this."

I have tried to set down this conversation as I remember it. My chief impression is of its thoroughly low level, the simplicity, the naïveté of the arguments, and the general low standard of judgment. Was that what our captains of industry looked like at a close view? I have never watched these men conducting their businesses. It is therefore not my intention to cast doubts on their ability in that sphere. But their level of political thought was no higher than that of subordinate employees, while the state of mind in which they embarked upon the National Socialist adventure was altogether primitive.

It was depressing to note the general feeling of disappointment and dissatisfaction after a year of National Socialism. They grumbled at the middle-class nationalists for their lack of resistance, and were unable to understand it.

"We have no say in what goes on," they complained. "How are we going to get out of it?"

3

A GERMAN INDUSTRIALIST

I CANNOT CLAIM to have known Fritz Thyssen intimately. But on the few occasions when I had more than a few casual words with him I gained an impression of him which was confirmed by his breach with Hitler shortly before the war. He was one of the many mistaken German patriots, and he was also one of the many international captains of industry whose ability and capacity of judgment desert them the moment they emerge from their own sphere and attempt to meddle with politics.

Thyssen must bear a large portion of the blame for the evils which have befallen us all. But his motives cannot be dismissed with the facile condemnation which part of the public has visited on him. It was preposterous to denounce him as a Gestapo agent when he left Switzerland for France, with the intention of going on to the United States. The man had made mistakes, as we all did. It matters little whether he erred a little more or a little less than the rest of us. But he saw his error, which is more than can be said of a good many of the people who denounced him. He tried to remedy his error and to prevent its consequences. He could not prevent the catastrophe, but at least he gave the world documentary proof that the German unity is far from complete, and that, however much Germany's present course may seem to have roused the whole nation to enthusiasm, many responsible men are co-operating in it with desperate repugnance. They are doing so under the influence of national discipline—a mistaken discipline, certainly, but one which is very hard for them to resist.

Even if anyone had wanted to offer opposition, for the vast majority it was completely impossible to do so. There was, indeed, no sense in it, because the result would have been that the objector's post would have been given to someone else, who in the competition for a share in the spoils would have done much more than was being demanded of the objector. Only a very few were in a position to offer opposition in a way that would become public and even perhaps effectual. One of these was Thyssen. Such opposition called for more courage than does barking at Hitler from a safe distance. Perhaps it also needs a good measure of naïveté, indeed of indiscretion. The so-called "sensible men," the "men who are alive to realities," will not only refuse to follow Thyssen's example but will even condemn it as senseless and useless. That is one of the reasons why it was possible for matters to

go to such extremes in Germany. But anyone who believes
this is only possible in Germany is mistaken.

In point of fact Thyssen possessed this ample portion of
naïveté. It is an amazing attribute for an industrialist of such
calibre. But is it really so amazing? Thyssen was summoned
as a member of the Reichstag to the session which was to
sanction Hitler's decision to risk war against Poland. He
remained away. He protested; he demanded that his reasons
should be heard and his opposition publicly noted. In so doing,
he spoke for German industry, or at least for the largest part
of it.

I do not feel at liberty to tell the full story of this breach,
which I have only at second hand from some of Thyssen's
intimate acquaintances. But the manifest point of his opposition was "no war." War with Poland meant war with Britain and France. This in the long run meant certain war with
America. In other words, a repetition of the last war. As for
the Russian alliance, Ribbentrop's diplomatic master stroke to
prevent a hostile coalition meant the Bolshevization of Germany.

It was naïve to imagine that the protest of a single member
of the Reichstag, even if his name was Thyssen, or indeed
solid opposition from German industry or from any other
quarter, could succeed in changing Hitler's decision. But this
protest gave vent to a long repressed feeling of having been
misused. For years these captains of industry, like many other
Germans, had suppressed their better judgment for "patriotic
reasons." They kept silence and acted against their own convictions. One of them, at least, had now been independent
enough to call a halt at the critical moment. Religious convictions also played a part in this protest. So far as can be
judged without inside knowledge, Thyssen was a believing
Catholic.

This growing belief that he had been misused colored the
conversation I had with Thyssen during a conference in the

spring of 1934. In the freer atmosphere of one of the ancient
North German Hanseatic towns, in between lectures and
entertainments, Thyssen gave me some indication of his
motives and his anxieties. In what follows I have tried to give
the gist of what he said.

"Did you ever hear such stuff?" he whispered to me after
we had listened to a confused open-air speech by Rust, the
Minister of Culture. "How can anyone of sense endure it?"
We went to have a meal together when the discourse was over.

"We've given our support to those fellows," admitted Thyssen, "and then they play the fool like that! I'm going home,
man. What a waste of time once more! Yet, you know, that
man Hitler made quite a decent impression. He used to have
some good ideas in his head once upon a time. He was a
modest fellow, too. That's the sort of man we can control, I
said, we can make use of him. But now you can't get a chance
to speak to him, or if you do, he just shouts at you. Tell me,
what's up with the man? I used to know him in the days
when he'd just stand there, shy and awkward. Now you've
got to try the backstairs approach if you want anything out
of him. And all of a sudden you find it's you yourself who
are shy and awkward, and can't speak up to him."

I replied that we all seemed to have underestimated him.

"Then there's that man Goering. He's quite a usable chap.
But he, too, can get nothing more done. It's going from pillar
to post all the time. Things can't go on like that! Tell me now,
whatever can we do? Nobody will risk burning his fingers.
The Reichswehr say it's not their business. They've no use for
further trouble. If you tackle them, they tell you you can't be
always hankering after something new. Should we let things
take their course? You say we've got to stop the fellows doing
any mischief. Well, just you try to stop them! The more you
talk, the less they'll listen to you. They shout at you and won't
listen to a word you say. So what chance is there of a reasonable discussion? It's like trying to handle a vixen of a woman.

Once she gets away with screaming and stamping her foot at you, she'll try some trick on you every day. That Hitler knows you get tired of him shouting at you."

"Not the sort of things we expected," I replied.

"We said to ourselves there's got to be an end of these everlasting Government crises, which make it impossible to know where you are. How can you make any business arrangements at all? You can't have your plans completely upset every couple of months. We need a stable Government. That's the first condition for getting industry on its legs again. That's what we said to ourselves—and now, just look at things as they are today. Do you think you can run your business under these conditions?"

"That," I said, "is the 'Umbruch' (renascence) and 'Gleichschaltung.' Lovely words!" (Gleichschaltung means co-ordination—a euphemism for making everyone "toe the line.")

"I don't want to hear the words!" Thyssen exclaimed. " 'No revolution!' I said to Hitler. 'No march on Berlin! That is our condition. We don't want a revolution. There must be a stop to that sort of thing. Any ass can see what comes out of a class war.' 'We shan't make a revolution'—the man swore it. Now they call it 'renascence' and 'co-ordination.' "

He relapsed into moody silence. I told him I had long had the same misgivings. "Revolutions are difficult things to manage. They are natural catastrophes, governed by their own laws. No one can foretell on what shore a revolution may wash up a nation."

"We thought Brüning was our man," said Thyssen, pursuing his own line of thought. "But we couldn't make out what he was up to. I ask you, what will be the end of it when they start confiscating and nationalizing? If private property is only tolerated, so to speak, there won't be much left after the next chap has come along and taken his whack. Brüning was obstinate enough to let half the business concerns go bankrupt, and that's what he called putting industry on a sound footing. Breaking the forces of revolution by timely reforms, he called it. And who backed him up? Not even his own party!"

I remarked that the aims and motives of Brüning's policy were known to very few people. Taciturnity had its merits in politics, but perhaps with Brüning we had too much of a good thing. But Brüning was perhaps the only man who could have coped with the situation. "That, at all events, is how it looks to me now."

"You can't carry on a Government so entirely without the support of the workers," resumed Thyssen. "Look at Papen. An able man. He has ideas. He is clever at bridging over differences of opinion. He's simply magnificent on a board of directors. But how can so shrewd a man overlook the most important thing of all? When they made him Chancellor, I said at once that the experiment would turn out badly. The Reichswehr soon stopped his game. Where would he have brought us? You didn't need to wet your finger to tell which way the wind was blowing. We should have blundered right into revolution."

I asked him how the astonishing alliance between Hitler and Papen had come about.

That was a business with many ramifications, he replied evasively. He knew only a part of what had happened. "Papen learned a thing or two," he said. "He saw you can't govern with the whole of the masses against you. He's not easily upset, and he means well, and he is certainly in earnest. He's ambitious, naturally. He wouldn't be a politician if he wasn't. Yet, just think of it, after the attacks of the Nazis he took all the blame on himself and then was ready to play second fiddle!"

I replied that I thought he had been playing a double game.

Thyssen laughed and said he would not deny that. "Of course Papen assumed he had taken a post where he'd have control. They thought they had Hitler and his crowd tied tight to their leading strings. 'If the man wants to take over the responsibility, let him have the pleasure of it,' said Papen to us. Sounds a wonderful intrigue when you tell the story. But after all it was just an ordinary political game. An artful dodge, if you like. Each man kept his own thoughts to himself and neither meant what he said."

There was little ground for satisfaction, I said, with the outcome of the struggle. Hitler had now shaken off almost all restraint and had really worked himself to the top.

"Yes, the man has the devil's own cunning. Where does he get it from, I'd like to know. He was a shy little idealist. Well," continued Thyssen, "should we let the National Socialists break their necks? And then have the whole tide of the masses come flowing back on us? That would be the end!"

Hitler, continued Thyssen, stated his terms. Hitler maintained that he could keep the parties together only if he was the one to form a Government. He almost let them go down on their knees to him. He would do it only for Germany's sake, he told them. If there were not enough influential men to put the only unexhausted forces in Germany where they ought to be, then he could do nothing. Then his part was finished. "Oh, that's a long, vexatious tale," said Thyssen, breaking off impatiently. "The man is artful—how artful I've only just discovered. He's got us all caught in his web. And how's anyone to know what he's really after? It'll soon be as bad as Bolshevism. Things are in a holy mess. They're ruining industry completely. And industry needs careful handling. After all, it's a delicate machine!"

He was silent for a while. "I'll tell you something," he resumed at length. "I'm in a bad mood. I can't see it going on like this much longer. I've just come back from Hitler. I told him off about the way he is treating industry. I asked if he thought the present state of things was what he had promised us. Did he really think it was a fight against Bolshevism, or wasn't it really just the way to promote Bolshevism in Germany? I said he had declared himself the protector of private enterprise, but if things went on as they were going there'd soon be no private enterprise left. Well, then he shouted at me that he knew best how to finish off Bolshevism. He didn't need any lessons, and least of all from the fine gentlemen who boasted that they had backed him up. Not one of them had known a single thing. They were all helpless against Marxism; otherwise they'd never have supported him. He knew very well what was going to happen to industry, and the big bosses could thank their Creator that he, Hitler, was looking after them. But no one cared a rap about his difficulties. Every day his own people were dinning it into his ears that they wanted to see a bit of the Socialism he had promised them. If we were going to be stupid enough to make further trouble for him, then he'd find himself forced to let his own people have their way with us. The real revolution had still to come, and it might break out any moment. Then he couldn't guarantee anything more. We ought to be grateful to him for giving us our lives and safety so far. He'd done that up to now. But he couldn't promise that one day things wouldn't take their course, as in Russia, which would mean that not only would they abolish private property but pack off its owners into the next world as well."

Thyssen had grown excited. "I couldn't keep my temper," he continued. "I said to him: 'Now, look here, Herr Hitler, is that all that comes of your fine promises? Is that your thanks? Is that how you keep your word? Is that what we financed you so long for?' 'I never made you any promises,' the man answered. 'I've nothing to thank you for. What you did for my movement, you did for your own benefit, and wrote it off as an insurance premium. You didn't do it even for Germany!'"

Thyssen paused, and I thought it best not to speak. "What a thing to have to swallow!" he continued. "After getting imprisoned by the French when they occupied the Ruhr. I did all I possibly could do for Germany and German industry. And where was this man Hitler in those days? He and his movement sat quietly at home, brewing revolution and scheming to get into power. Yes, that's what they were doing at the very time when things were at their worst in Germany. Did the man think of Germany then? Has he ever thought of Germany?"

4

A BARREL OF SAAR WINE

"DO SOMETHING TO help us, and I'll trundle you a barrel of the best Saar wine all the way to Danzig."

I replied that it was hard to resist the temptation of a light and luscious Saar wine, but that what I was asked to do in return implied an overestimation of my capacity.

"What! Why, you're forging ahead! You're successful. Help me to prevent it coming to a plebiscite in the Saar."

Röchling, a well-known Saar industrialist and a privy councillor, was sitting with me in the pretty Beauséjour Park in Geneva. We were discussing the kindred problems of Danzig and the Saar. I asked him whether he was really afraid of a plebiscite.

"It looks bad," answered Röchling. "Let us not be deceived. A year ago I would have prophesied a ninety-five per cent vote for Germany, but my answer now is that every month makes the situation more critical for us."

"But why?" I asked. "Has the French propaganda been so effective?"

"Not a bit of it. But the people don't want to join the Third Reich."

"As in Danzig," I told him.

"Yes, the Nazis have done us a lot of harm. I must say so

quite openly. It's a fact. I shouldn't be doing anyone any good by hushing it up."

For a while we drank our coffee in silence. It was a wonderful autumn day. One by one the chestnut leaves fluttered to the ground. The rustle of the Aar came up to us.

"What do you think will happen if there's no plebiscite?" I asked.

He told me of the efforts being made to obtain the consent of France to the return of the Saar without the plebiscite specified in the Treaty of Versailles. It would be a gesture of final appeasement. A renunciation of rigid insistence on obligations. A banishment of the spirit of Versailles. In short: reconciliation and a gift to the new, young Germany.

"Reconciliation!" I said. "At this moment? Have you noticed the feeling at the Council meeting? Is there any chance of it?"

"Very little," admitted Röchling. "That's why I want to interest you in the idea. It would help all of us. Just think what would happen if we got a bad knock. Perhaps only seventy per cent of the votes for Germany! Perhaps sixty or even under fifty per cent!"

"Are things really as bad as that?" I asked, in shocked surprise.

"It's quite impossible to tell. Anyhow, a result like that would only embarrass the French. They simply don't know what to do with the Saar. The politicians and the industrialists, I mean. From the military point of view, of course, the Saar is a key position. That's where we find the opposition."

I had a superficial knowledge of conditions in the Saar. I asked Röchling whether he thought that only the French military chiefs were interested in securing the annexation of the territory to France.

"Yes, they're the only ones. We can reach an understanding with the French industry. We could get an understanding in every sphere if the military and politicians had no hand in the game."

"A bad poll would mean the end of the Nazi regime."

"If that were all!" exclaimed Röchling impatiently. "But with it would go the last hope of a real understanding."

"An understanding with France? Is that really possible?" Some other men from the Saar territory joined us. The conversation drifted into details. But I met Röchling several times. The similar situation of Danzig and the Saar was a bond between us. We generally discussed the harm done in both territories by the Nazi policy, which had made the situation in both Danzig and the Saar perceptibly worse instead of easing the tension. But there was an occasion on which Röchling gave me an insight into his personal views. We were traveling from Geneva to Frankfort via Basle. It was the night express, and we were alone in our compartment.

"The dilemma is," said Röchling after we had discussed the ever growing tension in the international situation, "that England understands our position and perhaps really desires to reach an understanding with us. But how, I ask you? We can find a way out of our difficulties if we bring all Europe into a single fold, so to speak. At all events economically, to begin with. But that's the one thing England can't permit. Her theoretical good will is of infernally little use to us."

I remarked that British policy was always benevolent in matters of detail and ready for compromise, but that in its attitude toward the European continent as a whole Britain obviously held fast to the old traditional lines—a destructive policy.

"She can't do otherwise," replied Röchling, "unless she takes over the leadership herself and incorporates us lock, stock and barrel in her Commonwealth of Nations."

"And saddles herself with a whole pack of troubles," I said, laughing.

"In reality, it wouldn't be at all a bad idea," Röchling continued. "But it's technically impossible. The conceptions of the British Empire and the European-African region, the *Gross-*

raum or 'big space' now in process of evolution, mutually exclude one another."

"It's a long way to such 'big spaces,'" I objected. "Oughtn't we to make a more modest beginning?"

"What do you mean by 'more modest'? Huge economic regions are coming into existence. That's inevitable; no one can stop it. And how are we otherwise to get out of our universal difficulties?"

I said I thought Europe was more likely to cease to exist than to unite.

"Politicians certainly won't bring it about, if you'll forgive me saying so," continued Röchling. "Politics today means obstruction and creating obstacles to economic development. That's not confined to Germany; it's the same in all countries. That's why politics will have to take a back seat during the critical period."

I asked whether he meant that economic activities could achieve the things which politics had left undone.

"There's a sentence which has been in the mouths of Hitler and his agitators till one's sick of it, but it appears to be true— to the effect that politics and not economics govern Germany's destiny. That is right enough as a counterblast to the Marxist views. But such cheap slogans have only a semblance of truth. As if economics were not largely politics, and vice versa. A working agreement between French and German industry is an attainable goal. It is not limited to the heavy industries. It is only the political ambitions of little-minded people that have stopped its accomplishment. Parliamentary politics means nothing but keeping up the prejudices of yesterday. Are the Saar, German-speaking Alsace, and the Briey ore basin problems worth going to war about? There's a set of different problems to worry us. The adaptation of purchasing power to modern production possibilities, for instance. We've got to look at it that way, not the other way round. It's a question of the big market, isn't it? Well, doesn't that mean a common market? Are we to destroy each other's markets? We are living in a different world from the one we imagine. Our ideas are those of yesterday, but the problems that make up our real life are the realities of tomorrow. I am a German. If it comes to war, the Saar'll be a war zone. A good part of my mining plant will go up in smoke. But I ask you, are these really the things that matter? Is it so important whether this or that strip of territory is German or French, or, in your case, German or Polish?"

"I'm surprised to hear you speak like that," I said. "But frankly, I'm glad. I've come to the same conclusions about the Eastern question. It's damned difficult to make oneself understood on that point without being set down as a confirmed pacifist."

"Can anyone of sense fail to see that the days of petty nationalist particularism are over? I'll tell you something, although I wouldn't like to say it publicly. Versailles or no Versailles, it isn't this peace treaty that is the cause of our misery. But this man Wilson—an American, if you please, with no notion of European nationalism—saddled us, on doctrinaire grounds, in the name of justice and a mythical right of national self-determination, with a lot of miniature national States in Europe, and completely destroyed the few existing rudiments of great supernational regions. That is the cause of all the trouble! But at bottom all these sponsors of Versailles were well aware that they were helping the ideas of the day before yesterday to no more than a formal existence."

I mentioned Briand and other men with pan-European ideas.

"The French are not today in a position to make any serious efforts. Little men are ruling the French today, little litigious people, sticking to the formal letter of their rights with typical peasant cunning and with the obstinacy of the little man with his little savings. Those are not leaders with big ideas. They know very well, too, that they're unfit for leadership. Consequently their one idea is to stop others from coming to the top.

"Then," I said, "you can see next to no prospects in present developments. If there can be no understanding, it means a fight for supremacy in Europe."

"It's quite true and, indeed, a commonplace, that no nation can be allowed to have supremacy in Europe, but that the only possible thing is the equilibrium of many forces. I'm hoping for an understanding, but I don't place any faith in it. There must be a nucleus of power, round which a new order can form. First by compulsion: later the reins can be loosened a bit."

"Doesn't that mean war?"

"Between you and me, I don't see how war can be avoided. We can't polish off England in any way except by presenting her with a fait accompli. We'll juggle her out of Europe in a friendly way, but with some slight pressure. As far as the French are concerned, I'm afraid they'll need just one blow—but a strong one—to make them reduce their demands to the right level. A short war, as against Austria in 1866, and then a real settlement. The French feel in their hearts that they were not the real victors in 1918. They're a gifted, clever people, an amiable people, a hard-working, thrifty people, but one that has slipped out of history a bit, like the Spaniards. I know them well. They've given up wanting to be leaders of Europe. They'd be quite content with second or even third place."

I remarked that all this seemed to have been thought out somewhat on the lines of Bismarck and the "Wars of German Unification."

"Quite right," replied Röchling, "because a real European unity cannot be made merely by 'decisions.' It can't be realized by means of an assembly of States pressing measures by a majority of votes, in parliamentary fashion. Either this unity will be achieved by a couple of military strokes by a leading nation, or else it can never become a reality. Force is inevitable in such a case. And what nation except the Germans could do it? Afterwards the time will be ripe for reasonable, rational agreements. But there must be no attempt to oppress other nations. On the contrary, we must develop them and promote their purchasing power. What markets there'll be for us! Expansible markets, not merely in Europe but in Africa and Northern Asia as well! If we understand our job, there ought to be markets for the German, French, Dutch, Belgian, Swiss, Czech, and Austrian industries! But someone will have to take the business in hand. We're the leading industrial nation, in this region at least. There are enormous possibilities for all of us."

"But wouldn't this centralized leadership involve totalitarian, centralized planning?" I objected. "And wouldn't that mean the abolition of free initiative for private enterprise? Shouldn't we find ourselves irrevocably committed to a Bolshevist planned economy, with controlled production and consumption?"

"My dear sir, in any case we are only trustees for the public authorities. All this will happen whether we want it or not. What does property mean nowadays? It's only a polite fiction. Besides," argued Röchling, "there'll always be room for private enterprise. What has to be planned is the framework. But that will have to be a real plan. No getting round that. You're a farmer, and probably you are saying to yourself that all this is entirely incompatible with your 'back to the land' schemes for the German nation. Between ourselves, what your Darré says on that subject is nonsense. Don't take it amiss when I say that. You can't put back the industrialization process. Our strength and our future lie in our industries. Let us leave agriculture to the other nations in this region."

We went on talking of the necessary magnitude of a unified region, and the means of promoting its gradual development. Hitler, we agreed, had stopped halfway, but he was capable of making further progress. "The only opponent we need take seriously is Russia," he added. "We must liquidate her power before she liquidates us. Her territories belong to our region."

When we parted, it was almost morning. "Help us to clear away the first obstacle," he said in farewell. "Don't do anything stupid," he added. "Don't spoil your career. Don't make any unnecessary opposition. We've got to go through with it. We'll have to get rid of the inefficients. We can't abolish National Socialism; we shall have to co-operate further with it. The Nazis have one good point—they are realists. Be a realist too. There's a barrel of Saar wine telling you to."

5

THE EXACT PROCESS

IT IS CURIOUS to note how many engineers Hitler drew into his select circle. In economic affairs he never took advice from practical businessmen, but constantly from engineers. This fact is characteristic in itself. In his eyes industrialists represented only individual interests, and so they seemed to him completely incapable of grasping national economy as a whole. For trained economists he had a whole-hearted contempt. There were also occasions on which he expressed skepticism concerning the economic ideas of engineers. Nevertheless he continually had engineers in his company.

A couple of years before my meeting with Keppler I had become acquainted with another engineer who held similar views. His name was Plaichinger, and at that time he was a sort of special economic adviser to Hitler.

Plaichinger remained unknown. He died before the National Socialists seized power. He lived in Munich, where I visited him in the early summer of 1932. He was full of suggestive ideas, and for the rest a modest, gentle, intellectual man.

At that time we Danzigers were supposed to be following the example of the Reich by bringing about a program for creating employment. I was referred to Plaichinger, who was said to enjoy Hitler's confidence, and I called on him in his modest pension, close to the "English Garden." I found him in the midst of a wilderness of papers and maps. The first thing he said to me in reply to my inquiries was that Danzig's fate would be quite different from what I had imagined. "There," he stated, "we shall deliberately plan a metropolis— a great commercial mart. Danzig lies at the point of intersection of important routes, and is a junction of two great fields of energy. Within a few decades she will become one of the most important industrial centers in the Eurasian *Grossraum,* the vast territorial unit which is coming into existence."

I listened to these fantasies of future greatness with a somewhat skeptical ear. I cannot remember the details of our conversation, but I retain the impression of a man who was so sure of his subject that he took no trouble to try to convince me by arguments and remained indifferent to critical objections. He pushed such objections aside with a disarming amiability. It was from his lips that I first heard the expression "planned control of energy"—the system that was to replace liberalistic private enterprise. I must admit that at that time I failed to grasp his meaning; it was, indeed, only later that I realized that similar ideas were common to all the engineers from whom Hitler took advice, even though they might differ considerably in their conceptions of an economic system under technical direction.

The idea of "technocracy" had emerged in America as a strange new doctrine. In Soviet Russia a group of young engineers were beginning to replace the old Communist party bosses, throwing over the Marxist ideology as useless ballast. A rule of technocrats appeared to be developing out of the dictatorship of the proletariat, and meanwhile, in Germany, Hitler had assembled a staff of engineers. Was this a mere coincidence?

Undoubtedly Hitler has technical gifts. Every layman who heard him discourse on engine parts and processes was impressed. He could throw on to paper an admirable sketch of machinery. But it was no mere fondness for the engineer's profession that induced him to choose such a strikingly large number of its members as his intimate advisers.

There grew up in Germany in those years, drawing men from all camps, regardless of their political and social traditions, a sort of invisible order embracing all those who believed in the need for social and economic planning of a radical nature. Its members sank all their social and political differences in a new community of outlook that linked the Communist with the National Socialist, the cool, calculating General Staff officer and the scientific research worker with the youthful intelligentsia of all schools of thought. All were inspired by the ideal, propagated with infectious clarity, of the devotion of men's utmost efforts to a reasoned ordering of human life. Was Hitler also of their fraternity?

For all these people National Socialism, and even Germany's political rise, were only necessary stages on the way to a radical phase of the technical revolution. It culminated in the planning of man himself, the rational interpretation of his nature.

Can this be done? Can we plan a human being? Can we so train him for rational social and economic functions that he loses the original stamp of his nature?

Strange to say, the answer to these questions was a passionate "yes" from persons differing so widely from one another as Todt, the designer of the Autobahnen and the Siegfried Line, and one of the most intelligent political economists here in bomb-racked London. By means of suitable education the competitive instincts forming the psychological basis of the "competitive system" can be eradicated from human nature. But eight years before I met this economist I heard the following statement from Todt:

"We have entered the second epoch of man's self-domestication. The first was characterized by war and a continual shifting of the balance between social and predatory instincts.

The main feature of the second will be the education of mankind for rational functions in an exact process."

I asked Todt what he meant by an exact process. He replied:

"Man is about to divest the sexual impulse—the strongest of all natural impulses—of its mythical and spiritual significance and degrade it to a natural need, so that he can satisfy it in a regulated fashion without making any fuss about it. We shall also canalize the social and economic impulses of the masses. The care for the means of existence will no longer constitute life's principal concern but will become nothing more than an unconsidered trifle."

Then, I replied, we should have happily reached Utopia, the Promised Land, the millennium.

"Today we can do everything we want to. Practically speaking there are no more impossibilities for man now. We can lengthen his span of life, and we shall remove all sorrow from it—to say nothing of providing such an inexhaustible store of the world's goods for everyone that economic envy, resentment, and ambition will be extinguished. Man has come of age, he is lord of the universe."

I had a number of conversations with Todt. In my *Voice of Destruction* I have described the petty deception he practiced on Hitler in the matter of the Autobahnen. Now he is a great man in the Third Reich. At the time of the conversation I am setting down now we were drinking the usual East Prussian "May drink" (rum and hot water) in a small East Prussian town after the opening of an Autobahn section. I had expressed some skepticism concerning the Autobahnen and their profit-making capacity, and had even cast doubts on their practical utility as military roads. Todt protested that military considerations and the desire to reduce unemployment had played a large part in the scheme.

"We are taking advantage of the military interest in these roads as a means to the realization of our own plans," he said. In any case, he continued, there could obviously be no question of profits in the sense understood by private capitalism. Any businessman knew at least enough about the estimation of profit possibilities to realize that. But that aspect was irrelevant. "You must get rid of these prejudices of a bygone age. You must not imagine that the events which are in the news in Germany now really count for anything. But behind them there are things really worth working for. We're in the biggest revolution of all times."

We discussed the purpose of the revolution, of which Todt thought National Socialism was only the initial stage. The real task was to create the elements of a completely new order, and so the old order had to be entirely uprooted. In the future there would be no more talk of State or society, of economics or politics, and no more attempts to distinguish between them. All such conceptions of order originated from an epoch now approaching its end, and had consequently lost all validity.

"You must picture the future substitute for State, society, and the economic system as a network for the distribution of energy. The party and the dictatorship are nothing more than instruments for the liquidation of the old conditions and the preparation of the new ones. In themselves they are valueless accessories which we can cast away when they have fulfilled their purpose."

I replied that all this was entirely alien to my own ideas. It was more or less the opposite of what I had in view—a multiple order of self-governing bodies with delegated spheres of State authority. I had attempted to create such organisms of self-administration in Danzig.

"Don't attempt any such nonsense! It's ridiculous to think that what you call self-administration would be possible in these times. The next stage of development we have to attain," declared Todt enthusiastically, "we shall have to call the technically controlled State, or technicalized human society. It is a necessity that is forcing itself on us; by clearing a few obstacles out of its way, we can shorten the painful transition process. Take America as an example. The people there are well on the road to accomplishing in their own fashion what we are striving to achieve with the assistance of National Socialism. Ten million or more unemployed in this competent, industrious nation! Do you think that can go on ad infinitum? Do you really believe the economic process will absorb them of its own accord? Well, what then? We must get rid of slipshod economics and slipshod politics. So far it's all been just a playground for people who've learned nothing. Now our day has come, and the planning engineer will take the politician's place.

"If an industrial concern doesn't function properly," said Todt, starting off again, "you call in a mechanical engineer who overhauls the plant and finds out where things have gone wrong. Today it's up to us to overhaul the entire plant of 'human society and the State.' Unfortunately we find the whole plant is hopelessly out of date and can't be modernized by putting in extra machinery. So we are drawing up a plan for a new plant. Social and economic problems are the tasks to be attacked by the technical experts of a new order. Social processes are transformations of energy. Economic processes are changes in the network or the distributional area of our system of control of human energy."

Koch, the East Prussian *Gauleiter,* also took part in our conversation. I found it strange that he did not combat these ideas. Obviously they were more widespread among the higher officials of the party than might have been supposed.

6

TECHNOCRATS

AT A TIME when Danzig was involved in financial difficulties for which it was comparatively easy to find a solution in

Germany, I was advised to seek out Keppler, in order to enlist
Hitler's support. Keppler was then Hitler's economic adviser,
and later became Under-secretary of State. At that time Keppler had his office in a tiny attic on the top floor of the Chancellery. Here he kept me waiting a long time, and then adopted
a hostile, superior attitude. My interview was not a success, but
I obtained an insight into a world of thought which until then
had remained closed to me. Or perhaps not quite closed, for
previously I had imagined it to be a fantasy of otherwise
sensible experts. I was accompanied by one of my closest colleagues, a prominent engineer formerly belonging to an important firm in the German electrical industry, a man keenly
interested in economic policy, like many of our technical experts. This man was the cause of the interesting turn our
conversation took.

I gave Keppler a brief sketch of my ideas on the financial
assistance which the Reich could continue to give us. My colleague Be. explained the technical details of our program and
gave estimates of the return it would bring in. I noticed that
Be.'s somewhat pedantic manner irritated Keppler, for he began
to fidget with the numerous documents on his desk and finally
interrupted my friend.

"My dear party comrade," he said turning to me, "you are
worrying about troubles which are completely irrelevant and
can easily be got over. All you have to do is to hold out; do
what you like so long as you stave off Danzig's financial collapse. You don't need to worry about rebuilding Danzig's
industries. That is our affair, and we shall do it in quite a
different way from what you are proposing. The promotion
of private enterprise is not the line of our future policy."

We reverted to a discussion of the currency trouble, and I
expressed my concern at being forced to adopt the unpopular
measure of devaluing the Danzig gulden.

"There's the flaw in your economics, party comrade," interrupted Keppler impatiently. "Gold is ridiculously antiquated

as a currency basis and unit of value. If you don't drop these orthodox ideas of a bygone age, you won't get far. We shall very soon be instituting a new unit of measurement."

I replied that in that case the substitution must take place very soon; perhaps it had escaped his notice that the Danzig gulden was not an auxiliary German payment medium, like the municipal money tokens issued during the inflation, but a currency quoted on the international money market and bound to lose its value if the normal cover was reduced.

"We are getting over these difficulties," replied Keppler. "And I strongly advise you not to express such views in the Fuehrer's presence. You had better amend them as soon as possible." My job, he continued, was to wait until Germany was ready to make a fundamental change in Danzig's destiny.

I protested once more, depicting the political and economic risks which Danzig ran in pursuing so adventurous a policy. But Keppler reiterated that my ideas were out of date.

"You have no means of seeing what is going on, and what is on the way, as we have here in Berlin," he told me. Then he hinted at developments on a larger scale than, he said, I could possibly imagine. "We have resources which I can't disclose to you, and we are in the midst of a process so vast that it would be ridiculous to waste time on questions of the order of those you are raising.

"The help for which you are asking is just what we can't give you," said Keppler, dogmatically. "Besides, it's easy to see you've not had a technical education. Only a universal genius like Hitler, with his capacity to separate the essential from the irrelevant, can understand without a technical education that the economic process in all its ramifications, including distribution and consumption of goods, is a technical process, and must therefore be settled on strictly rational lines, from which politics and private interests—they amount to the same thing—must also be completely excluded." He turned to my companion. "You'll understand me at once when I say

we can only emerge from a state of permanent crisis by instituting technical control over the entire economic process."

My companion voiced emphatic agreement. I reverted to
our individual problems, and showed how our special position
affected our approach to labor problems, making it impossible
for us to create employment by the methods evolved in the
Reich.

Keppler replied that this universal problem of unemployment furnished the best of all proofs that it was no longer
possible to solve critical problems within the present economic
order. "Can you ever abolish unemployment in a capitalist
economy, in a free market economy?" he asked. "I'll save you
the trouble of a reply—it can't be done! But why not? I'll
answer that too. I hope you'll then understand why I can't
advise Herr Hitler to back your proposals. In plain words,
the reason is the progressive disproportion between the continually increasing output of our economic machine and the
continually diminishing purchasing power. But why this
shrinkage, you may ask. We're asking ourselves the same
question, and there we've hooked our fish. Purchasing power
is distributed in accordance with each individual's labor output. We call it earnings or wages. But if the process of production shows a continual decrease in the percentage of human
labor involved, what then? Well, we have a glut of products
on the one hand and markets unable to absorb them on the
other. But why does the process of production involve a progressively diminishing proportion of human labor? Simply
because technical advance produces increasingly automatic
methods of production. In the early stages of technical advance
machinery increased the productivity of human labor. Later
men were employed to operate the productive machines, but
now one machine operates another. The degree of participation of human labor in the process progressively falls. Consequently we have to find a new principle for the allotment of
purchasing power."

I remarked that this was presumably the way in which our Socialism was to be established.

"Call it Socialism if you will," continued Keppler. "It is, of course, Socialism. We can only accustom the masses to the coming changes by representing the new conditions as their Socialism. In reality, of course, it isn't, because Marxist Socialism simply can't exist. A redistribution of purchasing power on principles of an alleged justice or equality would be totally ineffective. It's not a matter of justice or equality, but of expediency. Quite a different standard, of course. It wouldn't be popular; the masses wouldn't understand it. That's why it can only be considered behind a popular fiction. We want a suitable allotment of goods, but that does not mean equal rights for all. On the other hand, it will rule out the inheritance of property, as we know it in the capitalistic system, for the simple reason that title deeds are promissory notes. I won't go into the futility of the creation of debts, on which all financial transactions have hitherto been based. But even if we are not sentimental Socialists, and consequently not doctrinaires out to create a 'just' social order, we happen to come close to Marxist Socialism on some important points. In the eyes of the masses we are becoming socialistic mainly because of the possibility, or rather the necessity, of an immense rise in the general standard of living, and because of our authoritarian control not only of production but of distribution and consumption as well."

I interposed that all this seemed to be very far from what had so far been expounded as National Socialism.

Quite true, said Keppler. One had to keep one's eyes open to distinguish between the popular fiction and the real developments going on behind it, he said. "The best element in our technique is one which we have not yet fully exploited. I mean our capacity to produce an endless glut of goods. Up to the twentieth century the characteristic feature of the world's development was a shortage of goods. Now there's a sudden glut. But there's a lack of purchasing power. Instead of tackling the problem at the right end, we talk of over-production. Instead of understanding the world revolution and grasping the fact that mankind's ancient trouble, shortage, has vanished, we creep back into the shell of our ancient notions and create an artificial shortage. All the economic policy of today has no other aim than the creation of artificial shortages."

My companion grew quite agitated in his eagerness to express his agreement. "Instead of accepting the vast transformation wrought by the industrial revolution, they all try their best to cling to the antiquated notion of want. It's grotesque," he said.

"The artificially enforced deprivation of goods," said Keppler in assent, "which characterizes our present economic system. We shan't solve a single problem of our so-called crisis unless we substitute for the present system another one— a logical, rational system of control, in which the engineer is no longer there just to fetch and carry for the businessman, but becomes himself the directing economic leader and statesman, to whose rulings all must bow."

Keppler went on to talk of the necessity of taking full advantage of the maximum output of the machinery of production, because this was the only way to assure an enormous cheapening of products and so to raise the general level of existence and introduce a complete revolution in our social standards. These developments would enable us to bring the class struggle definitely to an end, and to make the whole problem of poverty and insecurity meaningless.

I replied that this could assuredly be accomplished only by a general standardization of products and renunciation of individual tastes. The probable consequence of this would be the gradual decline of man from an individual entity to a general type, with a widespread conformity of needs and desires.

Keppler considered that in the future the influencing of the market, that is to say the consumer, by means of advertisements which involved deliberate deception of the purchaser, would no longer do. "We must find new means of guiding the consumer. National Socialism is busy developing them. We can no longer afford to base the distribution of goods and the demand for goods on individual appetites and the principles of the market hucksters of past centuries."

Keppler raised the question of the formation of industrial combines; these he declared to be of no assistance to rational planning because they grew up on a financial basis, with no relation to productive capacity or the aims of production. As an exception he quoted the famous German industrialist Stinnes, whose vast combine, organized on a vertical basis, he agreed was marked by evident knowledge of future needs. If Stinnes' plans had fully succeeded, they might have helped toward the achievement of the new order National Socialism was now trying to create. But military rearmament now afforded an opportunity, which would never recur, of establishing a total control of industry, so permitting the launching of a new economic process. "Then," concluded Keppler, "we shall live in an economic system so infinitely superior in productive capacity to the present one that we shall practically dominate the world through it. Don't waste your time on makeshift help for little crises during a temporary transition stage, and so hold up the great process of transformation which, among other things, will make all your small Danzig problems negligible."

Keppler then hinted at important inventions, the nature of which he regretted he could not disclose, but which, he stated, were of such vast significance, and would give Germany such superiority over all other countries, that a swift and fundamental change in our situation was no longer in doubt.

7

WORK IS A VICE

"IN A TECHNICAL order of society poverty is inconceivable. Poverty is not merely a crime against society, but mental indolence. Such assertions would naturally appear ridiculous to serious-minded captains of industry. Well, I trust that despite the contempt of these wiseacres we shall live to see the abolition of poverty. It is the technician's dynamic power that makes all formulae derived from the wisdom of our ancestors out of date. Faith has never yet removed mountains, but technical skill can do it. If any would not work, neither should he eat, was the maxim of former days. That was the appeal to envy with which Marxism ran its politics. 'Work and despair not' is the motto of all the apostles of honest labor. But our gospel is 'Thrift is asocial.' Spending is the good citizen's duty. Everything depends on the speed of the movement of goods. What did I strive to achieve with my doctrine of money, which was so pitifully misunderstood, other than a stimulus to quick spending? 'Be idle and do not despair' is the slogan nowadays. Work is not a virtue. Like everything else that is overdone, it can become a vice."

This was the gist of a private lecture given to me by Gottfried Feder when I visited him. Feder was the notorious inventor of the "Feder money."

Although Hitler, when he came into power, very quickly discarded his adepts in the theory of currency manufacture and hunters after a sort of economic perpetuum mobile, he retained a good part of the contempt for financial problems affected by old party comrades. Money is plentiful, they used to say. The question of money need never be an obstacle. Money problems are uninteresting. In this primitive fashion the *Gauleiter* and *Amtsleiter*, the regional and departmental party chiefs, echoed Feder's and Hitler's views.

"You see, I'm a victim of the situation," Feder told me, when I called on him after his dismissal. He was indignant with Hitler for having left him in the lurch, after telling him explicitly that in the main he agreed with his ideas. Hitler had added, however, that the time was not yet ripe for putting them forward. The party must first be more firmly in the saddle. Feder admitted that he had been too free in the exposition of the real economic intentions of the Nazis.

The former Under-secretary had shared the fate suffered by so many "men of the first hour" in all revolutions. In his speeches before the Nazis seized office he had often announced the measures he proposed to carry out as Minister of Economic Affairs and dictator of the currency bank. Nothing of this was achieved. His capacity to evolve plans was inexhaustible, but he was helpless in dealing with practical problems. Nevertheless, he was shabbily treated. He was a man of benevolent disposition, far removed from the usual Nazi type. He had sunk a large part of his fortune in the movement, in the early stages of which he wielded considerable influence. He remained the National Socialists' theoretician until the seizure of power.

His middle-class opponents of the Right were delighted to expose his floundering efforts to deal with practical problems. "They say I ventured too far forward. You see me," he complained, "the scapegoat of the agitated reactionaries who were frightened about their securities. I am ruining business, I am an obstacle to confidence in the new conditions, I am injuring our currency, etc., etc."

We discussed Luther, who at that time was still president of the Reichsbank. "It may be," he said, "that that is the sort of man who is wanted at the moment. Well," he added, shrugging his shoulders, "we shall be wanted when the time comes for real constructive work. Then they'll send for us."

They did not send for Feder, but the gist of his ideas, largely a welter of faddist notions, was the gospel of the end of the individualistic economic order, and the belief in this was shared by all the leading pioneers of National Socialism. Feder and others used the expression "exact control of energy" to designate the new, coming order.

I had come to talk about some of our plans for creating employment. I was oppressed by the feeling that all the attempts to end unemployment by means of programs for the creation of work, however ambitious, were clearly heading for failure.

"Your view of it is, of course, perfectly correct," said Feder.

"And the practical outcome?" I asked. "Can nothing be done?"

"Nothing! You can do nothing except let things take their course until the time is ripe for decisive action. A dangerous policy? Yes, but Herr Hitler wants it. The creation of work is never anything but camouflaged unemployment relief. It can't be otherwise. That's why I only gave way most reluctantly to the *Gauleiter* when they wanted a program of creation of employment. They only wanted it for propaganda purposes. I'll tell you another heresy," said Feder. "Unemployment is a measure of a country's technical level. The higher that is, the more unemployment. But instead of discovering the only way out of the dilemma, what do we do? We introduce conscription of labor."

I touched on other unfortunate attempts that were being made to abolish unemployment by artificial means. Certain people were beginning to cry out against machinery. They said, for instance, that street sweeping should be done by men with hand brooms instead of mechanical appliances. In rural areas the modern machine wreckers demanded that corn should once more be threshed with hand flails.

But that, Feder replied, could no more check the total mechanization of industry than the machine wreckers of a century ago had been able to stop the victorious onset of the machine age. "We can't barricade ourselves," he said, "against the logical evolution of the laws of technical progress. We can't abolish technical progress; we can only adapt our social structure to it."

Feder declared that politicians are incapable of grasping realities. "The rule of politics," he said, "is over. A future day will see the end of our own party's usefulness. During its early years I deliberately guided its policy in such a way as to enable the party one day to render itself superfluous. I do not at all approve of the advance of the party to its present dominating position. The time will come when humanity will at last get rid of the intellectual inadequacy that we call politics, and accept in its place the rational rule of science."

The only thing that could solve the unemployment problem, he continued, was a new economic system. I confessed that I failed to understand what was meant by a new economic system.

"It's all so simple," replied Feder. "All our poverty arises from the fact that goods are not produced directly but only indirectly for the consumers, and the direct purpose is simply the making of profits. This system has muddled along somehow in the past. But now has come the age of technical invention. This is a new element, but our society remains the same as it was three thousand years ago. The result is a misfit, a maladjustment."

I pointed out that these were two very different explanations. The first sounded very like Marxism. The second I could appreciate better.

"We shall certainly be unable to maintain private ownership of the means of production," Feder insisted.

"Well," I replied, "I begin to understand why Hitler won't accept these ideas. Your new order clearly implies, among other things, the socialization of the means of production."

Feder indignantly denied this. It was the application, he

said, of rational means of technical planning to human society. It was not a question of theory or doctrine, but of practice.

"And your money theory?" I asked.

"There," he said, "we come to the crux of our problem. The time for the agreed use of a commodity as a standard of value is over, no matter what you take, gold or cowries or anything you like. We have to find a new standard of general validity. That standard is the work done. However, by work I do not mean only human labor but all forms of energy. Incidentally we see how little human energy really counts in modern industrial processes in comparison with the vast supply of mechanically derived energy."

I objected that there is a difference in quality between goods made by hand and by machinery. But Feder denied it. Our conception of value is simply an inheritance from the age of barter.

"But man always makes valuations," I said. "Isn't it in his nature to do so? A valueless economic system and a soulless existence! Is that to be our future?"

When I heard a belittling of currency and financial problems from Hitler's own lips, I regarded it as a sign of his political levity. It was not until later that I saw the connection between these views and the ideas of Feder, Todt, and Keppler, and realized that this was not sheer amateurism but the expression of a definite outlook, kept secret at first, on the future economic order. Later events showed that Hitler remained faithful to his view that the linking of the needed standard of economic value with the commodity of gold is not a help but a hindrance to industry. He never tired of insisting that the value of money depended not on gold but on work.

8

A PLANNING OFFICE

A VISIT TO Königsberg brought me a most enlightening experience—a conversation that revealed the extraordinary ideas that were being confidentially worked on in Nazi quarters by the men who were in actual charge of the party's official economic research work.

I had gone to see Herr Bethke, who at that time was director of the Chamber of Agriculture for East Prussia. Bethke had put forward, before the Nazi seizure of power, a general plan for the extinction of agricultural indebtedness; the plan had been officially disavowed by the party, but later some of its suggestions were adopted. He took me to meet a young economist of Königsberg University, Professor von Grünberg, who was the actual author of his plan.

Professor von Grünberg had set up, under the special protection of Herr Koch, the *Gauleiter* of East Prussia, an economic planning office as a sort of institute attached to Königsberg University. In reality it was a party institution. Koch was keenly interested in economic questions, and in two particular questions above all. The first of these was economic and political association with Soviet Russia. There had long been an annual fair at Königsberg, the *Ostmesse*, in which Soviet Russia had always been the principal exhibitor. Here in Königsberg the feeling was strongly pro-Russian. The leading Nazis were divided as a rule between the three normal German points of view in regard to external policy. Some wanted an accommodation with France, some wanted to come to terms with Great Britain at the expense of France, and the third and most active group were trying to get an alliance with Soviet Russia against the whole of the West.

I knew that Koch was the chief advocate of this last policy.

He took pains to keep in personal touch with Russian emissaries. He wanted to go to Russia himself. Assuming that I had Hitler's ear on questions of eastern policy, he repeatedly asked me to put forward his ideas in talking to Hitler.

Koch did not get to Russia, but young Professor Grünberg did. In 1936 or 1937 he spent a considerable time in various parts of the country, in contact with important personages. I am unable to say what success he had with the propagation of his ideas. These were not difficult to surmise—to arrive at close co-operation with Russia by peaceful means, perhaps even to reach a complete symbiosis of the two regions, an objective which Grünberg and those who thought with him regarded as the natural basis of the welfare both of the Central European and the Soviet Russian peoples.

Koch's other great interest was planning the industrialization of East Prussia. This region, separated from Germany by the Polish Corridor, was economically backward and had a declining population, owing to continual migration to the western provinces of Germany. Koch's idea was to develop industries in East Prussia, in order to set up within the framework of the German system of autarchy a sort of small-scale East Prussian edition of that system. These plans fitted in with certain ideas of the army leaders for various reasons. Grünberg had been commissioned to work them out. What came of them was something altogether different.

I went with Bethke to Grünberg's office. It consisted of a whole suite of rooms, filled with specially drawn maps and plans. I glanced at these. Were they just bluff, hung up to make an impression? I could not decide. East Prussia came little into the picture; the maps covered the whole of Eastern Europe and part of Russia in Asia. I asked what they all had to do with East Prussia.

"All this," replied Grünberg, "is our natural hinterland."

I pointed to a map with unexplained marks and lines, and asked what they meant.

"That is one of the maps," said Grünberg, "in our survey of sources of energy—the necessary starting point for any reasonable system of planning."

"Are all these power stations?" I asked.

"Yes," he said, "that's it."

"But you don't suppose we can set up a joint power grid with Soviet Russia?"

"Of course we shall," he replied. "But, mind you, we don't include just the grid. When we talk of energy we mean, of course, every sort of factor in production, every source of energy, and all the materials of production. Coal and ores, for instance, and timber, and grain. Electric power and also man power; and, above all, industrial plant."

I asked why the political and national boundaries were nowhere shown.

"Boundaries? Frontiers? Don't interest us. Chance, arbitrary interruptions in existing fields of energy; we've got to get rid of them."

I did not know whether Grünberg was joking or meant what he said. "It would be fine if we could do it," I said.

"Do it we shall," was his reply.

I pointed to colored lines crossing a map. "Are these to be first-class motor roads?"

"That is the distributive network, the grid for the distribution of energy. Those are the routes of the future controlled traffic and regulated exchange of goods. These things can't be left to the commercial man's fancy; they have got to be planned, carefully and rationally. We can't go on leaving it all to chance; that is utter waste of energy."

I pointed to other signs and learned that these represented sources of energy and centers for its utilization. The whole thing struck me as fanciful and dilettante.

"Yes," interposed Bethke, "we are not merely planning East Prussia here; we are at work on the preparations for the coming Great Order."

"Isn't that looking rather far ahead?" I objected. "We still have in all these regions a lot of national groups, States and even whole systems of States. You can't just sponge out the whole human superstructure."

"That," said Grünberg, "is the very thing we're doing. We are showing on these maps what these vast regions look like when that's done—when you wipe out the ephemeral work of those arbitrary and incalculable fellow humans of ours who, as the phrase goes, 'make history.' Look at these two maps. They show up at once the absurd mess our so-called national civilizations have made of the world. This is an ordinary political wall map; here are the centers of production, the raw material supplies, and the existing transport routes. And here you have the same region as it would have been if it had been free of political and private interests and influences, if production and distribution had been rationally and logically organized on the basis of the natural conditions. See how the natural tendencies have been cramped and warped! We can't afford all this squandering of energy. Every bit of this waste is a bite out of our standard of living."

"Very instructive," I said. "It should help in the fight against the artificial restrictions on trade dictated by private interests." At the same time, I said, we could not expect that everything that had grown up around us in the course of history should simply disappear to make way for a rational new order. Man was not led by reason alone. His irrational element was part of him. It was not even an infantile element out of which he would grow. All this seemed to me just a new, modernized edition of the cult of reason of the French Revolution. "Here, I suppose, in these maps and plans, we have the symbol of today's conception of Reason. A four-year or five-year or x-year plan—it strikes me as a dry sort of celebration of the new Goddess."

"For all that," retorted Grünberg, "these Planning Chambers will take the place of the Parliaments of the past. There will

be no more political debates because there will no longer be
any representation of private interests. In these Chambers the
calculations will be made and checked and the tasks allotted
for the populations of the new Great Regions."

"In all this," explained Bethke, "we have abandoned the
customary standpoint of a social order rooted in exclusively
political ideas (the standpoint from which, as we all know,
our own party works), and we have set ourselves the task of
inquiring into the potentialities of a more serviceable order.
You see here the first results of our investigations. The first
thing to be done is to take stock of our sources of energy,
reckoned preferably not in fictitious gold values but in horsepower. What is already possible for us? How far have we got?
What further development is needed? That is the rudimentary
first stage in which we are working at present. The next stage
will be that of tentative sketch plans: what is needed, that is
to say, for the development of the system of energy of our
technically controlled society. In terms of private enterprise
that would correspond more or less to the conception of capital
investment. The third stage will be the consideration of the
volume of goods which we are able to apportion among the
whole of the population. In this connection far-reaching investigations are required in regard to the suitability and the
order of urgency of the goods to be consumed, their various
types, and the amount of play that should be allowed for
individual taste. This is a field into which we have not yet
entered."

"Why, this," I said, "is complete Bolshevism."

Grünberg replied a little tartly that that was a total misconception, though unfortunately a common one. "Bolshevism
is an intermediate stage on the way to this type of rational
order, just as are the ideas put forward at present by the party."

"Well," I said, "I am afraid I cannot keep company with
you along that road."

"A matter of generation, no doubt," snapped Grünberg.

"Anyhow, whether we like it or not it is our unalterable destiny, determined by the technical system and its decomposition of our society. We have committed ourselves much too deeply, advanced much too far already in that system, to be able to retrace our steps. It is the modern industrial society itself, as people call it, that compels us to march on. That compulsion is our new freedom. To do what has to be done, and to do it of our own free will—that is freedom."

"Freedom! Is it really freedom?"

"It is such freedom as exists for men."

"You will never overcome human inadequacy and irrationality."

"To overcome those things," insisted Grünberg, "is precisely our task. Human inadequacy is being cut out. The tasks we are setting ourselves are tasks for which there are exact solutions. Politics and private interests play no part in them, or none of any importance. These, among others, are elements of friction and resistance that can never be entirely got rid of, but they must be kept down to a minimum."

"Man is a rebel born."

"Yes, there is faulty material as well as good. The faulty will be eliminated."

"Does that mean that the man who is still inclined to individualism will be eliminated?"

"Certainly."

Grünberg pointed to some maps showing Great Britain, Western Europe, the United States, and Russia.

"If we calculate," he said, "the energy basis of each separate region, we arrive at exact results. Perhaps these maps will make our general idea plain to you. Judgments on a basis of this sort will hold water. The politician is blind, he has to feel his way in the dark. We, on the contrary, know. Look at England, for example. What is her energy basis today? As you see, it is slender, damned slender. A country of shopkeepers, a creditor country. But its time of greatness is gone, or will be soon. What sort of a part can these exhausted tin mines play, these coal mines, the water power or the agricultural sources of energy? Are they enough to live on? Enough for a world race to live on? They belong to the past. England developed her sources of energy long ago, in the days of narrow and limited spaces. That gave her an advantage—then. But what is it worth now, in comparison with the quantities of energy in the new Great Regions? England herself will have to send her population out into the Empire. England will become a little island, lying like a Heligoland off the Great Region of the Continent, a sort of Scandinavia. There'll be no living in the future on trade and finance and such things. Trade is only a function of industry, not an independent sphere of activity. Industry is a function of the available energy. You can see the end of England—here it is on the map! There is her horoscope! In a hundred years England will be a small country of at most seven to ten millions population. There it is in black and white—her fate!"

This, I felt, was all too fast for me. If there was anything in these ideas it would take not hours but days to establish it.

"Look at Russia," he continued. "There's no future, of course, in this Soviet business. But the country itself, that vast region! To potter about social problems in the way they have done is ridiculous. Naturally the masses must have their due. They will do well—they'll have all their hearts' desire: amusements, no saving, only buying and casting aside, no more darning stockings, every moment a new fashion! No going short, no want, everything in profusion. Magnificent, believe me!

"But, you ask, where does it all come from, and how do we manage it? A fair question! There's a limit, of course, to everything. It is all a question of the available energy, the quantity of horsepower, so to speak, at our disposal. Purchasing power can only grow in proportion to the quantity of energy released. That's obvious, and admitted. So don't mis-understand me—we're not out to plan Utopia!"

"So you consider that Russia will outdistance Britain?" I asked.

"Obviously. England has at best a generation of voluntary liquidation ahead of her. Russia is the land of the future."

"Fine prospect!"

"Not, of course, the Russia you are thinking of," said Grün-berg. "When I say Russia I mean the whole Eurasian region, Europe included. Only a vast region will make possible the sort of things I have just hinted at. That is why it is so important to set the right bounds to the new Great Regions. They must have within them the requisite quantities of energy. Obviously it's impossible to raise the standard of living arti-ficially. In India and China, for instance, it cannot be simply levelled up by decree to the English standard. Thus the Great Regions will have very good ground for their regional pa-triotism. (Don't laugh at the idea. There will be better ground for it than for national patriotism.) The quantity of energy within the Great Region determines the possible level of the standard of existence shared by everyone in the region.

"Take America, for instance. No question but it is the country in which all that I have been suggesting, in a very fragmentary way, will be bound to force itself into existence very soon on a grand scale. And in an altogether radical fashion! Much more so than in the German-Russian region. Just consider the sort of land it is—a land where the wild idea of a State prohibition of alcohol could be entertained! The United States the land of freedom—don't tell me! They have the courage for radicalism, and therefore the fantastic may become reality there at any time.

"I am convinced that America will be the first Great Region to become a technically governed Energy State. It has tre-mendous, almost unimaginable resources. Its energy basis will enable it to maintain the highest standard of living of all, with the minimum of working hours."

"The working hours will be different in the different regions?"

"Obviously," replied Grünberg. "The fewer the working hours, the higher the standard of living, and vice versa. There must be a separate calculation of working hours for each region. The more highly developed the productive organization, the less human working time, obviously, will be required. We shall be able in the social sphere to achieve really big reforms quite painlessly without any of the class antagonism of the nineteenth century. A fulfilment of Socialism such as no Marxist of any shade ever dared to dream."

"What sort of differences," I asked, "will there be in the working hours?"

"The American region may have no more than a twenty-hour week; the Russian-Asiatic region perhaps thirty-six."

I pointed out that in that case it would be very much to Germany's disadvantage to go in with Russia instead of the West. I admitted, however, that the answer to this objection was evident. Great Regions could not be arbitrarily defined; they were the product of the natural conditions that determined their shape and their limits. Failing those natural conditions, it was impossible to make an arbitrary delimitation. "Well," I concluded, "what are the natural Great Regions?"

"Apart from our own, which is coming into existence already, there are only two," replied Grünberg. "The Great American and the Pacific and South Asian."

"And what will be the future of the British Commonwealth?"

"That empire is the very type of a pseudo-Great Region, the product of arbitrary political action and chance private interests. It is an artificial creation, formed without regard to the natural conditions for Great Regions, and therefore now caught inescapably in a process of final dissolution."

In the course of our conversation I asked how it was supposed that such Great Regions could be brought under one control. Russia would hardly be ready to give up her independent rule of her own territory.

"Why not?" replied Grünberg. "It is a change that has got to come—there cannot be the least doubt of that. And the men at the head in Russia are as a rule shrewd and clear-headed realists, without a trace of sentimentality or feeling for the conventional and customary. Thus there is every reason for assuming that they will be broad-minded enough to enter into close collaboration with Germany, voluntarily and without war."

"And if they do not?"

"If we do not attain our end by peaceful pressure, a short war will place us in possession of the essential regions. But it would mean very bad political bungling if war had to come. Germany and Russia are complementary, not only in resources but in the characteristics of their peoples, so that there should be no difficulty at all in achieving a common control of pooled resources."

"But this would mean either a new sort of German domination in Russia, which the Soviet rulers are surely unlikely to tolerate, or a Bolshevizing of Germany."

"There is little need to fear either the one or the other. Bolshevism is a child's bogey. The things in it that frighten our elderly statesmen are far less radical than the things we ourselves are in process of introducing. And German engineers and technicians in Russia in no way imperil that country, for the simple reason that the nationalism of the nineteenth century has passed out of existence—gone as completely as all the glory of the bourgeoisie. We still go on talking of 'national values,' but it is only talk; examine it and you find it is completely empty."

My only reply was a skeptical silence. In a moment he continued: "That, anyhow, is the way the young intellectuals of all countries look at it. You just don't happen to have come into contact with them. That is their outlook in America as in Soviet Russia—and even in England."

"Why 'even'?"

"Because, owing to a curious shifting of phase in intellectual development, England is only beginning to reach the stage at which your generation came out of the Great War."

"You regard Britain as a backward country?"

"Backward—what does it mean? Let us just say honest middle class. It is the country that has preserved longer than any other the noble standards of the Good and True and Beautiful, in a word the ideal of the sturdy freeman. Whether that is a good or a bad thing remains to be seen. From our standpoint it is, of course, a disadvantage for England. For there is no halting the course of events."

"What course? The replacement of politics by technics?"

"I should put it more generally and more primitively—we younger men no longer take seriously the things for which your generation was ready to die. But nations and States have always been ruled by old men to this day. The fact is only noticed when complications arise."

"You mean homeland, nation, the ideals of freedom?"

"Exactly—that whole ideological superstructure. Including, of course, Socialism, the class war, and the classless society. And this is not confined to us younger men of the intelligentsia and the possessing classes. Ask some of the younger workmen; ask them why the Social Democrats have none of the rising generation in their ranks. All that stuff is out of date, antiquated, stuff for the oratory of the bosses of yesterday. We younger men of all classes and all countries mean now, once for all, to order our lives by reason and common sense."

"And what are you out for?"

"That," said Grünberg, indicating, with a wave of the hand, his maps.

9

A VISIT IN EXILE

SUCH WAS THE philosophy, the new outlook on the world, of what might be called a "new materialism." Obviously Grünberg had not been brought to these views by any social resentment. It was easy for me to understand intelligent young engineers like my friend Be. lapping up ideas like these. He had often told me what he thought of the system of "old men's rule," as he called it, in industry—the humiliation he and his fellow scientists felt at having to place their knowledge and their exact calculations at the service of arbitrary private business interests and of that mindless idol "the market." I had attributed these ideas and this line of criticism to the evident proletarianization even of the most highly qualified engineer, his economic enslavement, as soon as he had a family dependent on him and so was himself dependent on securing a permanent situation. But there could be no such feeling in Grünberg's case. Here one was met with a complete and radical breach with all tradition under no other compulsion than that of pure reason. How widespread was this attitude? Was one really of the older generation and incapable of appreciating the new ideas?

I have tried to record views of that sort so fully because they seem to me to be important and revealing. I am not sure that I understood them properly, and I may have oversimplified them. The technical world is beyond my ken except where it comes into practical contact with the farmer's profession.

Be. threw up his office in the Danzig Senate at the same time as I did, and he stayed with me for a long time on my farm. I always found it an effort to follow his argument. It seemed to me a queer mixture of clever intellectual gymnastics and incredible puerility. Intellectually all these men of the

younger generation—though Be. had been an officer in the
last war—had somehow failed to ripen. Their development
had stopped short.

This intellectual callowness revealed itself clearly in another
young man, whom the Danzig Storm Troop authorities had
recommended to me as a personal adjutant. In spite of his
official standing in the party he was a thoroughly decent and
loyal fellow; he was one of those students of our technical
colleges who go on and on and never manage to complete
their course. His outlook on the world was of a crudity that
would have been impossible in any student in the past. The
combination of technical knowledge with complete brutishness
of spirit is the atmosphere in which the gospel of the new
technical radicalism thrives and spreads.

It is a process that deserves close and anxious attention in
other countries besides Germany. In Germany it has spread
everywhere under the Nazi surface. I learned this from a visit
I received in exile in Poland in 1937. The young man who had
come to see me brought an introduction from my friend Be.,
who had secured an important post in the German electrical
industry, and had been through his training as an officer in the
new army. Be. had heard that I was writing a book against
National Socialism—my *Revolution of Nihilism*. He sent me a
message urging me under no circumstances to publish it—it
would serve no purpose, and would be dangerous for me. The
movement, he said, was irresistible. His view of the vulgar
Nazism had not changed. But he had now gained a better
insight into the real forces and real aims of the movement.
Germany had acquired such a lead, and such vast transformations were in progress in the country, that any defense of the
old order, even from the best and humanest motives, was to
be condemned. I must not cut myself off from all possibility
of return to the Reich. He could be of assistance to me.

Be. had waited a year in Danzig in the vain hope that conditions might change, and had then departed. On taking fare-well of me he said:

"If Hitler wants to be deceived, why should we not humor him? I shall do everything the party wants. I shall go to the meetings, and pay my contributions, and shout 'Heil Hitler!' as often as they want, and stand for hours with my arm stuck out."

I said that was not very grand. (Be. was nevertheless, I insist, a loyal and decent fellow, with an utter loathing for Nazi methods.)

"It's not a question," he replied, "of what's heroic but of what's sense. I'm going to daub myself with the same protective coloring as the rest. Then I shall wait and see what happens. I've no ambition for martyrdom!"

This was the typical attitude of the great bulk of the German people. Join in with the rest, practice protective mimicry, wait and see, make the best of the fraud, above all lie low; there's nothing to be gained by opposition; the whole crowd are a dirty lot and will come to grief by and by, so why worry?

That was in 1935, and two years later, I learned to my surprise from my young informant that my former friend had abandoned his waiting attitude and had become an energetic Nazi worker. My young visitor assured me that my friend, and many others with him, had not changed their opinion of the party in the least. It was still considered in Germany that Nazism was only of passing importance. At the back of it, however, immense changes were under way, changes in which it was essential to have a hand. Like everyone else in a key position in the practical affairs of the country, Be. considered that there could be no going back, and that the task before them was to direct the unceasing revolutionary process to relatively sensible ends.

I asked what was now regarded in Germany as "relatively sensible." In reply the young envoy gave me the sort of picture I have just tried to sketch in the account of my talk with Grünberg.

The sensible course, said the young man, was to get rid of the ideas of the nineteenth century. The sensible course was to make an end of nationalist ambitions and social utopias. All these things had become meaningless. It was paradoxical that a movement that had posed as socialistic and nationalistic should throw off these two very elements, on which it had seemed to depend for its existence, but that, anyhow, was the reality beneath all the tumult. This liquidation must be allowed to proceed to its natural completion. It would be wrong to place obstacles in the way of the Nazi movement; on the contrary, it must be supported.

"But," I said, "you cannot live on the liquidation of the past; you must of necessity have some positive aims."

"The reality," replied the young man, "is the technical revolution. Just as France's bourgeois revolution produced the nineteenth-century system of national States, which reached its culmination in the Versailles peace treaties, so the technical revolution will produce a new public order which will determine the character of human society in the centuries to come. This is hardly likely to come to pass without wars. We are alive to that, and are already making our preparations. But it is no longer a question of restoring old frontiers, it is no longer a question of turning to the west or the east; all these ideas are out of date. Nor does the fact that Germany, with Soviet Russia, has been the first country to grasp the message of the twentieth century imply that she is destined to become the leading world Power in the old nationalist and imperialist sense."

I replied that I had heard all this so often that I was afraid it had become no more than empty phrasemaking. What, for instance, was meant by "the message of the twentieth century"?

"Of course," he replied, "that is just a phrase coined for the dull of comprehension. All it means is that the technical system is no longer the servant of industry and profit but the controlling element that will plan out and determine all human relationships."

The young man returned once more to the object of his mission, the effort to persuade me not to publish my book. However justified, he said, its criticism of Nazism might be, it would not arrest the development in Germany, and would merely injure individual careers. There could no longer be any question of the successful formation of an opposition either within or without the party. Not only the army but other influential elements had identified themselves with Nazism, regarding it as the indispensable catalyst for the preparation of the new order, and intending to make use of it as such. Opposition now would be not only personally indiscreet but mere sentimentality. It was impossible for any political order to guarantee such human values as freedom, personality, the inviolacy of the sphere of private life, or individual moral responsibility. There was, indeed, nothing to be gained by harping on these things and holding them dear in the old bourgeois fashion.

That is the last I heard of my former friend. There are many roads to capitulation.

V

OLD GENERALS AND YOUNG
OFFICER ADVENTURERS

1

THE FETISH

"SO YOU, TOO, have landed safely in the arms of the Great Manitou," said someone at my side.

I had just left the Chancellery, and was walking down the Wilhelmstrasse toward Unter den Linden. I turned around, startled. It was the first time I had heard that decorative epithet for Hitler. An old acquaintance of my youthful days had caught up with me. Von H. was an officer in the military organization which represented the German General Staff under the Treaty of Versailles. He was a very capable officer, a coming man in the General Staff. He is now playing an important part behind the scenes.

I greeted him and stammered a few embarrassed words of excuse.

"Cheer up," laughed my acquaintance. "The mob must have its fetish."

I replied that I had been feeling some doubt whether what was so charmingly termed a "national uprising" was really the right course. I had just had an interview with the Chancellor which gave me much food for thought. "Where is it all leading us?" I asked.

"Getting cold feet?" asked von H. sharply.

"Not at all," I replied. "But we thought things would turn out a bit differently."

Von H. shrugged his shoulders. "No doubt you've the same opinion as we all have of this play-acting. Or do you believe in the swindle?" He made a contemptuous gesture with his glove.

Put in this direct, brutal way, the question was an awkward one. I answered that I had certainly regarded National

Socialism as a means to an end, but everything depended on the end. Instead of averting the long threatened revolution, it was beginning it in earnest. No one could say where this would end—perhaps in war, in disaster such as that of 1918, or perhaps even worse.

"No, my dear chap," said von H., cutting me short rather disdainfully, "it won't come to that."

"Then you fellows have got something up your sleeve? What is it?"

"Maybe we have. Wait and see. Why do you want to know it all in advance?" He laughed. "Do you think it will all go according to plan, with nothing left to chance? Cheer up, there's a chance for everyone. If you know a thing or two, if you think you can do something, go ahead. There's a chance for everyone, I say. Hitler's not bound to be the big noise. Why don't you enter for the race to the top? Someone's got to get there. Well, why not you?"

I was struck by his cynical tone. But it was general in Berlin. "We thought there was going to be an end of all these ups and downs," I said. "But things seem worse than ever. Who is the real ruler of this country?"

"It's a witches' Sabbath," laughed von H. "But it's not a kid glove affair. We've got to go through this mess, and anyone who's afraid of dirtying his white waistcoat had better stay at home."

It was lunch time; we turned into a well-known restaurant in Unter den Linden. When we had given our order, von H. fell to talking about our days in the cadet college.

"Do you remember that red-haired fellow in the 1st Guards?" he asked. "Do you remember that time in the swimming pool when he made us do the pike's leap over the barrier into the Havel? No one was let off; those who couldn't or wouldn't try it on their own had to go over with him. Head first! And afterwards there was egg brandy as a reward."

"Yes," I replied, "I remember it well."

"That's your national uprising, old man," he laughed. "Over the barrier and into the stream. Then swim for it!"

I knew the flippant tone of Berlin officers well enough to guess that there was something serious behind this trivial talk.

"Just look at that crew! A sloppy, crooked, undisciplined crowd of savages! What are they going to make of things? The German people are getting out of hand. If we give them their heads for a couple of years, we'll all go to the dogs! Old man, you needn't think that because we're playing a sort of revolution here there isn't a real one on. We're right in the thick of one."

"Yes," I replied, "and that's just the trouble—how to bring it to an end."

"But why, my dear fellow?" said von H. "A revolution is a damn good thing if you know how to use it. Besides," he continued, "what do you mean by ending it? How do you propose to do it? Can it be done?"

I told him that I was very well aware of the huge, ever-advancing technical revolution and all its social, economic, and political consequences. The revolt of the masses and the collapse of the spiritual foundations of our civilization were certainly symptoms of a great revolution which could not be ended so easily.

"Weren't we right to engage that lion-tamer and circus director?" laughed my friend. "We need someone to crack the whip and shoot off his revolver! You know that play of Wedekind's which begins with the circus director coming before the curtain and cracking his whip and firing shots at the audience? You know how the elegant mob gets a kick out of its terror? Well, that's Adolf, the Great Manitou!"

I was silent. Von H. noticed my depression. "Well, how did you think it was going to turn out?" he asked.

I indicated in a few words what I imagined to be the real

solution, the real way to counter the rise of the masses, by giving new life to a system of self-administrative boards, by decentralization and the transfer of functions of the State to autonomous bodies—in short, by building up a federative State. But when I tried to explain these ideas to this cold and unemotional man, I saw for myself how unconvincing and unreal it must all seem to his cool skepticism.

"Why not say a monarchy and be done with it?" he exclaimed, cutting me short.

I replied that I had certainly thought of a monarchical restoration as an important means of maintaining political stability in Germany.

"Don't let me destroy your childlike faith," he said. "But we're not interested in a monarchy. You really are very innocent," he continued. "You've no idea what's happening. We're playing for high stakes. It's we or the others! Monarchy, Republic, self-administration, decentralization—do you think you're living on the moon, man? Do you think you're going to cure the world's ills by studying all those academic questions? Don't you see we're hurtling down a foaming torrent? Do you want to pick flowers on its banks? Very charming, of course! Get that cataract in your eye operated, and then perhaps you will see more clearly what's happening in the world. A new world is being born. Yes, I know it sounds rather like what the second-rate writers say, but it's true, all the same. Our ideas of it can't keep pace with reality. There are tremendous chances. It's going to be us or no one! The days of liberty and equality are over. The days of the small countries are over. The good middle-class times are finished. We have no choice. 'Go through with it' must be our motto."

"That means war, then," I replied.

"Cheer up, old man. Why are you afraid of war? Have you become a pacifist? Probably we can't win through without war. Everything big and new must go through blood. We shan't seek war, but we shan't seek to avoid it."

"Who decides these things? Who's the real leader?" I asked. "Who is pulling the strings?"

"You want to know too much. You're assuming there must be a power behind the scenes."

"Why didn't the Reichswehr support Papen or Schleicher? Why is it supporting Hitler?"

"We're not here to back up reactionaries, my dear fellow."

"But to back up a revolution?"

"Yes, if you mean by revolution what we do. Yes, it's certainly a revolution. It's not the end, as you imagine, but a beginning. A guided and directed revolution."

"What do you mean by that?"

"Doing what has to be done!"

"And what's that?"

"Ask anyone you meet, and perhaps you'll get the answer."

"Yes, a different one each time."

"What we think about it counts for nothing, and what we propose to do counts for just as much and no more. There's only one course we can take. We are being driven along it. You may call it fascination by fate or simply lust for adventure, if you like. Perhaps it's our restlessness and dissatisfaction. Our fears, maybe! Anyhow, we've got to carry on. Keep at the top. It's our only chance. Anyone who doesn't take it will be crushed beneath the wheels."

I was depressed. I saw myself as an insignificant man from the provinces. Those Berliners could see the naked, brutal truth.

"But the Reichswehr?" I asked. "You people? Are you really going to go off into the blue like this?"

"We must be ready to, old man. 'The readiness is all.'"

2

THE POWER BEHIND THE SCENES

WERE WE WITNESSING the renascence of Prussian militarism through the spirit of the modern technical and materialist age? Was it the military who were pulling the strings in the background? Did the generals take over the leadership of the nation in order to rescue it from a morass of degeneration and national impotence, in the way that the French army chiefs claimed to do after the collapse of France in 1940? Or were they solely concerned with securing a political framework for rearmament? In any case, to all appearance they were not ready to take full responsibility for what was termed the rebirth of the nation. General von Brauchitsch (now Field Marshal) told me the reason for that. He was anything but a Nazi, at least at that time.

I make no secret of the fact that I esteemed and sympathized with this man. I had repeated opportunities for conversations with him when he held the Eastern Command at Königsberg. He was my guest at Danzig, and we also met elsewhere. He was a man of slender build, barely of medium height, reserved but amiable, accommodating, and of pleasing appearance, but his features did not bear the stamp of any extraordinary ability.

I have already quoted in the past some characteristic utterances of his which I was able to set down without compromising him. Now I should like to record what I can remember of our many conversations, and so to explain the part played by the armed forces in these fateful events. I have already related how I expressed to Brauchitsch my anxieties concerning National Socialist developments and my desire for help in controlling them, to which he replied with contemptuous coldness that this was none of the Reichswehr's business, because we, the National Socialists, had undertaken responsibility for them.

On another occasion he replied to me that the Reichswehr had no intention of letting themselves be forced into the part Ludendorff had once played and taking responsibility for everything. He also indicated the reasons why the army leaders would envisage a liquidation of National Socialism only with the gravest misgivings. The extent to which the Reichswehr leaders were, nevertheless, involved behind the scenes in the whole of the political developments was revealed to me at a meeting with Brauchitsch at which I was accompanied by Baron von Radowitz, the German Consul General at Danzig, with whom I was on friendly terms. At this talk, which took place a few days before the Roehm affair and the party "purge," von Brauchitsch explained to us the motives for the Reichswehr's attitude. The army leaders had no intention of tolerating the playing at soldiers of the National Socialist Storm Troops, or of allowing Herr Roehm's amateurish schemes to complicate their carefully prepared rearmament plans. They were going to stop any attempts to follow the example of the Italian blackshirts, who had forced the army to incorporate entire Fascist formations. Such interference would impair the necessary high standard of the new *Wehrmacht* (armed forces). Rearmament was too serious and difficult a business to permit the participation of drunkards and homosexuals.

It was clear to me that von Radowitz did not relish these blunt words. Moreover, they contradicted what the General had told me at Königsberg six months previously. At that time he made our political troubles the reason for the Reichswehr's refusal to intervene, depicting them as tedious civilian quarrels which did not interest the military men; now, however, he declared that the army's real mission was imperilled.

Later I took the opportunity to express my satisfaction at finding the Reichswehr taking over entire responsibility for developments. Von Brauchitsch denied emphatically that they were doing so. They were only teaching some people a lesson and trying to restore order. He said, in effect:

"Under no circumstances can there be any question of a military dictatorship. It would only attract attention of the politicians of the entire world and make our relations with them impossible. It would probably mean the end of our rearmament. We want political wings for our stage. We shall be quite content to see the persons occupying the center of that stage not taken too seriously, and to listen every couple of months or so to prophecies of the fall of the present regime. To a certain extent we welcome the emergence of evident difficulties and quarrels. They will give foreign observers the impression that we are weak. But if we emerge from the background people abroad will know at once what is happening."

Our conversation turned to possible alternatives to the existing regime. Von Brauchitsch did not entirely reject the idea of national middle-class leagues, such as the Stahlhelm, as potential successors to the National Socialist Party. Perhaps it might be necessary to fall back upon this organization if Hitler remained obstinate and tried to keep Roehm.

"What would you do?" I asked. "Would it mean civil war?"

"If you would call it civil war," von Brauchitsch replied contemptuously. "We should clean up the trouble in the streets within twenty-four hours. The only thing we need be afraid of is a split in the armed forces."

I could not refrain from remarking that if that was so the Reichswehr ought to intervene as speedily as possible.

"There are other difficulties which you fail to realize," replied the General. "Are you—are the German Nationalists in a position to hold the masses politically in check? The Stahlhelm is not a mass movement like the National Socialist Party. The discipline we need cannot be imposed and enforced from without. The masses must submit to it of their own free will. That's why we need leaders of the masses. They must make the imposition of discipline just as much their business as the workers do in their own organizations."

I asked whether in that case it would not have been wisest to support General von Schleicher's efforts, to use the trade unions and a part of the National Socialists as the basis for a national Government. Would it not be possible to revert to this experiment, with certain modifications?

General von Brauchitsch hinted that Schleicher was still working on those lines. He did not wish to exclude the possibility of success. But the trade unions were too ponderous and lethargic; and they had not struck root strongly enough politically in the younger generation. They were the organizations of the old men, not of the younger generation, which was what mattered. They lived in schemes which were beginning to date. Moreover, their international relations and their fundamental pacifism constituted a handicap. "We think it best," he concluded, "to keep the new armed forces entirely aloof from all political differences of opinion, and to cultivate in them a spirit of patriotism developed organically from our old traditions and recognizing no party ideology. They must therefore adopt an attitude of neutrality toward the National Socialist Party, which may be regarded as a temporarily useful instrument for the current political developments, but as nothing more than that."

I put the question whether the Reichswehr would not find it necessary in the end to emerge from its attitude of political neutrality and take full control. "The national revival," I said, "is itself the outcome of the spirit of preparedness for defense; does it not follow that the military leaders should dominate all manifestations of national life?"

This trend of thought was common at that time in all patriotic circles. It did not by any means envisage a "war of revenge," but was based on the simple fact that a nation which rejects the idea of self-defense and preparedness for war loses its national character.

The General replied that these matters were not simple enough for him to give a plain "yes" or "no." Naturally the restoration of military preparedness would involve attention to the moral situation and would demand the conquest of the egoistic materialism rampant in modern Germany. "We shall therefore not rely entirely on National Socialism for the cultivation of patriotic virtues. We are organizing associations of reservists who have been through the school of the new armed forces. From them we shall build up the skeleton of a future super-party national life."

This scheme remained a compromise. It was the cause of the ominous falsities which poisoned all the relations of the *Wehrmacht*. The Reichswehr elected to continue to remain the power behind the scenes and give only indirect guidance. Ever since the Armistice it had been a kind of complementary Government which hatched plans for the eventual restoration of military supremacy and of Germany's full sovereignty and equality of status with other Powers. But it shrank from taking full responsibility when the internal situation required it to do so, and that led to its surrender to National Socialism.

It was, indeed, von Brauchitsch himself who later expressed the desire to revert to the Schleicher plan. But then, two years later, it was he who, on grounds of military security, abandoned the scheme of forming his own reserve cadres, thus subordinating the armed forces entirely to National Socialism, to Hitler and the Gestapo.

Von Brauchitsch maintained his critical attitude toward National Socialism for a long time. He helped me in the circulation of a memorandum on German policy which I issued some time after my retirement, hoping to gain the support of influential men outside the party for a more moderate political leadership.

3

HITLER BOY QUEX

"WE HAVE NOW what we lacked in 1918. You see, Herr President, these are men we can make use of, men we can depend on. They are a rough lot, indeed a ruffianly lot. But they are splendid for all that. You should see them at work! It's a vastly different thing from the lame middle-class nationalism of 1914 and before—Navy League, Colonial League, and so on, with nothing but schoolmasters and professors as leaders."

The speaker was General von Blomberg, the newly appointed War Minister, who had invited me to visit him.

"Hitler boy Quex" was what Blomberg's intimates called him. Quex, of the Hitler Youth, was the leading figure in the first Nazi film—a lad burning with uncritical enthusiasm for National Socialism, who does everything for his "Fuehrer." Undiscriminating and without moral courage, perhaps without any sort of self-restraint—this new type of German officer, with nothing akin to the old Prussian officer, was uppermost in Blomberg.

My first impression of this tall, lean man, with his hair combed straight back in very unPrussian style, was a good one. His eyes were devoid of expression. He seemed to like making a speech, but his delivery lacked the terseness which we are accustomed to expect in officers of high rank.

The practical subject of our interview was the training of young men approaching military age and the creation of an effective military cadre for Danzig, which was forbidden by its Statute to maintain any armed forces. In the critical situation which had existed even before the seizure of power by the Nazis, the danger of Polish action against Danzig had been felt to be acute. Whether with good reason or not, I

276 MEN OF CHAOS

will not venture to say. In any case the Danzig Government considered, and was supported in its view by all parties, that it would be necessary in an emergency to offer military resistance to the Polish troops, and, if possible, hold up an attempted invasion for at least twenty-four hours.

I felt bound to state that in the event of a conflict between Poland and Danzig in 1934 the German Reichswehr, which was then in process of reorganization, could hardly have intervened in Danzig's favor with any hope of success. That was the background of the conversation I am recording here.

"We must set up our defense force as a popular organization. That is the essence of our task," continued Blomberg. "The people must identify themselves with us. The defense force must be really popular, not merely a showpiece, or a State within the State. We must never have a repetition of August 8, 1918, when the men struck and left us officers in the lurch."

Von Reichenau, monocled, then still a colonel, took part in our conversation. I was there in company with a member of our Government and an officer of our police force.

"Now take the middle classes," continued Blomberg. "What could you make of them? You will understand what I mean when I tell you that nowadays it would be impossible to build up a defense force on a basis of middle-class patriotism. We need the masses. Hugenberg and Papen failed to bring them over to us. The trade unions are equally useless. Decent fellows, but pacifists! They'll go with us up to a point, but when things get serious they'll break away. But the Fuehrer! That man is magnificent. A real gift from the gods. How he has got the whole nation behind him! He grips. And what a gift of the gab! He carries you away. He can do anything."

His audience made a few assenting remarks. Blomberg continued: "We must go with the masses." Then he began to talk of Russia and his impressions of what he called his study trip there. "I have seen in Russia what can be got out of the masses. I was not far short of coming home a complete Bolshevist. Anyhow, that trip turned me into a National Socialist. That may seem incomprehensible to you, but you ought to see what they do for their army over there. Everything, I tell you! No budget difficulties, and no red tape in the civil service. The people are all enthusiastic about their defense forces. No grumbling at barrack-room life as over here. Every proletarian regards the army as his personal affair, and he is proud of it. That's what we want. We mustn't have it said again that we are out of touch with the people. Our officers must no longer be aloof. Officers must cease to be representatives of one particular class; they must represent the whole nation. Prussian Socialism, eh! Well, I like the expression. Prussianism always was Socialism, because Prussianism means poverty and discipline. Prussianism means being hard to oneself and others, but chiefly to oneself. Prussianism means happiness in work and satisfaction in service. Prussianism means 'living and dying in harness.' "

Was Blomberg really as enthusiastic a supporter of Hitler as he pretended to be? Perhaps he was only one of the many who were ready to overthrow the Fuehrer the moment the time was ripe. He made a strange statement to us. It gave me something of a jolt. I can remember the tone in which he voiced it:

"It was a point of honor with the Prussian officer to be correct; it is the duty of the German officer to be crafty."

This craftiness, practiced in dealings with the countries which desired to keep Germany down and prevent her from rearming, was to be the guiding principle of every step taken in Germany.

We reverted to a discussion of rearmament and our own affairs. An officer had come in with an urgent paper. Blomberg had to give his decision in some armament matter. "This armament," he said a little theatrically, turning half to us and half to the officer, "this armament is a painful compromise between the necessary and the attainable."

I remembered these words later when we asked one another how it was possible for the armed forces to take the oath to Hitler after Hindenburg's death. The trick by which Hitler contrived to win over to his side all rival cliques in the services was his habit of granting in full, or even in more than full measure, every request in the matter of rearmament.

"We cannot satisfy all demands, even when we consider them absolutely justified," continued Blomberg. He then reverted to our own topic of discussion. "We are passing through a danger zone, and we must avoid everything that might complicate our difficult situation. At this stage we are as vulnerable as a crab changing his shell. We must creep into hiding until the new armored shell has hardened. Discipline, gentlemen, please! And keep the Poles at arm's length for us. They are the most watchful of all our neighbors." He added a few words of thanks for my political endeavors at Warsaw, which had helped to ease the tension. "Now we can pay more attention to the West," he concluded.

I should like to couple this conversation with a later one on the same subject. By then, however, the situation had changed: the exchange difficulties connected with the mark had made it impossible for Germany to give any further financial support to Danzig's defense measures. Blomberg had invited me to lunch, and we discussed the tense international situation. But there was another change. My first visit had led me to believe that Blomberg had something of the spirit of Scharnhorst, the creator of the Prussian national army in the Napoleonic wars. I gained an entirely different impression of him this time. I seemed to be dealing with a weak, inefficient, and not very intelligent cavalryman.

I drew his attention to the danger of Polish aggression. Leading Polish circles had never ceased to discuss the advisability of an early preventive war against Germany. We dis-

cussed the possibility of having to face war on several fronts—
with Poland, France and Czechoslovakia; perhaps even with
Russia thrown in. But Blomberg scouted the idea of a preventive war being launched by such a coalition. "France won't
march," he declared.

I reported my Warsaw impressions, and the skepticism
shown by leading personalities there about the possibility of
French aid.

"France is finished," said Blomberg. "They have held fast
to a wrong conception. There's no mutual confidence between
French officers and men. The higher officers are cultured men,
but too old. The army has grown unpopular in France. The
masses will no longer co-operate willingly with it."

I replied that I was unable to form a judgment about
France, but that past history showed that she possessed astonishing recuperative powers. France could undergo miraculous
changes overnight.

Blomberg denied this, and said that he and his friends were
well informed about affairs in France. "Any French regeneration is a long way off. Besides," he continued, "Germany is
already taking measures which she deems necessary for her
safety, although they will probably meet with a bad reception
in the political columns of the foreign press. Possibly there
will be complications."

"All the more reason to avoid unnecessary melodrama," I
replied, and I went on to report the intrigues and excesses of
Nazi elements in Danzig, and to ask that representations
should be made to Hitler with a view to their being checked.
I added that I doubted the wisdom of similar Nazi machinations in Austria. Germany, I said, was facing perhaps the most
momentous turning-point of her history. We could get all we
wanted, provided that we acted with the moderation which in
all history had been the mark of strength and greatness. By
acts of violence we might possibly, thanks to the element of

surprise, achieve a number of successes, but in the end we should suffer irreparable disaster.

"We shall prevent war as long as possible," replied Blomberg, "but at certain points on Germany's upward path there is danger of a conflict. I don't believe in war, but we must be prepared for it. It is our duty to postpone it as long as possible, and our political measures must be aimed at preventing under all circumstances a second big coalition against us and a war on two fronts. That is why the relaxation of the Polish tension is so valuable."

"What is your objective?" I asked.

"Whatever we can get," was his evasive reply.

"And what does that mean?"

"To go to the limit of the attainable," he answered. "We are always putting out feelers to test the resistance to us, and so we can never say in advance how far we shall get. Germany is facing her hour of destiny. But 'hour' is just a poetic phrase. Her 'hour' is a long, difficult time, during which there will continually be new decisions to make."

I came once more to the subject of Austria, and warned him of the possibility of fresh complications. I felt it my duty to convey to him the ideas and proposals of a prominent Austrian who had asked me to do so. They seemed to me to accord particularly well with the interests of both countries.

But I soon noticed Blomberg's dislike of them. "Austria is German," he argued.

"Yet," I pointed out, "Bismarck always urged his Austrian visitors who were inspired with similar sentiments to drop the idea of a union between Germany and Austria."

"There is no comparison," replied Blomberg, "between the Dual Monachy of Bismarck's days and the small rump State of German Austria today."

I urged Blomberg to ask Hitler to make an end of his Austrian activities—which later, it will be remembered, provoked Italy's menacing step.

"I have a sort of jester's freedom to say anything I like to the Leader," replied this German General. "But I shall never dream of saying anything to him about Austria, and I strongly advise you to steer clear of the subject yourself. Austria is his weak point. It's a matter on which he is hardly sane. He won't allow anyone to influence his decision on the Austrian question."

This naïve admission, this self-revelation from the leading German General, this description of the elementary duty of a German Minister of State to warn his leader as a "jester's freedom," seemed to me so eloquent and so depressing that I desisted from further efforts.

It is said that Blomberg's mental powers are seriously impaired at times—owing, if I am not mistaken, to injuries to his head which he received from a fall from his horse.

4

THE POINTS

VON BLOMBERG CANNOT be said to personify the whole German officer corps. His nickname shows that his comrades found it queer, and indeed ridiculous, to champion the cause of the "lance-corporal of the world war" so emphatically. They considered it a whim, or a pose, useful to his own career, though also assisting the fiction, so industriously maintained, that the fighting services must not take sides in politics but must leave that to other elements. Later I frequently heard it said in service circles that they desired nothing better than to have Hitler thrust himself into the foreground as he did, and so take responsibility for all measures, virtually representing them as his own personal ideas and decisions. "If the man insists on doing it, and if it pleases him, well, why not? It makes our work easier," was the ironic

comment of many an officer each time Hitler prefaced some
hard and unpopular decision with the words: "*I have now
resolved . . .*"

The judgment passed on the generals by a military relative
of mine was: "Never will those men step in and overthrow
Hitler. They must have someone to give them orders. If they
can't have their old king they'll find themselves a new one,
even if they have to drag a pimp out of a brothel for the
purpose!"

In the ranks of the higher officers there were other men,
with a sense of responsibility, who felt it to be a genuine
patriotic duty to recover for Germany what William II called
her "place in the sun." Such men were far from any idea of
preparing for another war, because they were only too well
aware of the risks and sacrifices it involved; but it was inconceivable to them that Germany should permanently play a
subordinate part to nations like Poland and Czechoslovakia.

Men might be for or against England, for or against France,
pro-Russian or anti-Russian, but these differences in regard to
practical policy were irrelevant to the general political aims
and to technical military questions. Possibly there were two
aims that found general acceptance. They were the so-called
"wiping out of the disgrace" and a minimum demand for
security for Germany against all possible combinations. It was
believed that these could be achieved by building up a strong
nucleus of power.

At the suggestion of a friend, a highly placed civil servant
of the old school, I called on Baron von Fritsch, the new chief
of the High Command. At that time Germany seemed to be
heading for disaster in home and foreign politics alike, and I
wanted to get a clear idea of the actual controlling elements
at work. I hoped to discover an authority capable of checking
developments and diverting them into other channels.

The accommodation then provided for this important department was meager and even primitive. The adjutant who

announced me asked me to be as brief as possible, but the talk
became a very thorough discussion, ranging over the whole
field of current issues.

The General was short and thickset, a sturdy figure with
a frank, almost jovial, somewhat rotund face. The outstanding
thing about him was his bright, clear eyes. He wore an eyeglass. His words were few, explicit, and definite. He put
questions. He preferred gathering information to giving explanations. He was the exact opposite of von Blomberg.

I gave my general impression of National Socialist developments, touching on the new difficulties which had arisen, and
emphasizing that some of them were gratuitous, arising out
of our rearmament and the new, strongly nationalistic policy,
but caused by heedless and unnecessary provocations.

"What are the aims of your Polish policy?" asked von
Fritsch.

"I am sorry to see," I said, "that the new German policy
toward Poland is generally regarded only as a temporary tactical expedient. Unpopular as a settlement with Poland may
be, I regard it as indispensable to any German recovery."

"What do you mean by a settlement?" asked von Fritsch.
"Recognition of the present German frontiers, or their revision
in Germany's favor?"

I replied that it would certainly mean war if we started off
with frontier revisions. But such revisions might perhaps
round off a long period of improving relations. That would
avoid war. To the best of my knowledge Brüning, the former
Chancellor, had secured the consent of Britain and the United
States to a revision of our eastern frontiers. Even in Poland
there were influential circles which had grown accustomed to
the idea of frontier revision. It would naturally be a minimum
concession. But it seemed to me better first to attack other
questions, the settlement of which would eventually lead to or
at least substantially facilitate revision.

"What questions? Political, economic co-operation?"

"Precisely so."

"You think war with Poland can be avoided? You consider its avoidance desirable?" asked von Fritsch.

I said I should consider it a bad start to assume in advance that war was inevitable. Such a conception would cripple our whole political effort. I was aware, of course, that the Nazi leaders not only regarded the risk of war as one which might have to be run, but in their policy were deliberately steering for war. That was, in short, the reason for the anxieties which occasioned this visit. So much more could be gained by avoiding war. That meant limited aims and discreet methods. "But," I concluded, "are we out to achieve political and military successes just in order to win popularity for the new regime, or to win permanent recovery for Germany?"

"Do you think political and economic co-operation with Poland is possible? Do you think it will last?"

"That depends on Germany," I replied. In my opinion everything depended on whether our Foreign Ministry was there to assist in the establishment of a starting point for advantageous military operations, or whether it was there to find solutions for the problems themselves.

"Is the aim," I asked, "to conquer, partition, and annex Poland, and perhaps other countries as well? Or is it intended to win them over and treat them as partners with equal rights and interests?" I went on to say how sorry I should be if the Government had decided on the first course. Unfortunately, I felt certain that this was the attitude at least of the Nazis. In a protest against my political leadership which the Danzig Senate had made to Hitler, the main contention of my colleagues was that I believed a real settlement with Poland to be possible and was acting accordingly.

I concluded by stating that I saw no good in regarding the Poles as vermin or sub-humans, as Forster, the Danzig *Gauleiter,* did, and continually threatening to deal with them accordingly when the time was ripe. From the military standpoint it might be an easy operation to overrun and occupy Poland when the German rearmament was completed, but I doubted very much whether such spectacular successes would bring a permanent solution. I had to admit that this was not the only problem in which I had the impression that the German Government was out simply to secure quick and conspicuous successes.

General von Fritsch was silent for a while. "I believe," he then said, "that the Government's policy at the moment is only to gain time and that it is not attempting to solve any problems. I think that's right. At the moment they have no means of getting to work on the actual solution of current problems."

I replied that I considered this to be only half the truth. Even if no broad general solutions were possible at present, our situation still gave us good opportunities of preparing for decisive solutions.

"Why do you attach such importance to Poland?" asked the General.

I answered to the effect that Poland was not merely a military power that was not to be despised, but as a State was very little less than a Great Power. People were too ready to belittle Poland and ignore the fact that behind party quarrels and other manifest weaknesses there remained an ancient historic nation with whole classes of great intelligence and capacity. Poland was in such a difficult situation that we might succeed in winning over these intelligent and capable people from their sterile resentment against everything German, and persuade them to work for a radical change in Polish policy. Poland was very skeptical about the reliability of France as an ally. Pilsudski and his Foreign Minister, Colonel Beck, were realists. Under certain circumstances they would be ready to look for a new starting point for Polish policy.

"I've been told that Marshal Pilsudski sees Poland's future in the East," said von Fritsch, interrupting me. "Is that correct? If so, it means he's anti-Russian. Could we base a policy on that?"

I replied that to the best of my knowledge the Polish Marshal's policy was not dogmatically fixed, but that both his past career and his present political reflections certainly induced him to regard Soviet Russia as an enemy with whom he would one day have to reckon. It was my conviction that as long as the Marshal lived there was a chance for Germany to replace France as the principal partner in a Polish system of alliances.

"In your opinion, what political and military advantages does that offer us?" was the General's next question.

I said that I attached importance to a real and not merely a tactical settlement with Poland because, with this new State as a partner in a joint rise to power, we could, for the time being, not merely baffle Britain and France, as the rapprochement between Hitler and Beck did, but break out of our political isolation by purely political action, without military complications and simply by the means which had hitherto been the monopoly of political democracies. An alliance with Poland would enable us to break France's political monopoly in Europe without giving the wise men of the Council of the League of Nations the opportunity for a single word of criticism. That was a development that would serve the interests of Germany and Poland alike. It would break down the French system of alliances in Central Europe, and French domination of the so-called Succession States would be shown up as the fiction it really was. These States would then have no choice but to attach themselves to the German-Polish nucleus of a great central and southeastern European system of alliances. I regarded a German-Polish alliance as the starting point for a broad development toward a political and economic system of alliances within which all partners would reap the advantage of association in a great common region. It would be the repetition on a higher level of the slow but purposeful work represented by the Prussian Zollverein, which laid the real foundations for Bismarck's edifice of the German Empire.

"Good," commented the General. "A useful idea. But how far is Poland a reliable partner? Would there not be reason to fear that in a crisis France would seduce our partner and isolate us politically?"

I replied that in any case the risk was less than that of the war which, if another course was followed, would become inevitable. The men in touch with the Fuehrer felt a need for quick and showy successes, but they were also convinced that Germany's future lay in domination over other nations, instead of leadership in a group of allies. They rested all their hopes on acquisitions through superior force, evincing a type of realism that ignored one of the most essential real factors, that of good will and voluntary co-operation.

"I agree with you that an attempt to base Germany's rise purely on superior force would be a repetition of past errors. But," continued General von Fritsch, "my objection is that you want to help Poland, a potential enemy, out of a precarious situation and then present your claims on her. We have not had such good experiences with a policy of making concessions in advance as to be prepared to continue that policy voluntarily. Is not your proposal against every rule of political common sense?"

I replied that France seemed clearly to follow the principle of not making concessions in advance, but that our own experience threw doubt on the wisdom of such a policy and the chances of success it offered. To keep a political opponent down until he fought his way up again despite all obstacles seemed to me to be one of the most futile of political conceptions.

The General turned to the Russian problem, indicating that, for reasons of military policy and for other kindred reasons, he had regarded a modern continuation of the traditional Prussian policy of reinsurance by means of friendship with

Russia as the manifest political line for the future. Certain considerations had led him to revise his opinion. "Are you aware," he asked, "that your political scheme must lead to war with Russia?"

I denied this. Hitler's anti-Bolshevist propaganda, and especially Rosenberg's slogan of a crusade against Russia, seemed to me absurd, but Hugenberg's resumption of General Ludendorff's pro-Russian policy was also in my opinion a deviation from the course we had to take. "We can't skip any stages of development. If we indulge in fantastic visions of world conquest in the way Herr Hitler does, even purely speculatively, we shall inevitably get into great difficulties. Our immediate task is to achieve the political and economic unity of Central Europe and the Danube Basin. This can be achieved without military complications."

General von Fritsch agreed that Germany's recovery depended on the limitation of German aims. He regretted the tendency to unlimited, fantastic aspiration evinced by Hitler and his followers. "At first I was inclined to ascribe Herr Hitler's wild ideas to youthful exuberance," he said, "and to view them with sympathy—because, after all, only the man who attempts the impossible gets anything done. But now I regard this reckless hustling as our greatest danger. It corresponds exactly to what we used to call a 'forward retreat' in the war—recklessness that passed for courage. It caused us great losses and may have lost us the war."

This seemed an opportunity for launching a general attack on Nazism and its leaders. I asked to be permitted to speak frankly and confidentially. The past year's experiences, I said, had been so devastating that it seemed necessary either to restrict the functions of the Nazi organization to the very minimum, and to reform it, or, better still, to regard the historic function of Nazism as fulfilled, and to justify its liquidation to the public on that ground.

The General replied that he could express no opinion on

this very important question, because it did not come within his competence. He could say, however, that similar suggestions had been made to him by all sorts of people. "The crucial question, Herr President," he continued, "seems to be this: have you any idea of what to put in the place of National Socialism?"

I replied that in my opinion some moderate form of military dictatorship was inevitable. After what had happened it would not only be tolerated by all classes of the nation but felt as an immense relief. It would have to be a temporary measure, pending the re-establishment of legality and constitutionalism centered on a legitimate authority instead of a spurious one.

The General protested vigorously. Under no circumstances could there be any question of a military dictatorship. The army was in a most vulnerable phase of reorganization. It could not undertake the responsibility of political risks in addition to its own risks. "It is the army's duty to remain in the background and observe neutrality in politics. Otherwise it cannot fulfil its own mission."

"In the old parade drill, as I remember," I replied, "there was a word of command, 'Points forward!' The two men who advanced in obedience to it served as the directional points for a march. It seems to me we need such points. But what directional points are we really following? I have the impression of complete confusion. Are we not marching just for the sake of marching? Like those senseless National Socialist night marches?"

Von Fritsch smiled a little at my remark; then he grew serious again. He had risen and was pacing up and down the room with vigorous strides. The afternoon sun of a warm spring day shone in from a courtyard garden.

"I agree with you," he said. "We lack those directional points. We haven't yet found them again. The German nation has lost more than a war. It has lost itself. With the loss of Christianity it lost its morality and with the loss of the mon-

archy it lost its political steadiness." He came to a halt and
stared at me while adjusting his eyeglass. "You spoke of a
genuine authority to replace an artificial one. I assume you
mean the monarchy. I regard the restoration of the monarchy
in Germany as the decisive factor for the maintenance of balance in home politics. Unfortunately we cannot achieve unity
on this question. Moreover, we are in the difficult position of
having no suitable claimant to the throne. I am afraid we
missed the right moment for the restoration of monarchical
institutions. We are informed that the masses have accepted
Hitler and that the idea of a monarchy as a successor to a National Socialist dictatorship would be regarded as a political
retrogression. If ever the monarchy can be restored," he concluded, "it will be only after a victorious war."

I protested against this. On the contrary, I said, monarchy
was only possible as the mandatory of a new social and political equilibrium and a state of peace. At this very moment an
overthrow of Nazi party rule, which tended ever more to a
dictatorship of violence and lawlessness, would offer the justification of that mandate. It would place the monarchy at once
in possession of manifest functions. Its restoration would be
equivalent to the fundamental act of a re-establishment of the
State and society.

The General reflected for a moment. "Do monarchical institutions fit in with the plan for a wide 'living space' of which
industry is always talking, and which you think necessary, if
I'm not mistaken?"

He broke off and, looking at his watch, regretted his in-
ability to continue the conversation. Summing up, he said that
it must be our task to avoid misleading tendencies and refuse
to be carried away by successes and opportunities, but at the
same time not to become slaves to our own hopes and feelings.
"Let us build up a strong nucleus of power, round which a
new order can form. And let us limit ourselves to the immediate task."

I left von Fritsch with the feeling that I had met a man of candid and sincere character, but not a deep or even an independent thinker.

✔

5

LOST BALANCE

IN THE REICHSWEHR under the Republic and in the new army of the Third Reich, the chief virtue of the old Prussian army was lacking—an original combination of discipline with the independent spirit of men of strong character. The fact that there is nothing of this sort in the Third Reich is for me one of the strongest arguments against crediting the durability of the Nazi regime and the moral strength of the new army.

The change in the members of the officers' corps in Germany has long been noticed by thinking officers. I discussed it with an old friend in Berlin after the first great crisis of June 30, 1934. He had advised me to go to see General Schleicher, in order to get a clear view of the possibility of a drastic change.

I did not know Schleicher, and another friend had warned me not to go near him. His residence, my friend said, was being watched day and night. In any case, he was finished, and he had now lost his following in the corps of officers through his weak and inefficient conduct of affairs as Chancellor.

Schleicher was a strange mixture of sentimentality and harshness, sensitiveness and schoolboy callowness; spoiled and superficial, and with it all a cynical intriguer. Thus he seemed to me to be the very type of a modern officer with no steady principle of living.

Nobody knows to this day how Schleicher managed to make his way to the summit of power. His unceremonious, disrespectful treatment of many of the senior officers can only be

explained by assuming that he knew that he held the whip
hand. One of his colleagues gave me to understand that the
General had secured his power through acquiring intimate
knowledge of the personal affairs of the officers who counted.
He did in any case make some use of the tactics later developed to such a pitch under the Nazis, of getting hold of
compromising material concerning important members of the
opposition before beginning to negotiate on material issues.

The question whether Schleicher actually got into touch
with prominent leaders in other countries, in order to over-
turn the common enemy, Hitler, is difficult to answer today.
It is very likely that he tried to make sure of France's benevolent neutrality in the event of a new sanguinary coup d'état.
He had no formal objection to introducing foreign Powers in
this way into an internal German conflict. But many of his
army comrades were extremely sensitive on this point. That
explains the generals' passive acceptance of his assassination.
It is not permissible to take the representative of a foreign
Power into one's confidence and, by making him a present of
one's criticism of developments in one's own State, to place a
weapon in the hands of the enemy. Revolutionary as was the
general attitude of the army of the Third Reich, it had preserved a strict sense of correctness that made the generals regard Schleicher's efforts to overthrow the Nazis as a complete
and final loss of balance.

6

A NECESSARY WAR

EVEN IN THE time of the German Republic it was considered that for an officer to be mixed up with politics was beneath his dignity. Von Schleicher was thus looked upon with
suspicion in important military circles. Schleicher's regime was

tolerated as a transitory phase. When he seemed to have compromised himself he was abandoned without regret. His views were shared only by a small clique, though for a time a powerful one.

Other ideas were actively sponsored by a wide and relatively moderate circle. I learned something of them from General Raumer, an officer with whom I had several talks about our policy. He was not a prominent man, or at all events he is so no longer. But he held views which were shared in both military and non-military Conservative quarters. These views may make it easier to understand why Germany attacked Russia, instead of concentrating all her forces on an invasion of the British Isles.

Raumer would probably still call himself a disciple of Schlieffen, the German Chief of Staff who conceived the plan of attack against France by means of a great flanking movement along the French coast. He had the strategic problem of a war on two fronts to solve. An attack on Russia was, in his view, a difficult military task of which the solution depended on a prior rapid overthrow of France. Raumer disagreed with me when I contended that with Germany's existing political course she would soon or later have Britain against her if war came again.

"Believe me," he said, "there is not a single man in the *grosse Bude* ("the Big Shop"—the General Staff) who would ever dream of having another war with England hanging round his neck. We shall avoid anything that might lead to a new war with England. There are problems of which there is no military solution. One of them is a war entered into by Germany, the continental Power, against Great Britain, the maritime Power, or vice versa."

"But today," I said inquiringly, "there are gossipers inside and outside the party who declare that with the resources we now have any action against England could be risked."

General Raumer scouted the idea. "Not a word of truth in

it! The essential condition is lacking in England itself. There is no depth, no room for maneuvering. The best elements of our tactics would be impracticable. I say again, don't be deluded, it's all rubbish! I know where your apprehensions come from. Those airmen. They declare there is nothing they can't do. They look upon us as old-fashioned chaps. Of course I don't underestimate the possibilities of a new air warfare. But you won't attack England in the air alone.

"Or perhaps an improvised attack? That might even be the only military chance. Push on against them as they flee, in the midst of the confusion of the retreat of the British forces to their islands. But it is impossible to build up a whole plan of campaign on a chance like that. There is no such plan. The thing has been worked out over and over again in the war games. Over and over again we have found that we get no further than the occupation of a certain zone and a few coastal towns. An entirely new plan of tactics would have to be developed—operating in the most confined of spaces, with practically the whole of the enemy forces ready to march against any point."

Thus, I suggested, the only chance, if I had got the drift of it, was a surprise thrust at a moment when there was no organized defense of the islands. Would it not, then, be the natural thing to pursue the British forces and to stampede the unready defenses of the islands, instead of first attacking the French armies and occupying Paris?

The General laughed. "That sort of thing might be risked," he said, "by a lieutenant. Imagine it—an enterprise like the invasion of England, with an unsecured left flank, and the whole of the French armies in readiness to make a tremendous flank attack at the moment of acutest crisis. Such risks are for bar room strategists only. An enterprise like that demands security."

I may mention that it was the recollection of this and similar conversations that led me to declare with confidence, after the overrunning of Holland and after Dunkirk, that Hitler's next blow would be directed against France, not England. It is possible that Hitler may have proposed to proceed the other way round, but if he did he met with the most determined opposition from the General Staff.

The same argument applies to Germany's attack on Russia. For so hazardous an enterprise as an invasion of the British Isles, the attack on Russia was indispensable, in order to secure Germany's rear. Here again it was easy to foresee the course that was actually taken. But there was a further ground for it.

"Our principal task lies in the East, not the West," my friend had repeatedly insisted. He summed up his meaning approximately in these words:

"It will always be possible for Germany to come to terms with Britain. If we are reasonable, there are few sources of friction between the two nations, one a maritime and the other a continental Power; common sense suggests that they should be politically complementary, not military antagonists. War with Russia, on the other hand, is unavoidable. Just as Britain insists that no single naval Power or coalition of naval Powers shall be allowed to be stronger than herself on the sea, so Germany's security imperatively demands that in our precarious central situation there shall be no possibility of any coalition of military Powers stronger than Germany."

That, I replied, was evidently what Hitler was getting at when he said that Germany must not permit the emergence of a new military power and must destroy the existing one, France.

"France," said Raumer, "is no longer a big problem. If there were no risk that she might fall upon Germany's rear one day, she might simply be left to herself. The only task which Germany must solve militarily, and can solve in no other way, is the smashing of the gigantic Russian forces, which otherwise would soon make a bid for world domination, and at the very

least would weld Europe and North Asia into a single vast
block.

"Look at the efforts," he continued, "that they are making
in Russia. A giant Power is coming into existence such as has
never before been known. At present it is all just for defense.
But in a few years' time they will be in a position to swarm
over all Europe. The Russian steam roller of 1914 and 1916
offers but a faint suggestion of what will be waiting for us
then. Up to now the Russian soldiers have been good, but the
leadership miserable. Why should not the leadership become
efficient one day? The men over there have new ideas, and
they are intelligent. When that day comes, God have mercy
on us!

" 'We will ride to the eastern land,' 'Crusade against Bolshevism,' 'Living space in the East'—all these slogans are bosh!
What is really essential is the removal of the dangerous giant
force of Russia, that first of the Great Powers in the new sense.
A mortal danger lies in wait for us there. We must counter it.
There is no way in which this can be done except through
war. And this I think is just as much in the interest of Great
Britain as of the other European countries. If we are prevented
from doing it, it's a bad outlook for the future. But I cannot
imagine that the politicians will be so afraid of German hegemony in Europe that they will prefer to see an Asiatic tyranny
from the Behring Sea to the Atlantic."

I heard the inevitability of a settlement with Russia by force
of arms insisted on with arguments of this sort in other Conservative quarters. The motive was by no means simply desire
for war against Bolshevism and revolution. It was much more
the deep fear of Russia as a vast reservoir of human and material forces. The formulation of the idea as a campaign
against the world-enemy Communism was accepted because
that seemed a popular and effective slogan. But they saw perfectly well that it was really Germany's self-preservation from
an enormous future peril, with little time left for organizing

any successful defense. If that defense, however, was undertaken in time, and not disturbed by French intervention, there
was every prospect of rapid and complete success.

The Russian problem, I agreed, had again and again become
threatening. But what, I asked, was his conception of a satisfactory solution? Conquest in the ordinary sense seemed to
me inconceivable.

"Any solution will do," replied the General, "that prevents
a new centralization of the latent energies of the Russian territory."

That, I commented, would also presumably mean preventing the restoration of the Czars.

"The solution I should best like to see," he continued,
"would be the division of Russia into a series of territorial
States with full sovereignty, or at least a wide measure of
autonomy."

"A sort of Russian *Libertät*," * I said. "The sort of policy
that Britain and France have followed in regard to Germany
for the last three hundred years—the prevention of the centralization of power in Germany."

"There is certainly," admitted Raumer, "a similarity between
the threat to us and to the small States from a centralized
Russian Power, whether Czarist or Bolshevist, and the threat
to France from a great and united Germany under the Hapsburgs or the Hohenzollerns, under Wallenstein or Gustavus
Adolphus. Only the Russian peril with which we are threatened is incomparably greater than was any German peril in
the seventeenth or eighteenth, or even in the nineteenth, century."

We came back to the outset of our talk. "Does that not
mean," I asked, "that the whole problem is incapable of a
military solution? It is a political problem. And does not that

---

* "German liberty"—*Liberté allemande*—was a French political catch
phrase, implying the prevention of the uniting of the independent sovereign
states of Germany to form a single State.

show that war with Russia is useless and even harmful to us?"

"How would you propose to find a political solution for a situation of this sort? A German-Russian war cannot itself get rid of the problem, but it will be indispensable as the preparation for a political solution," said Raumer. "The entry into this war in sufficient time, and the political preparation for it, so that other countries shall realize the necessity for it, is the justification for the whole experiment with a new national government, on which in other respects we are bound to look with a good deal of skepticism."

7

MILITARY SECURITY

SECURITY RANKS HIGHER today than ever before in the world's history. Earlier ages were aware that the security of human institutions will always be a knotty problem. But our more enterprising age has no liking for resignation of that sort. Can the army leaders be blamed for being no exception in this respect? Security has, of course, a special meaning for them. They understand it as the hundred per cent security of military success. Their ideal is the elimination of chance, or, as unenlightened ages called it, destiny. Their particular security has reference to the possibility of attack from other quarters.

Every nation must feel threatened so long as war remains an accepted instrument of policy. Can it really be entirely eliminated? If as much as the shadow of a chance of war exists, the military assume the worst as the starting point of their consideration. The call for security is not confined to the West; a glance at Germany's past history is enough to show that she, too, has a legitimate claim to it. That was why I placed on record my friend's opinion. It is an opinion widely

held by German patriots, and not confined to the narrow circle
of nationalist imperialists. I confess that I shared it myself,
and that my friend's views seemed to me to be obviously right.

At the same time, I remember that I replied to him that
it did not seem to me to be entirely true that in 1914-18 the
German military leaders had had no ambitious plans of conquest and had been concerned merely for defense. There were
people who regarded access to the Atlantic as essential for
Germany. As regards the East, I knew from a good source
that Russia's complete defeat would not have been followed
by an acceptable peace even with the Czardom. Authoritative
military circles had declared as early as 1916 that important
territories must be detached from Russia and placed under
German overlordship. These included not only the Baltic
provinces, the Ukraine, and the Caucasian oil regions, but also
a Greater Finland. The Russian peril was to be liquidated once
for all. There was also a plan for a close alliance with Turkey
and the drawing of Persia within the German sphere of influence. The whole of Africa, too, was declared to be a German sphere of interest. All this went far beyond Germany's
needs for her future security.

"Yes," replied Raumer, "such ideas were undeniably put
forward. But it was a long way from such talk to an ener-
getically pursued plan. However, if you go closely into it, the
need for security very easily lends color to the most extravagant ideas. 'Security' is not merely a matter of good strategic
frontiers. It involves a whole system of requirements. Why
should not the same principle of security be applicable for
Germany which is assumed as a matter of course for Great
Britain and for Russia? But this brings us devilish quickly to
the plausible demand that Germany must assure herself by
conquests and firm alliances of a sphere of independent existence so great that it can virtually no longer be overwhelmed
by blockade or attack."

All this was nothing but an explanation of the political

conception which later worked such havoc as the doctrine of
Lebensraum or "living space." My friend made no use of
that term, but he, too, was convinced of the enormous scale
of the revolution going on around us.

"It is difficult today," continued Raumer, "to form any
conception of the great changes which are certain to come
even if war is avoided. Even France, in spite of her great
empire, belongs in the new sense to the small nations in search
of support. As for Germany, she is faced with the question
whether it is possible for any other leading world Power than
Russia to exist in Eurasia. This question is as yet undecided.
Does Germany too belong, perhaps, to the middle-sized nations that have to seek union with a greater State in order
to gain security and continued existence? Has she, perhaps, to
choose between Great Britain and Russia? But England would
not dream of undertaking such tasks on the Continent. The
question is thus pointless. There would be no question of
capitulation to Russia without war. This means that Germany
must push ahead and work herself up to the rank of a world
Power of equal status with Great Britain and Russia. She will
do so in the interest of the other nations of Central and Western Europe just as much as in her own. Protection, security,
is not to be gained by conquests, as the purely military thinkers
suppose, but only in a great coalition of peoples. Yes," my
friend concluded, "we are on the eve of great crashes and re-
buildings. They are not of our designing; they themselves
force us to act."

If this was the view at which this moderate man arrived,
this General on the threshold of old age, who had proved in
difficult situations his strength of character and his intellectual independence, then it was a view that carried great
weight. His argument seemed to me not only plausible but
unanswerable. That is not true, however, of the military conceptions that aimed at giving practical effect to these ideas.
These ideas could be discussed, but the conceptions based on

them were the beginning of tragedy. It is not for me to trace
the origin of the new military ideas in Germany. Who "invented" Blitzkrieg methods, total war, mechanization? Any
such search for an individual is pointless. Ludendorff was not
the only one to develop out of the experiences of the last war
the theory of total war. General von Seeckt was not alone in
conceiving the idea of special, highly trained shock troops,
thus upsetting the tactics of massed armies. The military
leaders were carried by the conception of military security into
a region of illusions and pseudo-security.

8

FROM SCHLIEFFEN TO TROTSKY

A FEW WORDS by way of comment on this talk, which
otherwise might seem a sort of apologia for the German-
Russian war.

In order really to understand what are set down by foreign
opinion as the abominable practices of Prussian militarism,
it is necessary to realize the view the military expert is bound
to take of the problem of Germany's defense. He has no escape
whatever from facing extremely difficult if not almost insoluble
problems. It is impossible for the military expert to say: "Nor-
mally there is no military solution for these problems; accordingly we must resign and make way for the statesmen, who we
hope will attempt a political solution." He is thus driven to
attempt radical military expedients that burst the bounds of
past strategy.

My friend, himself a close colleague of Count Schlieffen,
the last great German military Chief of Staff, gave me, in
answer to my questions, glimpses of the world of ideas of the
old General Staff, which made intelligible to me the inevitability of the development from Schlieffen through Ludendorff

to the radical ideas of the German General Staff under Hitler. These remarks, which have remained in my memory from a number of conversations, seem to me to help to explain the present German-Russian campaign. One of the elements that promoted it is the fear of the growing menace of Russia's superior power. The other is the opinion held by a section of the German General Staff that they now have a tactical method, and weapons of proved value, which offer prospects of success, in spite of Schlieffen's ideas, in an attack on Russia.

What was called the "specter of German encirclement" was an extreme but very real state of menace with which the political and military leaders of imperial Germany had to reckon, and which formed the starting point of their political and military thinking. The nightmare of encirclement darkened the later years of Bismarck and of Moltke. It arose from Germany's geographical situation. The German General Staff was compelled to take into consideration the possibility of a war on two fronts with the greatest military Powers of the Continent, France and Russia.

"Dominate Europe? Conquer the world? Not a bit of it! It is simply fear, and justified fear, that lies at the back of the Schlieffen Plan—the fear of having to face a coalition which under normal conditions is too strong for us." So my friend said one day when we were talking of Emperor William's sabre-rattling tirades and their effect on foreign opinion.

He explained that Schlieffen's strategic plan grew out of the reflection that under normal circumstances Germany cannot successfully withstand a simultaneous attack from France and Russia. Consequently a special situation must be produced that will enable first the one and then the other of the two opponents to be put out of action. "That means rapidity and the exploitation of advantages that can only be secured by infringing rights of other States which at any other time must be respected."

I say nothing as to the justice of my friend's contention. In his view a war on two fronts was hopeless from the outset without the infringement of Belgian neutrality. The necessary speed in action against France was to be gained only in that way. Besides, he said, the original Schlieffen plan envisaged the entire abandonment of southern Germany to French invasion, thus making the right wing of the German armies marching through Belgium so strong that a veritable second Cannae would have been won at Paris.

But the essence of the Plan was the clear recognition and demonstration of a Russian peril that grew ever more menacing. The essential thing was, from the first, not the overthrow of France but the securing at the earliest possible moment of the ability to concentrate all Germany's forces against Russia. For that war contained incalculable factors and would be impossible to bring to an end within a time limit. My friend had himself worked in the Operations section under Schlieffen, and described to me how Schlieffen had represented the Russian problems as insoluble with the military resources then available and had envisaged a long war of attrition on that front.

The recognition of Germany's difficult military situation enticed the leading generals step by step into accepting such desperate acts as the march through Belgium, the conception of "total warfare," and finally the "lightning war," conducted with the utmost brutality.

"Not a soul among us," my friend declared, "ever dreamed of world hegemony; we were much too sober-minded. Put any member of the French General Staff in our situation, and he will arrive at the same ideas! Defensive through offensive operations! What these men were after was nothing more than security for Germany. They had to make their plans for the defense of Germany, and a war on two fronts absolutely required a swift decision on one front, to enable us to hold out on the other."

Schlieffen would have refused to launch an offensive against

Russia. He would have occupied strategic key positions and allowed the Russians to attack. Under his plan the factor of time would have been allowed to operate on the Eastern front, instead of entering into a struggle with the factor of space. With the new technique and the new tactics it has been possible to rob the factors of time and space of their fundamental importance.

The German General Staff has long abandoned its old theoretical principles. It has not only become a sort of engineering office, but has received into its arsenals ideas and weapons that have come from alien sources. I remember a high officer saying to me once, in the early days of the Nazi regime, that the task of the moment for the military leaders was the assimilation of the operative ideas and the revolutionary tactics of the Soviet Union, just as in Napoleon's day the Prussian army adopted the revolutionary tactics of that time.

We had been talking of the way the Prussian and German armies had always received their crucial suggestions from external sources, and had never themselves shown creative impulses. They had always merely taken over and logically developed ideas introduced from without. My friend agreed with this criticism, and commented that it was not so important to have original ideas as to turn new ideas from anywhere to good account. He went on to describe the elements of the Russian and revolutionary tactics which in his opinion were new and of importance—things with which we have made practical acquaintance in the European campaigns of 1940-42.

Such ideas have certainly exerted a strong influence over Hitler. They certainly helped to suggest his ideas of political strategy, of a "widening" of strategy. I mentioned this in *The Voice of Destruction*. But the military experts also began to entertain ideas which could not be harmonized with past military theory and practice. These ideas must have produced a certain confusion and incoherence in the conceptions of the

German General Staff. That body, which had found strength
in the past in the sober and logical elucidation of the tasks
set it, was caught by tendencies that were in diametrical conflict with its nature. The revolutionary strategy of Nazism is
not the final logical outcome of Prussian militarism, but the
liquidation of all the elements of discipline and leadership that
had been of the essence of the Prussian spirit. The German
Wehrmacht, in its pursuit of absolute security, has been misled
into the adoption of expedients that will destroy it from
within.

When Napoleon attacked Russia, émigré Prussian officers
and politicians passed on to the Russians the idea of their
"Parthian" strategy of the time. It brought defeat to Napoleon.
When the Versailles treaty was imposed on them the German
officers borrowed from the Bolsheviks military ideas which
Trotsky had worked out in their civil war. From these ideas
the German General Staff developed its new technique of
brutal offensive warfare. It established machinery of political
attack. But all this was not an original conception, it was
merely a copy.

9

HANNIBAL'S ELEPHANTS

"DON'T KEEP TALKING of the Reichswehr and asking
'what is the view in the Reichswehr'! There isn't such a thing;
to quote 'Reichswehr opinion' is to deal in false generalizations. If you are referring to political ideas, everyone has his
own, though good form makes him keep them to himself. If
you mean opinion on military matters, there are of course
various 'schools' and rival faddists who tear one another's hair.
It's only to be expected."

We were sitting in the garden of my old friend, Wassmuth,

in a fair-sized town of northern Germany, where Wassmuth was organizing a new Division.

"But surely," I argued, "the General Staff must have formed a settled opinion on Germany's situation?"

"The General Staff!" said my friend, laughing. "Don't make such a romantic picture of it. No, old man, there are no personalities nowadays, only a mechanism. It's an engineering office!"

"But," I insisted, "you must have come to some opinion on the issue."

He shrugged his shoulders. "Our job is to determine the conditions for military success, and perhaps to provide them. Our job is to calculate. Whether for a crisis or in the ordinary course of work doesn't matter to us at present. Our job is just to apply our exact methods of calculation and to go on perfecting them."

"But here we are," I urged, "right in the midst of the crisis!"

"Are we!" he asked ironically. "Well, well, the hour has come. Anyhow, we know our job. We have worked out the lessons of the last war, and technical advance has yielded us new means of warfare. The cul-de-sac of trench warfare belongs to yesterday. We are ready for the new methods; from the German standpoint war no longer presents insoluble problems. Assuming, of course, that we are given time to accumulate the needed armament."

"So you and your colleagues are bent on war," I replied. "That was what I was getting at."

"No, no," said Wassmuth, laughing, "it's not so simple as all that. We are just experts, experts reporting professionally on the things within our competence. And as a professional man I can at all events say we know our job. Whether we are to be allowed to use a chance to prove it is another question. That is for you political gentlemen to decide."

"If I have rightly understood General Ludendorff's theory," I replied, "the decision lies rather with the 'Generalissimo.' Is not politics just the prolongation of the totalitarian plan of the General Staff into the sector of civil life?"

My friend felt that that was going rather too far. "But," he admitted, "from the professional standpoint I could not conceive a better moment than the present for the resumption of the suspended hostilities. That is the general view in our circles, and it may be that the knowledge of this has an influence on political developments."

But that, I urged, was as good as saying that all this drama of the "national rising" had been staged merely to come into possession of the technical means for assuring a future military superiority. "Thus we are being pushed into war because the solution has now been found for military problems that twenty years ago seemed insoluble!"

"Let's keep off these tremendous generalizations," protested Wassmuth a little impatiently. "In any case, we can never expect such an opportunity again. We have the advantage today over the military leaders in every General Staff in the world. We have learned by experience, and we are in a position to make such use of the new technical resources, which the others have left untouched, that we can get something done with them in a military way. We have the advantage of possessing no obsolete arms. Ancient arms tempt men to think in categories of antiquated warfare. They create the temptation to adapt operational ideas to the available technical resources, instead of the other way round. We have the independence of mind that has enabled us to capitalize the revolutionary changes to which the fortunate "victor States" have closed their eyes. We can so develop our technical resources that they will enable our new operational ideas to be carried out. Not to profit by this advantage seems to me to be false modesty—not only from the standpoint of the keen professional man, such as we all are nowadays, but also from that of the good patriot."

We came to the lessons drawn from the last war, and the

analysis of these was so illuminating that it deserves separate mention.

"We know exactly what the others' ideas are," declared Wassmuth. "It's amazing how dull they are in drawing conclusions from that war. Any damfool layman could make at least two points. The utter helplessness, to begin with, of the old style infantryman against the modern mechanized arms. And secondly, the importance of the single specially trained soldier firing from a shell-hole or the machine-gun nest, operating on their own initiative without supervision. They can hold up whole regiments. And what are the conclusions to draw? One is that mechanization must be pushed to the farthest limits, with tanks and infantry airmen (there, by the way, the potentialities of the air arm have not yet been anything like exhausted) and intimate co-operation between land forces and airmen. Remember the crude tactics of the Entente in the last year of the war, the way they threw material into the struggle with no real sense of the possibilities of the new weapons; and imagine all that new material now really intelligently applied!

"I tell you, no front will stand firm against it, no Maginot Line will hold out. The second point has reference to that front itself: it won't exist any longer. Not, at all events, in the old sense. The thing we are aiming at is the system of totally dissociated groups, each man or group with a separate special duty. Sent out, of course, quite ruthlessly. We shall deliberately sacrifice whole units; the 'doomed detachment' of mercenaries of the past will be used once more. There are tasks that can be achieved only by sacrificing every man assigned to them. Regrettable for the victims, of course, but much less costly to the forces as a whole.

"In general, future campaigns will entail amazingly few casualties. Remember how few we suffered in capturing trenches when shock troops had been given practical training beforehand on models. Bear in mind, too, the distinction be-

tween shock troops and troops of the line, and generalize it—
in other words, a highly skilled professional army and occupying forces. And, above all, speed, speed! Keep up the pressure.
Attack ruthlessly, without sparing our own resources. Any
consideration for our men is false sentimentality, and in the
long run more costly than what may seem the most brutal
pouring in of forces. Each task considered by itself and worked
out with precision—that is the new style. Concentrate on the
offensive—it's the one thing that matters. But the prepared
offensive, prepared down to the last detail! Precision to the last
detail. There are a few tips for you on the way we go to work
today."

We spoke of the revolutionary character of the new tactics.

"I might call it," said Wassmuth, "the ubiquitous front, the
dispersed order, the tactic of special duties. Future campaigns
will bring a decision in a fantastically short time."

I mentioned Hitler's idea of a broadened strategy, of the
use of revolutionary erosion of morale as a preliminary to the
military offensive.

My friend did not entirely reject the idea, but was inclined
to qualify it. It was, he thought, just one expedient among
many others, and no panacea. The political sowing of discord,
the recruiting of paid or politically secured auxiliaries in the
enemy country, offered great possibilities, but it was impossible
to erect this method into a whole system. "The thing that
really matters is altogether different—the military profession
has become a transport industry."

"You're joking!"

"I'm not. I mean it literally."

We talked of England and the danger of a war with the
British Empire. He considered it incredible that the political
leaders should so blunder as to bring about another British-
German war. The General Staff were prepared, nevertheless,
even for that. Party leaders, I said, talked of a military landing

in England; what was the Staff view? Was it seriously envisaged?

"Why not?" said Wassmuth with a shrug of the shoulders. "Navy? It's no longer a decisive factor."

"But military friends tell me that all the exercises carried out by the Staff in mock invasions of England have failed. A measure of initial success has been achieved, but never anything beyond that."

"Perhaps we cannot get so far yet," he replied. "But in a few years' time a landing will no longer offer any insoluble technical problem. This, of course, is a case to which what I said about the totally disconnected front is particularly applicable. We shan't attempt, needless to say, a landing maneuver of the style of 1864. The new style will savor more of a tactical 'higher mathematics.' It is only made possible, of course, by our new methods of wireless communication and our transport industry."

Wassmuth admitted, incidentally, that a war with Britain might mean pretty well the end of all things for both nations. Especially if Britain was allowed time to organize her vast resources. "The Englishman as raw material—there's nothing to beat him! Once it begins, a war between Germany and England may be a war of annihilation. It's not easy for a politician to realize today the destructiveness of the new weapons. However, it has not come yet and perhaps it won't."

One or two campaigns here and there on a smaller scale were all that was needed, he considered, in order to establish Germany's position, and they would be extraordinarily bloodless. Britain had practically disarmed, and could not go to war. In France there had been no thought but for the defensive. "There's not going to be any war," he concluded, "anyhow not war as we understand it. So cheer up, old chap!"

"But," I asked, "suppose it does come, and we have to face a big coalition once more?"

"Then," he retorted, laughing, "remember Hannibal's elephants!"

10

TECHNICIANS OF DESTRUCTION

I DID NOT come much into contact with the younger generation of officers. The brief meetings I had with a few of them gave me the impression of a complete aloofness in their outlook on all human values. Their occupation with military problems as a sort of technique independent of national and patriotic aims of any sort was characteristic of these officers. This was the "new realism." They considered that their duty was to think out their problems to the end in the practice of a sort of military Art for Art's sake. These young staff officers and experts were a courteous but cold generation, of unprecedented ruthlessness, but also perhaps of unprecedented professional capacity. Shrewd and bold, with a mathematician's clear-sighted directness, supple and yet hard as steel, entirely rejecting all sentiment, they belonged to a very different type from our jovial and rather brazen young officers of thirty years ago. Those youngsters, ready as they were to kick over the traces, had been one of the elements of the German tradition. Their successors of today, clear-eyed and cold, deliberately cut themselves adrift from every tradition, spiritual, historical, or even patriotic. They were revolutionaries—the pillars of a hitherto unknown military radicalism.

The technical side, the logically developed processes in which each component could be exactly calculated, as the changes of energy can be calculated in an internal combustion engine—this was the side of the world's work in which these young military experts were absorbed. With this absorption in the technical went a love of adventure, complete ruthlessness, and revolutionary dynamism. The technical and the revolutionary—these were the two elements, and the only two, that inspired their imagination. And, with all their realism and cynicism, these young men worked *in vacuo*. They were no longer patriots in the old sense, or nationalists. They were technicians of destruction incessantly at work. Alongside their doctrine of purposeful and calculated frightfulness and their technique of military terrorism, the Nazi efforts in these directions were the bungling of amateurs.

I had to talk on official business with one of these young men. He was on the staff of the Supreme Army Command for East Prussia. I had had occasion to protest against all the playing at soldiers in Danzig. The Colonel responsible for the military training of our police cadres, a man of fine intelligence and a patriot of the most honorable type, had been disgusted to find political complications resulting from our military exercises. He refused to be drawn into political activities; he insisted that he was a soldier and nothing more.

Thus I had to explain the position to the command headquarters, who had seconded this officer for our needs, and to ask for the officer's recall. I will try to record some of the remarks made to me by a young officer, Major von P. (I do not want to give his name; he may since have changed his views). I tried to explain, as man to man, why I was not prepared to make Danzig the scene of military experiments. I was not concerned so much, I said, about the risk of political complications with Poland, or with the League of Nations, as about the wrong turn taken in the general political course, a movement which I could not support.

I put this in the friendliest possible way, but it was not of the slightest use. On the contrary, when von P. noticed how I was trying to make a personal appeal to him he grew all the more reserved and hostile. "If, Herr President," he said, "you give us no help in bringing Danzig within our armament program, I am sorry, for the Herr President's own sake. But I

venture to point out that we shall not abandon our plans, but
shall find other ways of carrying them out."

I let that pass, and went on to talk of the last war. I said I
was struck by the self-assurance and the harshness with which
Germany's mistakes of that period were judged. Such mistakes, said von P., would not be repeated. The war had been
badly prepared for, and had started with political blunders,
but that was not all: the great opportunities of making good
the earlier omissions had been allowed to pass unused.

"What opportunities have you in mind?" I asked.

"Our predecessors of that time were slow in recognizing the
revolutionary part that technical progress could play in the
whole conduct of the war, and we failed to take full advantage
of the opportunities which that progress afforded. Are you
aware," he continued, "that most of the innovations which
today are at last being adopted by the Supreme Command,
and are making it possible for us to rearm on the basis of a
completely new tactical scheme, were actually put forward as
proposals in the first two years of the last war?"

That was news to me. "And so we of the older generation
made a mess of things then? On what exactly do you base
your confidence that you will do better?"

"On the logical pursuit of the plan of delivering smashing
blows at the enemy and of the conception of mobility of
forces," replied von P. "We have been compelled by military
developments to make radical changes in our general ideas.
We have entirely cast aside the traditional doctrines concerning the phenomenon of war, and have thought out the essence
of it for ourselves. The Herr President can have no idea of
the great gulf that separates our modern ideas of the essentials
of war from those generally current, whether among patriots
or pacifists."

"Well," I said, "what do you think you can achieve with
the new methods?"

The Major evaded the question. "Ludendorff," he said, "was

the first to envisage war as an elemental process, and to free
the conception of it from all that is of secondary importance.
But he had not the technical knowledge needed for drawing
the right practical conclusions from his conception. The result
was that he became one of the principal obstacles in the way
of the perception of the new military realities. His vision of
total warfare remained quite incomplete."

"One thing," I objected, "the total warfare that Ludendorff
tried to popularize did reveal plainly—that things are beginning to be demanded of human beings that go against their
whole nature. That's just where Ludendorff came to grief."

"Human beings are raw material, with their specific degree
of response to manipulation like any other material. Preparation for war includes the proper selection and use of material.
Modern war consists of exact processes such as are implied in
any industrial activity, processes in a system of co-operation
and control hitherto inconceivable."

What seemed to me to matter more, I said, than all these
general considerations was the extent to which tanks and aircraft had changed the conditions of military success.

"We are developing these along lines that will render entirely obsolete every existing conception of warfare. For the
first time in the history of war, the army commander is liberated from considerations of material, and can make any
dispositions required by his operational idea."

Where, I asked myself, is all this leading? These young
men, intoxicated with the power to solve all their military
problems where past generations failed, and dazzled by the
revolutionary overthrow of age-old traditional rules of warfare, have delivered themselves over, rationalists though they
call themselves, to an unbounded romanticism. In their military field they were certainly working in harmony with a new
intellectual fashion that had captured every field of life.
Adventuring with the aid of infallible technical resources.
These men were indeed modern. Yet they were not personally

ambitious; they were simply under the influence of boundless professional ambition, obsessed by the cause they served.

11

THE LIMITS OF THE POSSIBLE

A FRIEND REPEATED to me something he had heard General Keitel (now Field Marshal and "Chief of the Supreme Command") say: "Rather than not go down at all into history, I would go down as the greatest destroyer of all time." In reality the cynicism of Germany's military leaders is less vivid but more serious. Personal ambition naturally plays an important part in army circles, but much more significant is the fact that among the more intelligent of the younger officers ambition plays a much smaller and less personal part than among the older and senior officers with the Hohenzollern tradition. There has been a strange and, indeed, a perilous reversal of the normal rule that the dross of personal ambition is cast off with increasing years and that duty comes then to be taken simply as duty. In the new German army it is the younger of the thinking officers who sacrifice their personal ambitions to a really inhuman concentration on duty.

It is this that makes them the decisive factor. They are so unsentimental and so radical that personal ambition is in their eyes a sort of nineteenth-century bourgeois failing. I know this from many conversations with young men who attached very little importance to their personal careers. In Germany today, and perhaps elsewhere, there is a class of older men who have not made the plunge from tradition into radicalism, but they are no more than the outward symbol of a military leadership that really passed long ago into the hands of the young, radical, rationalizing experts.

In army matters as elsewhere we are in full flight to a sort of technocracy. What do Generals von Keitel, von Brauchitsch, von Fritsch, von List, von Blomberg, and the rest, amount to nowadays? None of them is what he appears to be, a leader. Each is the executant of definite tasks and no more. Personality no longer counts; the leadership is in the hands of the anonymous machine. No one among these generals "turns the tide of battle"; no individual personality carries on the war. The military machine does that. Can the machine do anything more than decide particular issues? It can issue instructions for action under specified circumstances, but can it draw up a plan in general terms?

Other nations in war may rely on their great gift of improvization; if the Germans do not it is not because of their passion for organization. Their experts work out their plans to the last detail, from conviction. They regard the gift for improvization as a desirable quality, but one of only secondary importance. Improvization, in their view, can never take the place of an exact plan. The present-day General Staff believes in an exact plan of campaign, worked out as a separate unit, prepared down to the smallest detail, and then carried out to a fixed program.

But this sort of thing is possible only for the offensive. Is not the new German strategy built up entirely on the idea of the offensive, and must it not fail in the defensive? In its endeavor to avoid the conditions of the last war, is not the new German doctrine of war a one-sided doctrine of the offensive movement?

"The future German strategy will consist of separate assaults, explosive assaults, with shorter or longer pauses in between them. War will no longer be a continuous process." So von Krönig, an officer staying temporarily at Danzig for special duties, said to me one day when we were discussing the danger of a new war. He was an intelligent, amusing, jolly fellow.

"Are you fellows determined to have war at all costs?" I asked him. I had said I was afraid there was going to be another great universal war, and that nobody could say how long it would last. His only reply was a laughing *"Immer feste, feste"*—"That's all right! Here we go!"

I replied that it seemed to me a very simple conclusion that Germany would be forced on the defensive and thus would be unlikely to determine the limits of any war. Krönig laughed and said that it was, after all, not such a simple matter as that.

We discussed the lines of a broad political plan. I mentioned the possible restoration of the institution of the Monarchy as a factor in the maintenance of internal and international peace. Krönig did not like the idea. "A monarch," he contended, "is an element of insecurity."

"Then we are to rely on our military machine as a safety valve?"

"Of course everything depends on the machine. The one solid thing in these times of upheaval is the expert military organization that sets before us the detailed problems and their solution."

"Just consider each question as it arises and otherwise let things take their course?" I suggested.

"I should prefer," he replied, "to put it a little differently: keep the situation open, so as to be able to move at the right moment. It's the only thing we can do—keep ourselves ready and prepared for all sorts of situations. Our opportunities may be more restricted than we imagine, but they may equally well be wider than the most we dream of at present."

That opinion was shared by almost all the people one met, by politicians and high officials of every shade of opinion, by army officers and economic experts. Don't tie yourself down too soon! Keep on the move! Watch out for opportunities! In every question of public affairs men's attitude was undergoing a gradual change of which the significance is only now beginning to become plain. Their plans were dictated by the chances of success.

That might seem a healthy principle. In reality it is the most revolutionary of principles of action, since the limits of the possible have been extended so widely by technical advance and rationalization that they seem no longer to exist at all.

Today "the limits of the possible" is almost identical with the attainability of the impossible.

12

HITLER'S DODGE

"THAT MAN," SAID General von Blomberg to me once, full of enthusiasm, "that man tears down all the paper obstacles. He teaches us to detect the papier-mâché where we thought we saw iron and steel. He has the penetrating glance of the truly great leader, who sees through human weaknesses and knows how to make use of them. Surely you, too, want to see Germany great and strong! But we shall not manage it amid the encouraging applause of those swine of international journalists, or with the patronizing benevolence of the members of the Council at Geneva. Don't worry; Hitler is not going to land us in a world war."

The War Minister had been answering doubts I had expressed about the military training at Danzig. I was reminded of his words later when a friend gave me his impression of the change in the outlook of the leading generals. "They tell us," he said, "that we must stick to it and steer a steady course. It's no good shilly-shallying; we must go right ahead. There's no going back, only forward into a new stage. It's impossible to take the revolution in tow for our own purposes and at the same time to stay tied up to old traditions."

"In other words," I asked, "Hitler is now the real commander of the army?"

"Make no mistake about it—that man really has exceptional

abilities. He has managed things amazingly well. But Nazism
is neither here nor there—we've altogether different fish to fry.
We're not interested in the slightest in Nazism. We are the
heirs and the defenders of the revolution. The revolution runs
in our blood, in the blood of all of us, down to the junior
captain on the Staff. We are carrying out the greatest of
military revolutions, and this affects our intellectual and political outlook. It makes it impossible for us to continue as tradi-
tionalists and monarchists. Our patterns today are the young
generals of the French Revolution. Our model is Napoleon,
with his pace and his complete change in tactics. It is logical
that we should seek in our armies the revolutionizing fanaticism of the sansculottes. And no more of the bourgeois patriotism of 1914. Do you follow the line of thought?"

"I follow it only too well," I retorted. "It has the typical
flavor of the laboratory and of the unnatural cocksureness that
is the failing of all the super-clever people, whether in literature or politics or the army."

"Ah! Don't take it all the wrong way," my friend protested.
"We really haven't all suddenly got Hitler-drunk. We can see
the man's limitations and weaknesses clearly enough. But there
are two considerations that compel us to accept Hitler and his
cohorts. To permit the tension to go on between Nazism and
some other form of German patriotism would mean keeping
open a cleavage that would be very dangerous if there should
be any likelihood of war. And, still more important, we are
the executors and the beneficiaries of the revolution, the universal, worldwide revolution, and perhaps it is we who will
make an end of it."

"Everybody," I replied, "knows how to cover up his capitulation with fine phrases. It is clear now what has happened.
At first we all said, 'Let's hold our hand. When the man has
done his job we'll see whether to sack him or keep him on.'
And the simple truth now is that in our irresolution we have

allowed the man to get so strong that there's no longer any possibility of deposing him."

"May be," replied my friend, "but that's not quite the whole story. We had our cautious colleagues. They were all against experimenting; they were for setting limits to our aims and claiming nothing beyond the restoration of our pre-war position. They were the disciples of the Bismarck school, the semi-revolutionaries. We also had the men who imagined they were revolutionaries. Their idea was to go ahead tentatively until firm resistance was discovered. But when would that be? Where is it going to show itself? And finally we have the radicals, who answer that there is not going to be any real resistance. 'The existing order is in process of collapse. Apart from that, we are masters of a technique with which we can break all resistance.' That is their contention, and logic is on their side, for progressive radicalization is the law of all revolutionists. Hitler manages always to work himself to the head of the radicals. Anyhow, whatever explanation we may reason out after the event, the fact is there and there is no altering it. The only thing left to us is to play the revolutionary game. There's no more possibility of opposition."

"So he's done the trick, the German Napoleon!" I exclaimed. "He has made every opponent toe the line!"

"Shall I give away his dodge to you? He has simply agreed to whatever anyone has asked. He has even given men more than they asked. Thus he has laid them all under an obligation to him. He has made all rivalries pointless and reconciled all differences. Finally, he has driven everyone into the arms of radicalism. For if you voluntarily and lavishly provide the wherewithal for the expert to do his job, he finds one job after another practicable where he had given it up as a wild dream. In this way Hitler has brought all the rival schools and personalities to his side, by giving help to them all and accepting everyone's ideas. These generals who have been used to hearing nothing but sour warnings from the civil side about the need for economy, have come across a man who says to them every day that their plans and demands are entirely inadequate, that we have got to get twice as much, ten times as much done. I'd like to see the officer who will say 'No, thanks,' instead of 'Let's have it, let's have it, we'll take it on.' "

"Yes, our mistake was in imagining that the military chiefs were anything more than experts. We imagined that they were out to take the lead in our national revival, and they were merely experts, experts run wild."

The expert becomes obsessed by his profession. It becomes his home and faith and country; he is ready to sacrifice all three to it.

13

A PEACE PARTY

ONLY THE INITIATED can speak with authority about the cliques and coteries in German army circles. Whether the knowledge is of any great importance may well be doubted: the thing that has really mattered is the victory of the extremists in the army over all other schools.

Even after the formal surrender to the National Socialists, however, there was opposition within the army which remained an important factor up to the outbreak of war. It was visibly exemplified in the dismissal of General von Fritsch.

It was not merely an opposition to Nazism; it was also directed against military radicalism, which, I should like to repeat, has little to do with Prussian militarism. Military radicalism in reality represents the application of the most modern notions of rational planning and mechanization to the military sphere. Consequently it approximates to the trend of thought of that political radicalism in all countries which advocates a future rationalized world order.

There was a definite peace party in the German army under the Nazi regime.

In Paris in the summer of 1939, I was invited to meet with certain anti-Nazi German officers in Switzerland, to consider ways and means of preventing the threatened war. About the same time a French friend brought me news that a highly placed French General, enjoying the complete confidence of Daladier, the French Premier, was ready, in accordance with the Premier's desire, to take part in strictly confidential conversations with a German General Staff officer of equal rank. My friend urged me to second these efforts.

I found certain French circles inclined to regard the German army as a trustworthy partner in an eventual agreement. This tendency was to have fateful consequences a year later. I had been informed of remarks alleged to have been made in the autumn of 1938, at the time of the Czech crisis, by certain German military men, to the effect that it was impossible to carry on any confidential negotiations with the corrupt French political clique, because, despite all assurances to the contrary, everything would be known to the Gestapo in Berlin within forty-eight hours. Anyone who trusted French politicians would be risking his life. Confidence could exist only between military opposite numbers.

I cannot say whether German intrigues had deliberately pulled out the stop of the "mutual chivalrous respect of the ex-combatants of Verdun," in this attempt to reach an understanding at the eleventh hour, or whether certain Frenchmen who realized their country's unpreparedness clung of their own accord to the idea that an appeal to the chivalry of military men might stave off universal disaster. So far as the German efforts are concerned, I did not go to the preliminary rendezvous in Switzerland. It is scarcely conceivable that a political émigré could play any part in missions of such political importance. But I made efforts to ascertain the conditions which, in the German view, would enable peace to be assured.

The military peace party informed me that they were not interested in the restoration of the monarchy. They were going to overthrow National Socialism, and the opportunity was offered by the threatened plunging of Germany into another war, which would develop with mathematical certainty into a world war and would be bound to end in a second German defeat. In Germany there were only small cliques in the party, in the army, and in certain other quarters, that really wanted war. A new Government, acting as the trustee of the nation, would advise the army on political matters. This Government would be formed from representatives of the main political and industrial elements, and would establish a constitutional state of affairs as soon as possible. Special importance would be attached to the restoration of the administration of justice, and of equality before the law. Special attention would be given to the Christian basis of the future State.

In regard to foreign policy I was informed that Austria would have to remain with Germany, as well as certain parts of Czechoslovakia, which must enter into a formal alliance with Germany. Poland would be expected to cede the Vistula Corridor and certain frontier districts in the Posen region, particular importance being attached to the return of Bromberg. It was hoped to reach a peaceful agreement with France concerning Alsace. Moreover, the persons concerned would be ready to participate in a general European peace conference, at which the necessary economic and military agreements would be concluded. A limitation of armaments would be acceptable, provided that it was declared to be binding on all parties. The resumption of international exchanges of goods and international currency dealings was desired, but with the reservation that a continental economic block should be established in conformity with existing common interests. A further condition would be either the restitution of the former German Colonies or the administration of all colonial possessions of European States by autonomous economic boards, on which all nations would be represented.

I passed on this information. So far as I know, it was given no further discussion. But this effort for peace is significant, if it was not merely an attempt to delude on the part of the leaders of Germany's political strategy, which I do not think likely. It shows that German government circles and the German army contained elements which were trying to prevent war and to overthrow the Nazi regime. I can offer no estimate of their strength.

Shortly before, when in London, I had heard from an old acquaintance from Berlin of a rather similar project, to make the imminence of war the occasion for overthrowing the Hitler regime. "Let them get on with their mobilization," said my acquaintance, "for it's the only chance of getting rid of Nazism. Keep on telling the people here and in France to stand firm; there'll be no war. We'll see to that."

I have known this man for many years, and his sincerity is beyond all question. He was in close touch with authoritative military circles. He certainly correctly represented their opinions. But why was there no revolt at the moment of the outbreak of war? Were he and his companions illusionists?

I admit that I was firmly convinced that the more thoughtful elements in the army and certain other men in the background were ready to take over responsibility at the critical moment and use the opportunity for a coup d'état. Their failure to do so is due to many reasons which can be easily explained today.

One reason was the political and military inactivity of Britain and France, who should have taken important action in both spheres. Another reason was the fact that the so-called men in the foreground, and those behind them, who intended to lead were in reality very far from being leaders, and were, indeed, entirely incapable of interfering with what was a gigantic mechanism in motion. In face of the vast organization of the Nazi State they were simply private individuals, whose personal views carried no weight at all. The course was determined by the machine, and no personal human responsibility came into play.

Ananke, the Greek Fate, in the form of modern rationalized mechanism.

EPILOGUE

WE PARTED OUTSIDE the block of flats. It was late at night. A policeman was standing at the next street corner. I had made up my mind to go abroad. I had been staying only a few days longer in Danzig, to put my affairs in order. My friend, who had come to say farewell, had been one of my closest colleagues—a National Socialist of long standing. He had gone, like me, into opposition.

"Now, you must give the people outside some idea of what this filthy business is like. The League of Nations has missed a great opportunity. Hitler would have had his first really big setback if they had been more alive. But the people seem determined to make Adolf a great man by main force."

I said it troubled me to be going, and leaving my friends behind. "Difficult times are ahead of us."

"Well," he said, squeezing my hand once more, *"auf Wiedersehen!* We'll meet in the German Province of the United States of Europe."

"Auf Wiedersehen," I said, and went indoors. It's a long way, I thought to myself, as I mounted the stairs to my flat, a long way to those United States. Was it high treason that the man had been talking? What had brought that old Nazi to such a revulsion in his ideas and aspirations? "We set our hearts on the wrong thing," he had said to me. "Hitler has deluded us!"

A little before this an old Social Democratic party official had left me. An intelligent, politically experienced man, in the printing trade. He had lost his job. The Nazis had refused to give him work. For months, while I was staying in Danzig for medical treatment and not going back to my farm, he had

326

visited me almost every evening. He constantly brought "prohibited literature," Konrad Heiden's and Rudolf Olden's books on Hitler, and many others. We used to have discussions. He had sound political judgment. He was not troubled about my former membership in the Nazi party. "We must all keep together," he said, "now."

He too had bid me farewell. I passed on to him all the literature I still possessed. "Thank you," he said, "it will circulate among us. Eager readers! They soak it up like a dry sponge."

We had discussed the situation once more, and the possibility of an early change.

"Things will grow more serious in the future," he said. "It stinks of war. I tell you Adolf will go to war. If the wise men of the West go on just calmly looking on, I can see the worst coming. Well, Herr Doktor, that's your business now. If you don't make the people see the truth in good time, we shan't be much longer about it."

"My dear friend," I said, "is not the only thing I can do to keep silent and make a modest fresh start with farming somewhere? For me, politics are finished."

"Ah, don't say that," said my friend eagerly. "That's what they all say. In that case, what chance is there ever of any change? They all have their dreams. They all want to be President of the Senate. Nobody will do a thing."

"Can a man go against his own nation? Can a man play the informer?" I replied. "Where is the line to be drawn between contemptible treachery and permissible struggle against what one regards as loathsome?"

"Now, don't bring up those questions, you too, at the last moment. I hear that argument every day from my German Nationalist customers, when I take books to them. Herr Doktor, they will soon give in, and our Catholic Center party too. Well, just tell me, who else is there left? If nobody will put a spoke in Adolf's wheel, we may as well give up."

"Yes," I said, "in the West they are making the same mistake that we made. They underestimate what is going on here as we did. Or else they refuse to see it. They are shutting their eyes to it. Is it not incredible? We ourselves know by now that there can be no coming to terms with Nazism. Don't the others know that yet?"

"Exactly," replied my friend. "So we are just waiting, but not much longer. Our men, poor chaps, are falling away all round us. When I go now into the market and drop remarks as usual—whispered slogans, you know what I mean—a year ago, I can tell you, they spread like wildfire, but today scarcely anyone will listen any longer. 'Shut your mouth,' they say— old women! Already some of them have begun to defend the Nazis. 'It's all very well,' they say, 'but Forster and his lot don't merely talk, like you.' Herr Doktor, Herr Doktor! Not seldom I grow anxious and alarmed at the way the people are beginning to change their tune. Is it that they are afraid to be against the Government? It all falls on us few who are left. What will be the end of it?"

Very different had been the line taken by one of my farm workers a few days earlier when I left my farm. He had driven me to the station. In the past he had been a Communist official, an intelligent, conscientious man. He was a village craftsman, and as a Communist had been boycotted and compelled to work as a casual laborer. After that I had taken him on in a permanent job, and he was grateful. While I was living in complete isolation on my farm after my resignation as President, he brought me his radio, and made me listen to the Moscow broadcasts, which my own set could not get. "Herr Doktor," he would say on a holiday evening, as if it was a thing of great moment, "today there is an important broadcast again. Shall I come along?" He would come and then, amid the whistling and crackling of static, we would catch now and then a few words, so far removed from one's own ideas and hopes, and yet in a way familiar and moving, because they aimed at a freer and worthier existence.

We had reached the station a little early for my departure. In the windswept little enclosure, amid the pawing and stamping of the horses, he tried to put courage into me. "The Herr Doktor will have a difficult time," he said. "But the Herr Doktor must not lose courage, however rotten it may be. It will all be different by and by. This is only a passing phase. Adolf won't last long. We are ready. Then will come the true revolution. That is as certain as anything can be. Adolf is doing the rough work for us. It is bound to be so. Herr Doktor, remember what I am saying. However short or long his time may be, Adolf won't last for ever!"

We spoke of Russia's future part. "War," he said, "war, Herr Doktor, that is as sure as anything. They know it in Moscow. They are prepared. And then! This time we shall manage it!"

He could see that this did not afford me much comfort, and had another try. "There is nothing for the Herr Doktor to fear. We shall not touch anybody. There will be no bloodshed. We are not Russians. We shall settle our account with the Nazis, eye for eye, tooth for tooth. We've got them marked down. But that's all. Anything beyond that is fairy tales. You are leaving Warnau," he went on. "That's hard luck. But you have not been having much of a time. Nothing but trouble, and how to get together the money for wages and charges. I'm saying no more than the truth. The Herr Doktor won't be offended? I'm only saying, what's the good of such a big property? When it brings nothing but anxiety! Kulaks, Herr Doktor, won't exist in the future. But for that very reason there'll be peasant farmers, and each one shall have his own farm. Landless peasants—that doesn't work. Our people know that perfectly well. And when we have achieved—got to that stage, the Herr Doktor need have no hesitation, but can come straight back again. You'll have your twenty acres, I promise you, I assure you. You have got to have that, like each one of us. Then you can farm in happiness and content. That will give you time and leisure for studying and writing. Nobody will dream of interfering with you!"

What has happened to that good fellow? I do not know. He brought up his children well. He was the most careful and honest of my workers. "We are all in the party," he admitted to me once. "But we are just the same as ever. If the Herr Doktor knew how we have everything fixed up in readiness! When the time comes, we shall be on the spot!"

It was early morning when I set out on foot for Danzig Station. My steps rang out on the pavement of the empty streets. The spies, official and amateur, were still in their beds. The policeman at the corner had gone.

On that cold autumn morning I recalled these and other similar impressions and experiences of recent years. Old acquaintances had become strangers to each other, and strangers had become close friends. New friendships had grown up in entire disregard of conventional barriers, and bitter enmities were tearing families asunder.

When I had crossed the near frontier into Poland, I breathed again. I had not been arrested. Not until later did I learn that I was to have been prevented from leaving. I had been fortunate in choosing so early a train. As the train proceeded through the woods and heaths that had been familiar to me from my earliest childhood, all formerly Prussian and now Polish, I asked myself what it was that gave this revolution its deep, indelible stain. Were all great historic crises, seen at close quarters, similarly horrible events, beyond contemporary comprehension? It might be so. And yet that was an inadequate explanation. There lay something unprecedented. Other revolutions had been scarcely less cruel and destructive. All of them had been dominated by terror. But the wrongs done, the existing rights destroyed, were incidental to the effort to create a better and juster order. Here, however, the men at the head, cold and cynical, or irresponsible and mocking, or skeptical and without hope, were throwing away all that distinguished man from all other creatures. They set out to be blond or brown beasts, and that was what they were. Humanity had begun to lose its meaning.

Where were the men who were standing out against this evil? Where was the other Germany? Was it only a fiction? Where were those who would overcome this revolution? Where was the great, patient people? Had only an individual here and there kept his senses? Did those meetings and talks that I had had offer any explanation at all? Where did the actual roots of this process lie? Where were all the men of science, of art? Where stood the women now? What were the churches doing? Where were all those honorable men who had stood for democratic freedom? Had all these elements merely gone brown by way of protective coloring? Was the color less than skin-deep, did it need only a little scratching to expose the genuine reality of old? Or were they all corroded from within, and had the whole spiritual and moral fabric of a great nation collapsed?

Those were the questions that crowded on me during my journey. Only as I approached my future place of refuge did I begin to realize how deeply I had myself changed during these experiences. It may be that we are all undergoing a vast process of cleansing. Cleansing or self-destruction. As those talks had proceeded, so these thoughts ended—to quote the words of a political thinker of a hundred years ago—"in the poignant sharing of the sense of a time of peril, and in the recognition that all devices for delivery from it were alike open to grave objection!"

INDEX

INDEX

A

A., Herr von, 143-146
Aar, 224
Actium, Battle of, 60
Administration, public: Frick and, 18, 62-67; importance of for power, 16; Strasser and, 17
Adriatic Sea, 100
Afghanistan, 189
Africa, 59, 78, 127, 229, 299
Agrarpolitischer Apparat, 32
Agriculture, 22-23, 32-42, 247. *See also* Peasants
Air force, 19-20, 294; Goering and, 77-79; importance of for power, 16. *See also Luftwaffe*
Alsace(-Lorraine), 100, 226, 323
America (United States), x, xii, 81-87, 99, 135, 183, 187-188, 202, 216, 217, 231, 235, 252, 254-256, 257, 283
American(s), 14; farmer, 34; tariff, 210
Amtswalter, 109
Ananke, 325
Antony, 141
Arabs, 184, 189
Aristocracy, and Nazism, 28-32, 142-147. *See also* Junkers
Army, German, 9, 141, 172, 265-325; cliques in, 321; General Staff, character of, 306-307; Goering and, 17; importance of for power, 16; officers of, new type, 275-278, 291ff., 311-318; peace party in, 322-325; Roehm and, 17; war plans of, 298-301. *See also Wehrmacht*
Army, Russian, 277
Asia, 78, 126, 127, 209, 229, 248, 296

Asia Minor, 59, 127, 183
Atlantic, importance of, 299
Aufbruch, 58
Austria, 59, 100, 197, 203, 228, 279, 280-281, 323
Autobahnen, 232, 233

B

Baltic States (provinces), 57, 299
Basle, 225
Bavaria, 93
Be., 236, 258
Beauséjour Park, 223
Bechstein, Frau, 148
Beck, Colonel, 73, 171, 285, 286
Behring Sea, 296
Belgium, 100, 127, 198, 303
Berchtesgaden, 78
Berlin, 70, 72, 74, 78, 111, 113, 166, 174, 184, 197, 219, 237, 322, 324
Bethke, Herr, 247, 248, 251
Bielowicz, 74
Bismarck, Prince, xiii, 100, 165, 228, 280, 287, 302, 320
Blomberg, General von, 275-281, 283, 316, 318
Bohemia, 23, 100
Bolshevism (-ist), 44, 47-48, 51, 56, 58, 85, 103-105, 108, 139, 147, 193, 221-222, 251, 256, 296
Boncour, Paul, 163
Brauchitsch, Field Marshal (General) von, 270-274, 316
Briand, Aristide, 227
Briey, 226
Britain, *see* England
Brown House, 20
Bruck, Möller van den, 138
Bruckmann, Frau, 148
Brüning, 138, 155, 198, 199, 202, 219-220, 283

335

Bülow, Prince, 178
Bülow, von, 172-180, 185
Burbank, Luther, 87
Burckhardt, Jacob, 125

C

Caesarism, 124-125
Canada, Ribbentrop in, 196
Cannae, 303
Capitalism, 238-239
Capone, Al, 30-31
Catholic(s), 26, 60; Center Party,
    136, 327; Church, 135-136
Caucasus, 183, 299
Chamberlain, Houston Stewart, 191
China(-ese), 86, 254
Christianity, 98, 134, 199, 207, 289-
    290, 323; aristocracy and, 143;
    Hindenburg on, 140-141; struggle
    against, 38-41
Cicero, 124
Civil War (American), 81
Colonial League, 275
Colonies, German, 323-324
Communism(-ist), xi, 26, 43, 47, 60,
    75, 193, 195, 296, passim
Concentration camps, Hess on, 60-61
Condottieri, 71
Conservatism, Christian, 138
Conservative Revolution, The, xii
Conservative revolution, xii, 142
Conservatives, xi, 123-124, 138, 141;
    ideology of, 37
Constitutional state, theory of, 139
Corwin, Edwin S., x
Croatia, 100
Cromwell, 200
Currency, 242-246
Czechoslovakia, 26, 59, 203, 282, 323
Czechs, 100, 210

D

D., Frau von, 148-150
Daladier, Edouard, 322
Danton, 71, 80
Danube Basin, 288
Danzig, x, xii, xiii, 15, 20, 25, 52,
    60, 61, 64, 75, 93, 94-95, 99, 121,
    132, 156, 162, 166, 170, 175, 181,
    184, 223, 225, 231, 234, 235, 236-
    237, 241, 258, 259, 270, 271, 275-
    276, 278, 279, 284, 312, 316, 326,
    327, 330
Darré, 18, 20, 30, 31, 35, 39, 229;
    and peasants, 32-42
De-Germanization Policy in Poland,
    The, xii
Democracy(-ies), 102, 128-130, 199
Denmark, 100
Deutsch-National, xi
Dictatorship, military, 289
Die Wahlliste der Nationalsozialisten
    in Danzig, xivn.
Dohna-Schlobitten, Prince, 29-30
Dollfuss, Chancellor, 55
Dostoevski, 43
Dunkirk, 295
Dynamism, 59-61, 169, passim

E

East Prussia, 247, 248
Ebert, 160
Economic units, Hugenberg on, 127-
    128
Egypt, 127
Emmy (Goering), 151
"Energy States," theory of, 248-257
Engineers, and Hitler, 230-262
England (Britain), xii, 13, 14, 48,
    57, 99, 106, 122, 126, 127, 149,
    150, 164, 171, 177, 217, 225, 228,
    247, 252-257; Germany and, 78-
    79, 188, 189, 193-203, 283, 286,
    293-305, 309-310, 324-325; inva-
    sion of, 293ff.; Rosenberg and,
    190-191; tariff in, 210
Essen, 211, 212, 213; Mines Associa-
    tion, 213
Europe and world revolution, 39-60
European federation, 91

F

Far East, 59, 60, 127, 183, 184
Fascism, 44, 58, 139
Faust, 43
Faust, 110
Feder, Gottfried, 63, 242-246
Fichte, 212
Finland, 299
Food situation, Koch on, 87-88

Foreign Ministry, German, 7, 155-161, 172, 178, 182, 183-184, 187-190, 195

Forster, *Gauleiter*, 14, 42, 52, 53, 70, 75, 173, 284, 328

Fouché, 8

Foundations of the Nineteenth Century, 191

France: and Germany, 13, 14, 26, 48, 59, 77, 90, 99, 100, 126, 127, 128, 149, 171, 177, 192, 198, 199, 201, 202, 216, 217, 224-229, 247, 261, 270, 279, 282, 292, 293ff., 300, 302-305, 310, 322ff.; and Poland, 285-287

Frankfort, 225

French Revolution, 14, 66, 70, 138, 250, 319

Frick, 18, 62-67

Fritsch, Baron (General) von, 201, 282-291, 316, 321

Funk, 109, 113

G

Gauleiter, 18-19, 63, 65, 68, 88, 91, 92, 104, 244

Geneva, 45, 163-164, 171, 223, 225, 318

German people: attitude of to Nazis, 7-9, 11-15; character of analyzed, 4, 5, 8; *passim*

German-Polish agreement, 58

Gleichschaltung, 219

Goebbels, Dr., 18, 25, 38, 74, 109, 151, 163, 195; character and ideas of, 42-51

Goering, Hermann, 16-20, 51, 218; and army, 17; character and ideas of, 67-80; and police, 18

Goethe, 150

Great Britain, *see* England

Great Regions, 251-257

Great States, 127-128

Greenland, 127

Greiser, Artur, 15, 20-21, 25, 94

Grenzund Auslandsdeutschtum, 181

Grossraum, 225-226, 231

Grünberg, Professor, 248-257, 258, 261

Gustavus Adolphus, 297

H

H., von, 265-269

Hagen, 103, 105

Hammerstein-Equord, Freiherr, 9-10

Hannibal, 311

Hapsburgs, 297

Haushofer, Karl, 58

Heiden, Konrad, 327

Heligoland, 253

Helldorf, Count, 196

Hentig, Werner Otto von, 178, 185-189

Herrenklub, 135, 137

Hess, Rudolf, 17, 71, 72; character and ideas of, 51-61; flight of to England, 56-58

Heydrich, Heinrich, 23

Himmler, Heinrich, 17-18, 19, 57, 71, 76, 194, 195; character and ideas of, 21-32.

Hindenburg, Marshal von, 138, 140-141, 189, 160, 161, 189, 278

Hitler, Adolf, vii, viii, ix, 3, 7, 15, 26, 32, 38, 50-51, 53, 54, 57, 59, 61, 63, 65, 89, 155, 160, 185, 198, 200, 248, 260, 266, 288, 295, 309, 326, 327, 328; and America, 82, 85-86; attitude of German people toward, 13; compared to William II, 191; and engineers, 230-232; and money, 242-246; Party control by, 16-21; power system of, 19-21; religion of, 97; responsibility of for war, 4-6; and Russia, 193; relations with: army, 274-278, 280-282, 302-305, 318-321; Beck, 286; Blomberg, 280-281, 324; Darré, 33; Forster, 93-108; Fritsch, 288-290; Goebbels, 46-47, 48; Goering, 68-80; Himmler, 23-24; Hindenburg, 140, 141; Hugenberg, 124, 131, 132, 133; industrialists, 164-165, 166; Keppler, 236, 237, 238; Neurath, 164-165, 166; Papen, 134-135, 136, 137, 141, 142, 220-221; Plaichinger, 230-231; Rauschning, 166; Reichswehr, 269; Ribbentrop, 194; Schacht, 117-118; Schleicher, 291-292; "society," 147-

152; Strasser, 17; Thyssen, 215-
223
Hitler Youth, 189, 275
Hochschaukeln, 169
Hofmannsthal, Hugo von, 142
Hohenzollern(s), 297, 315
Holland, 100, 127, 198, 295
Horst Wessel, 106
Hugenberg, Alfred, 35, 89, 122, 208,
288; character and ideas of, 123-
134
Hungary, 100

I

Iceland, 127
India, 183, 254
Industrialists, 8, 27, 90, 112; attitude
of toward Nazis, 7-8, 207-230; po-
litical views of, 207-215; responsi-
bility of, 5
Industry, 211-215
Ingolstadt, 93
Italy, 127, 280

J

Japan, American war with, 85
Jews, 22, 37, 41, 52, 61, 107, 108,
109, 110, 207, 211; Forster on,
98; Goering on, 72, 79-80
Junkers, 5, 6, 8, 27, 89, 145; in S.S.,
29-32

K

Kalkreuth, Count, 7-8, 35
Kamchatka, 86
Keitel, Field Marshal von, 315, 316
Keppler, 3-4, 230, 246; character and
ideas of, 236-241
Koch, *Gauleiter,* 15, 103-108, 235,
247-248; character and ideas of,
81-93
Königsberg, 89, 92, 247, 270, 271;
University, 247
Köster, 158
Krönig, von, 316-317
Kuhlmann, von, 4-5

L

Labor Front, 17, 19
Länder, 66

League of Nations, 155, 156-157,
163, 167, 182, 183, 286, 312, 326
Lebensraum, 210, 211, 300
Lenin, 43
Leonhardt, H. L., xiii
Ley, Dr., 17, 109-110, 111, 112
Liberal state, 139
Liberté allemande, 297n.
Lisbon, 155
List, General von, 316
Loesch, Karl C. von, 181-183
London, 78, 184, 191, 324
Lorenz, *Obergruppernführer,* 25
Ludendorff, von, 57, 85, 271, 288,
301, 306, 313, 314
Luftwaffe, 19-20. *See also* Air force
Luther, 243

M

Maginot Line, 308
Marx, Karl, 111
Marxism (-ist), 26, 33, 56, 75, 111,
208, 222, 239, 242, 245, 255,
passim. See also Communism (-ist)
Massacre: of June 30, 165; of S.A.,
18, 20
Medicine, "Aryan," 109
Mediterranean, 127
Mein Kampf, 79, 192
Meissner, Under-secretary, 160
Middle classes, 110-113, 117, 129,
276
Militarism, 270-274; Prussian, 301ff.,
321
Military: caste, 90, *see also* Junkers;
radicalism, 321ff.
Minorities Treaty, 171
Moltke, von, 73, 180, 302
Mommsen, 110
Monarchy, restoration of, 138, 140,
268, 289-290, 317, 323
Moravia, 23
Moscow, 328, 329
Munich, 78, 230
Mussolini, 73, 190
Myth of the Nineteenth Century, 191

N

Napoleon, 71, 200, 202, 304, 305,
319, 320

Nationalists, 26-27, 35, 94, 103-108, 117, 124, 132, 144, 164, 172, 195, 197, 208, 272
National Land Union, 35
National Socialism (Nazism), ix, xiii, 68, 69, 71, 91, 265-266; agriculture and, 22-23, 32-42, 247; army and, 270-283, 288-290, 291-330; aristocracy and, 28-32, 142-147; Bolshevism and, 47-48, 51; elements in, 103-108; engineers and, 232-262; Forster on, 94; Frick on, 63-67; Hindenburg on, 140-141; ideology of, 3-10; industry and, 207-215, 241ff; middle class in, 110-113; and money, 242-246; von Papen and, 136-137, 139, 140, 142; Rauschning and, ix-xiv; and religion, 97-98; religious element in, 56; and revolution, 234; Rousseauism in, 96; "society" and, 147-152; strife in, 15-21; technocracy in, 231-262; trade unions and, 273; and world revolution, 58
Navy, 16, 310; League, 275
Nazi Conquest of Danzig, xiii
Nazi Party: agriculture and, 22-23, 32-42, 247; aristocracy and, 28-32, 142-147; army and, 172; attitude of German people toward, 11-15; background of, 3-10; bureaucracy and, 6-8; Catholic Church and, 135-136; character of, 11-21, 88-89; composition of, 25-27; Conservatives and, 123-125; elements in, 103-108; Foreign Ministry and, 155-161, 183-184, 189-190; industry and, 205-215; internal strife in, 15-21; Nationalists and, 164; von Neurath and, 167-173; peasants and, 32-42; policy of in Europe, 181; Saar and, 223ff.
Nazism, *see* National Socialism
Near East, 184
Neurath, Baron von, 161, 173, 199, 201; character and ideas of, 162-172
New Deal, x

Nibelungen Ring, 103-104
Nietzsche, 60
Norway, 99, 127
Nudism, 109

O

Obersalzberg, 52
Olden, Rudolf, 327
Ostmesse, 247

P

Palestine, 135
Papen, Franz von, 9, 26, 89, 155, 220; and Hitler, 220-221; character and ideas of, 134-142
Paracelsus Institute, 109
Pareto, 3
Paris, 294, 303
Peace, 57-58
Peasants, 22-23, 32-42, 89, 112, 328; in Poland, 173-174
Persia, 299
Pilsudski, Marshal, 73, 180, 285-286
Plaichinger, 230-232
Poland, xiff., 26, 57, 77, 90, 91, 128, 132, 188, 210, 213-214, 217, 259, 329; agrarian reform in, 173-174; and Germany, 73-75, 99-101, 119, 170-171, 180, 275-276, 278-280, 282, 283-287, 312, 323
Poles in Prussia, 131
Police, Prussian, 16-17, 20
Polish Corridor, 248, 323
Pomerellen, 100
Posen, 131, 323
Possessed, The, 43
Power, fight for within Party, 15-21
Prohibition (U. S.), 83, 84, 85
Prussia, 16, 87, 287-288; East, 247, 248
Prussianism, 277
Prussian militarism, 301-305, 321
Prussian Settlement Commission, 131
Public administration, *see* Administration, public
Public service, character of, 5

Q

Quex, Hitler boy, 275

R

Radicalism, 9; military, 321ff.

Radowitz, General von, 138, 158, 271

Raumer, General, 293-301

"Red Front and Reaction," 105, 106

Reichenau, von, 276

Reichsbank, 117, 118, 120, 244

Reichslandbund, 35

Reichsleiter, 65

Reichstag fire, x, 62, 68, 69

Reichstatthalter, 63

Reichswehr, 161, 218, 220, 269, 270-274, 276, 291, 305

Reparations, 211

Rettelsky, 135

Revolution, German: army and, 266-270; causes of, viii, 4-10; Frick's ideas of, 62-67; Hess and, 58-61; nature of, 261; peasants and, 32-42. *See also* World revolution

Revolution of Nihilism, The, 11, 259

Rheinbaben, von, 155-157

Ribbentrop, 7, 56, 76, 161, 172, 190, 191, 217; character and ideas of, 193-203

Robespierre, 80

Röchling, 223-230

Roehm, General, 16, 17, 18, 19, 29, 48, 271

Rome, 105

Rosenberg, Alfred, 7, 161, 184, 288; character and ideas of, 190-193

Rousseau, 95

Ruhr, 222

Russia, 47, 55, 56, 57, 74, 78, 90, 92, 103, 126, 127, 150, 168, 191-193, 199-203, 217, 222, 229, 231, 247-256, 276-277, 279, 282, 287-288, 293-305, 328, 329

Rust, 110, 112, 218

S

S.A.: importance of, 16, 17-18; massacre of, 18, 20

Saar, 223-230

Scandinavia, 253

Schacht, Hjalmar, 117-123

Scharnhorst, 278

Schleicher, General von, 155, 273, 291-293

Schlieffen, 293, 301; Plan, 302ff.

Seeckt, General von, 301

Shirach, Baldur von, 109, 110, 112

Siberia, 100

Siegfried, 103, 105

Siegfried Line, 232

Simon, Sir John, 163

Skoropadsky, 184

Slavs, Forster on, 99-100

Socialism (-ist), 47, 51, 56, 79, 89, 90-91, 103, 106, 107-108, 239, 255, 277

"Society" and Nazism, 147-152

South America, 59

Spengler, 125

S.S., 19, 20, 21, 22, 25, 144, 145, 146, 190; Himmler's training of, 27-30; importance of, 16-18; purpose of, 29; élite of race, 30-32

Stahlhelm, 272

Stavrogin, 43

Stein, Baron von, xiii

Steiner, Rudolf, 25

Stinnes, 241

Storm Troop (-ers), 16-18, 19, 26, 28-29, 52, 60-61, 271

Strasser, Gregor, 15, 17, 20, 89

Streicher, Julius, 38, 109

Stresemann, 155, 214

Succession States, 286

Sudan, 127

Sulla, 105-106

Sweden, 99

Switzerland, 100, 197, 198, 216, 322

T

Talleyrand, 8, 71

Technocracy, 231, 235-262, 316

Thyssen, Fritz, 213-223

Todt, 232-235, 246

Trade unions, 17, 111, 208, 209, 273, 276

Trotsky, 43, 305

Turkey, 299

U

Ukraine, 183-185, 299

Umbruch, 3-10, 58, 219

Unemployment, 244-245
United States, see America
Unter den Linden, 159, 265, 266
Upper Silesia, 213

V

Versailles, Treaty of, 121, 169, 178, 183, 198, 200, 211, 224, 227, 305
Vienna, 110
Vistula Corridor, 323
Vladivostok, 86
Voice of Destruction, The, 5, 69, 233, 304
Volksgemeinschaft, 209
Völkischer Beobachter, 191
Volk und Reich, 181

W

Wagner, 42
Wagner, Frau, 148
Wallenstein, 297
Wall Street, 85, 86
War, 86-87, 90-92, 101, 118, 122, 201, 268-269, 275-281, 283-288, 293-314, 324, 327-330

Warnau, 328
Warsaw, 74, 278, 279
Washington, D. C., 85
Wassmuth, 305-311
Wedekind, 267
Wehrmacht, 19, 57, 77, 270-274, 305. *See also* Army
Weimar Democrats, 122, 157
Weimar Republic, 8, 12, 22, 66, 110, 111, 135, 150, 151, 155, 157, 160, 190, 291
Weizsäcker, 200
Wilhelmstrasse, 58, 265
William II, 72, 191, 282, 302
Wilson, Woodrow, 227
Workers, 9
World revolution, German idea of, viii, 58-61, 124-125, 234-236. *See also* Revolution, German

Y

Yugoslavia, 213

Z

Zollverein, Prussian, 287
Zurich, 11, 197

6